ROBIN HOOD

ROBIN HOOD

A MYTHIC BIOGRAPHY

Stephen Knight

Cornell University Press *Ithaca and London*

First published 2003 by Cornell University Press

Printed in the United States of America

Library of Congress Cataloging-in-Publication Data

Knight, Stephen Thomas.
    Robin Hood : a mythic biography / Stephen Knight.
      p. cm.
Includes bibliographical references and index.
    ISBN 0-8014-3885-3 (cloth : alk. paper)
    1. Robin Hood (Legendary character). 2. English literature—Middle English, 1100-1500—History and criticism. 3. English literature—History and criticism. 4. Outlaws—England—History—To 1500. 5. Outlaws in motion pictures. 6. Outlaws in literature. I. Title.
    PR2129 .K585 2003
    820.9'35—dc21
                                                          2002152751

Cornell University Press strives to use environmentally responsible suppliers and materials to the fullest extent possible in the publishing of its books. Such materials include vegetable-based, low-VOC inks and acid-free papers that are recycled, totally chlorine-free, or partly composed of nonwood fibers. For further information, visit our website at www.cornellpress.cornell.edu.

Cloth printing   10 9 8 7 6 5 4 3 2 1

For Margaret

Contents

Figures

Introduction

The good outlaw: the idea attracts attention in every culture. Someone rejects conventional law, breaks it, is exiled from it, is pursued and imprisoned by its agents, but somehow always escapes and somehow always represents a system of social and personal order that is better than what we have now. The good outlaw tests contemporary law, reveals its weakness, and holds out a promise of greater freedom. The myth has undiminished importance.

Myths of this utopian kind can be personalized: a single figure can bear the meaning of resistance to oppressive circumstances. These figures may be imaginary, like Santa Claus, who promises merriment and generosity in the painful depths of winter, or real, like Martin Luther King, that resister of modern racial repression who is potently mythic for all because of his actuality.

Robin Hood's myth has existed for more than six hundred years, spreading around the world from its modest beginnings in shady corners of English medieval culture. When you start looking for him, he is everywhere: scribbled in the margins of medieval manuscripts, gamboling through the cheap chapbooks of early modern literary markets, entombed in turgid Victorian prose, referred to in many modern journalistic headlines; the forest of the Robin Hood electronic network reports new sightings of the good outlaw almost every day.

Modern or medieval, the references all have the same focus: Robin Hood represents principled resistance to wrongful authority—of very different kinds and in many periods and contexts. The good outlaw is a figure with as much mythic force as other heroic figures, but the unusual thing about him is that he has much greater variety than the customary personifications of value. Mythic figures tend to have a clear area of operation: the threat of winter or racial repression in the cases of Santa Claus or Martin Luther King, a specific time and place and a limited range of possible meanings in the case of figures such as Jesse James or Sherlock Holmes. Only figures bearing the full power of religion seem to have more meanings and manifestations than Robin Hood. Yet even though Jesus Christ and the Lord Buddha lead the field in mythic multiplicity, in many ways Robin Hood seems to have at least some of their compulsive flexibility and enduring sense of positive force.

He, like them, and indeed like all potent mythic figures, implies through his vivid energy and our need for identification an insistent sense that he did live and breathe. Though the power of heroic figures is inherently mythic, we also yearn for them to have a human presence. Obsessed with our own identity, or our quest for it, we need figures of myth to have some biographic standing. That is why this book is—has to be—a mythic biography, an account of a figure who is always represented as fully human, is always located in a certain form of earthly, and indeed earthy, life, and gains much of his force from that quotidian link. But this mythic figure is also a figure of wider-ranging, deeper-laid force than one human being could ever be.

Yet people—scholars as well as the sheriff of Robin Hood lore—try to contain Robin Hood, constrain the complex mythic figure into a narrow physical compass, biographical, not mythical. On November 17, 1992, the American supermarket tabloid the *Sun* reported the discovery in Sherwood Forest of a body wearing green tights and carrying a medallion in the name of Robert of Locksley. Readers could admire the mummified body, complete with hood and allegedly wearing green tights. The historical expert, in T-shirt and dark glasses, looked more like a *Sun* journalist than the Cambridge don he was stated to be. Of course, the journalists were amusing themselves (the Robin Hood byline went to one John Coffin), but they were mocking a modern obsession with reductive biographic empiricism—the first question for any journalist and many members of the public is "Did Robin Hood really exist?"

The opposite end of the interpretive forest, where a determinedly nonempirical form of existence flourishes, is occupied by the myth-only people. The most startling example, with its own appropriate element of playfulness, is found in that bible of English biographic pomposity, *The Dictionary of National Biography.* Among all the forgotten politicians and forgettable aristocrats lurks the outlaw hero; an entry written by Sir Sidney Lee, the coeditor of the massive project, insists that the name Robin Hood refers to a "mythical forest elf" whose name could be Hodekin and who was probably related to the Norse god Woden. This mythic figure inspired place-names and village rituals before he became an outlaw hero.

Lee's scholarship may be brighter than that of the U.S. *Sun,* but his premise is just as slender—the idea of a "forest elf" at the basis of all the outlaw material is as insubstantial as the notion that a medieval outlaw carried personal ID. These two extreme cases epitomize the limitations of mono-interpretation: Robin Hood cannot be constrained by any single view of reality or unreality. Neither solely a myth nor merely biographic, Robin Hood combines both ways of understanding a powerful figure, and this book will trace the remarkable range of variations to be found in the context of the good outlaw and his stories. This book is a mythic biography in two ways: it deals with both the human and the superhuman manifestations and meanings of the figure; but it is also a biography of a myth, that is, a single study of a figure who has over centuries and in many places and many genres had a varying but powerful identity. The myth can be read to reveal both the multifaceted potency of the figure and the remarkable ways in which different periods have, through this recurrent myth of resistance to authority, represented their own ideas of what constitutes oppressive authority and how, in dreams, wishes, or even reality, that might be resisted.

Despite the variations, Robin Hood retains some structures of coherence. This is not a field where meaning is in ultimate free play, or free fall, as postmodernists tend to prefer in their playful search for ultimate freedom. In terms both of period and of genre—ballad, play, novel, film and television in particular—certain coherences make it possible to discuss the outlaw's mythic biography under four headings, which are the chapters of this book. These chapters relate to a large degree with chronology: Robin the social bandit appears before

Robin the distressed gentleman—but the separations are not simple or total. The social bandit thrived in seventeenth-century ballads after the distressed gentleman bestrode the Elizabethan stage—and he continues: the chiseled profile of Michael Praed in *Robin of Sherwood* in 1984 re-created in many ways the social bandit in the contradictory but compelling form of a young radical, in touch with magic as well as ecology and swaying to the sounds of electronic folk music. Each of the four archetypal Robin Hoods I have identified as foci is still with us and can appear, or even coalesce, in sometimes disturbing, sometimes exciting ways. The family-oriented Robin Hood Esquire of the Victorian novels emerges surprisingly at the end of the 1991 film *Robin Hood: Prince of Thieves* as Kevin Costner embraces his lost and formerly hostile half brother.

Such connections and overlaps are part of the complexity of meaning in the outlaw myth and are key elements in its consistent self-renovation. Errol Flynn in 1938 is both a distressed gentleman and a social bandit-like trickster. At the end of the important American Romantic essay "Walking," Henry David Thoreau quotes from the four-centuries-old poem *A Gest of Robin Hood*. For Thoreau, as for John Keats, Walter Scott, Alfred Tennyson, and many lesser writers of the nineteenth century, the greenwood where Robin Hood walked bore a powerful message about value in the modern world, a myth for their own culture's biography. Yet Robin Hood's greenwood had meant something crucially different hundreds of years before: it was, in part at least, a medieval townsman's image of possible social liberation, rather than the more modern idea of personal feeling and freedom. The multiplicity and variation of the Robin Hood myth are central to its own continued life and its own varying biography, and this book aims to show both how various, and how variously vital, the myth is through its capacity to change.

The Robin Hood tradition is popular not only in terms of widespread acclaim but also in terms of generic form. Unlike other literary figures who survive from the medieval period to the present—King Arthur or Tristan and Isolde, for example—Robin Hood has not been re-created by high-art authors in timeless masterpieces, whether medieval poetry or modern opera; equally he played no part in the elaboration of the five-act drama or the sophisticated novel (though he does appear, with limited success, in both forms). In artistic terms, the outlaw tradition is a low—and free—form of life, and so is all the more variable, all the more flexible, all the easier for a re-creator to re-create. It may be that film and television have made Robin Hood an international figure and have contributed to the tradition at the level of masterpiece, and that as a result present and future versions of the good outlaw will be somewhat more constrained than previously by the impact of Errol Flynn, Michael Praed, or Kevin Costner. Despite such possibilities, few signs point to canonical constraints surrounding the free-ranging hero.

Always a fugitive, disappearing suddenly in the forest as he does in the bookshops and video stores, always hard to contain in any jail, town, or textual tradition, Robin Hood resists the constraint of precise explanation as well as other unwelcome forms of authority. The hero of a mythic biography is not dead.

Indeed, the life of Robin Hood sometimes takes surprising turns. In the summer of 1999 the London *Sunday Times* published a story that suggested Robin Hood might have been gay, starting a media flurry around the world. The idea came from a conference paper in which I passingly suggested that the subtitle of Joachim Stocqueler's 1849 novel, *Maid Marian, The Forest Queen,* might not in fact refer to Marian, who played little part in the novel, but to the doubtful sexuality of the outlaw hero. The story caught on—it was the press's "silly season"—and my suggestion was pursued around the world, from *Der Spiegel* to the *South China News,* including radio stations with Scandinavian weight and Australian hilarity. The gay media were thoughtfully interested, the Nottingham press predictably outraged, and I received a gratifying amount of hostile mail, in small white envelopes with neat handwriting.

Two conclusions could be drawn. One was that Robin Hood still caught the attention of the public on a massive scale—not a surprise to anyone aware of the continuingly massive production of Robin Hood material in many genres. The other, more surprising conclusion, embedded in the interviews and the letters, was that it was not his possible homosexuality that outraged the opponents but the fact that sexuality of any kind had been imputed to the worldwide good outlaw. Almost all of my personal correspondents complained that the story had breached innocence, rather than lamenting that it had perverted masculinity.

Analysts of the Robin Hood tradition have always sensed the depths in his myth that match its remarkable breadth, whether they are political, magical, historical, or, as now appeared, sexual. My own epistolary encounter with the strength and range of feeling about the hero prompted me to set aside a planned book of remorseless academic inquiry into the niceties of the tradition, addressing such questions as what were the real connections with Scotland, why did Ben Jonson abandon his sparkling *The Sad Shepherd*, and so on. Instead, I set out to write something that did not merely chart the topography of the Robin Hood world but tried to plumb its meaningful depths, to explore the myth itself.

Like most of my generation, I first encountered the outlaw hero in the robust shape of Richard Greene in the 1950s television series *The Adventures of Robin Hood.* But I had no more than a general interest in the myth until the early 1970s, when I was teaching a course on ballads at the University of Sydney and discovered that the available criticism on the Robin Hood ballads amounted to little more than general appreciations and F. J. Child's valuable but laconic introductions in his *English and Scottish Popular Ballads.* No detailed inquiry into the dates, origins, variety, or relationships of the texts existed. The lucid introduction and edition by Barrie Dobson and John Taylor, *Rymes of Robyn Hood,* which appeared in 1976, helped me realize that this was a substantial tradition which deserved a literary historical study beyond the necessary limits of their edition. So I began a long process of gathering the ballad texts, reading the out-of-print dramatic and fictional materials, and sorting out the patterns and contexts that emerged and overlapped in this extensive but elusive corpus. That eventually led to a set of publications intended, in the spirit of my original ballad teaching, to make available to students of all ages and kinds the riches of the Robin Hood tradition. The publications comprised an analytic survey in 1994 called *Robin Hood: A Complete Study of the English Outlaw* ("Complete," which I was tempted to spell "Compleat," was meant to indicate the traditionalist methodology as well as the wide range); an edition (compiled with my "good felawe" Tom Ohlgren) of the major early texts, *Robin Hood and Other Outlaw Tales* in 1997; an edition of the remarkable 1993 discovery of a seventeenth-century manuscript with new versions of familiar ballads, *Robin Hood: The Forresters Manuscript* in 1998; and to complete this set of outlaw study aids, in 1999 *Robin Hood: Anthology of Scholarship and Criticism*, reprinting often unobtainable essays in interpretation, literary, historical, and mythological.

Other scholars were at work in the same field. In fact, the most dynamic feature of recent years has been the establishment of a biennial conference where I could hear what others were thinking about the tradition and receive colleagues' comments on my further explorations in papers and lectures. These ideas often meshed with the illuminating comments made and essays written by students in the course on Robin Hood that I established at Cardiff University in 1996. This work all pointed toward another scholarly book, but there remained in my mind, like an arrow-splitting shot, a comment made by Douglas Gray after I gave a paper to his seminar at Oxford. Douglas, who in 1984 had published a searching essay on "The Robin Hood Poems" (one of the almost unobtainable items that made the anthology seem so necessary), commented that in spite of my insistence on the contextual reconstructions of the myth over time, I was, he felt, still implying that there was an essentially surviving identity of the hero. The historical cultural studies approach, he was politely noting, still depended on a humanist premise; or to rephrase it more damagingly into the theory-speak that we at Cardiff so admire, a myth of presence was at the heart of my deconstructions.

I did not have a suitably defensive response to Douglas's comment; but now I would see it not as a damaging analysis but one that in fact bespeaks the character of the myth and its constant appeal. A presence that can be humanistically imagined is indeed at the heart of the tradition, but the crucial feature is that this presence is radically reconstructed in different periods and genres. The four identities that are the titles of the four chapters of this book—Bold Robin Hood; the Earl of Huntington; Robin Hood Esquire; and Robin Hood of Hollywood—are the four major, though not the only, repersonifications of the myth of the good outlaw, and all have been crucial to the continuance of Robin Hood. Unlike Sir Guy of Warwick, Sir Bevis of Southampton, or indeed King Arthur, the outlaw hero has been reconstructed in succeeding (and often overlapping) periods and genres into a presence for the present—and the process goes on, as feminist authors are shaping a very different Robin to facilitate the new heroism of Maid Marian.

The tradition of Robin Hood combines an aura of antiquity that bestows a sense of timeless value with consistent cross-temporal variations which embody contemporary concerns. The past is the validating false consciousness of the present. Sometimes evidence can be very tangible, and this plangent but consoling contradiction is evident in the very address at which this book was completed. Wood Green, with its rural sound, is today a multicultural hub and hubbub in North London, enjoying a major bus depot and a necklace of mercifully non–Anglo-Saxon restaurants. I look out on an intersection that epitomizes the mixture of myth, mobility, and material concerns that characterizes the Robin Hood tradition from its beginning to its future. White Hart Lane, rich in magical suggestions (as well as the male games of a famously quixotic football team, Tottenham Hotspur), meets the equally mythic Green Lanes, down which cattle were driven to the voracious urban world that, as in the early ballads, both threatens and sustains its rural hinterland.

No drover works alone, and in assembling and propelling forward this herd of ideas and interpretations I am as always reliant on my colleagues on the international Robin Hood trail. In addition to acknowledging the many librarians, students, and respondents who have stimulated and shared thoughts, I mention those who have traveled with me on many a puzzling, dusty, though not always dry, journey and generously shared information: Sally Bentley, Marilyn Butler, Seymour Chatman, Peter Coss, Gavin Edwards, Peter Gill, Dawn Harrington, Kevin Harty, David Hepworth, David Lampe, Tom Ohlgren, Michael Parker, Helen Phillips, Jeffrey Richards, Lucy Sussex, and at Cornell University Press Bernhard Kendler, Karen Hwa, and Karen Bosc. I would like to single out for special thanks Tom Hahn, who has been outstandingly generous with his comments and advice in this field (as in others, as many scholars know). His help, with that of the people I have named here, has improved this book substantially. One of my best experiences, academic and social, has been the heuristic company of what Lorraine Stock memorably called the "Merry Men and Women" of the Robin Hood network. No doubt they—and, I am confident, some at least of the lively-minded students I have had the pleasure of teaching in this field—will continue explorations in the outlaw myth. As the shadows of international politics and local bureaucracy fall more darkly over activities that are insistently intellectual and critical, any work which both explores and celebrates the long-standing and still compelling idea of resistance to oppressive authority must be not only a matter of pleasure and excitement, but also—to reassert the central values of the tradition of the good outlaw—a matter of liberty and equality.

STEPHEN KNIGHT

Wood Green, London

Note on References

This book uses endnotes, found at the back of the book, to give sources and occasionally further comment, but for both clarity and compression specific references to lines and pages quoted have been given in the body of the text after each quotation: a full reference is given in a note when the source is first quoted in each chapter. In order to facilitate further reading in the myth easier, reference has been made whenever possible to readily available sources. The sources for many texts used is *Robin Hood and Other Outlaw Tales*, ed. Stephen Knight and Thomas Ohlgren, 2d ed. (Kalamazoo: Western Michigan University Press, 2000). This book contains a newly edited large selection of the ballads as well as early plays and chronicle references. Another selection of ballads, with some material on place-names and proverbs as well as a particularly full and valuable intro-duction is *Rymes of Robyn Hood*, ed. R. B. Dobson and J. Taylor, 2d ed. (Sutton: Stroud, 1997). The only complete set of the Robin Hood ballads is to be found in F. J. Child's massive work, *The English and Scottish Popular Ballads*, 5 vols. (1904; reprint, New York: Dover, 1965). The Robin Hood ballads occupy most of volume 3. Also with the aim of making material accessible, I have quoted a number of the important essays that have been written on the outlaw tradition not from their original elusive locations but from the collection *Robin Hood: Anthology of Scholarship and Criticism*, ed. Stephen Knight (Cambridge: Brewer, 1999).

ROBIN HOOD

 CHAPTER I

Bold Robin Hood

Bold and Strange

He lives in the greenwood and is expert with a bow; he leads a group of doughty fighters who resist the corrupt church, the sheriff, and his minions but remain loyal to the king. He rescues prisoners, celebrates at forest feasts, uses disguise to trick his enemies, and survives the dangers of town and castle.

The main features of Robin Hood's mythic biography are recognized around the world. They also all appear in the earliest stories that survive about the outlaw hero, late medieval ballads detailing in brisk, vivid style the adventures of Robin and his small band of fellow outlaws. The simple but powerful adjective *bold* sums up this hero, suggesting physical and ethical courage and success in his encounters with strong, oppressive enemies.

But the modern person also will find surprises in the early stories. The bold medieval Robin is not an earl or even a knight, he has no relationship with a lady, is not a Saxon confronting Normans, does not live in the time of bad Prince John and (allegedly) good King Richard, does not lead a large band, and, in particular, never robs the rich to give to the poor; he looks after himself and his close associates.

Bold Robin of the early ballads is consistently called a yeoman, the meaning of which has been much debated by historians.[1] Essentially, the term indicates a free man who is not a bound serf. He may own land or run a business, but he is usually a skilled worker of some kind. Although he may develop a good income, the yeoman is essentially linked to life in the lower orders of society; he is not inherently a member of the gentry, those landowners of substance who fought on horseback and to some degree aspired to the elaborate chivalric culture outlined in medieval romances like those about King Arthur and his knights.

If the early bold yeoman Robin is not a lord, he also does not have a lady. No woman plays a significant role in the early outlaw stories; the Virgin Mary is the closest Robin comes to a female object of devotion, and Marian never appears. Nor is Robin thought to be noble in ethnic terms: any difference between Saxon and Norman is never mentioned. The conflict of 1066 had been largely forgotten by the end of the twelfth century, more than two centuries before the first Robin Hood texts were written. He never meets Richard I: though a king appears several times, he is named only in one early text and only as Edward, without any defining number. The reigns of the first to fourth Edwards ran from mid-thirteenth century to late fifteenth century; the best candidate is Edward III, who reigned from 1327 to 1377. Bold and free though he may be, Robin is firmly faithful to whichever king rules in the early stories.

Differences also exist between the early yeoman and the later lord Robin. Though in many of the later ballads and stories Robin leads more than a hundred men, early on he is found with only three or four—just like real outlaws of the period. Such a group was likely to rob for its own purposes, as bold Robin originally does: though his actions have an ethical direction, the yeoman outlaw robs the rich to give to himself and his friends, not to be generally charitable to the poor. Other features also distinguish the early texts from the later image of Robin Hood. The early outlaws do not automatically wear green clothing—and certainly not leg-revealing tights. They tend to fight with swords and staffs, using archery as more a matter of game and display between men. The jovial friar is not one of their group, and—another surprise—they are by no means always active in Sherwood Forest and the North Midlands town of Nottingham.

Although early ballads gave rise to some surprising elements in both myth and biography, they—a little-known fact—were by no means the only form in which the early fame of the hero spread—and indeed they appear to be neither the original nor the dominant genre in the early myth of the forest hero. Plays, village rituals, passing references (legal, historical, moral), and even proverbs all seem originally at least to have been more widespread than the ballads. An analysis of these other forms illustrates the variety and complexity of bold Robin Hood in his first period of fame and helps define the values and meanings of this first formation of the good outlaw's mythic biography.

Glimpses of an Outlaw

In 1998 the Nottingham City Council debated whether Robin Hood was really the best public image of the town. Some felt that having an anti-rich figurehead was not the best way to attract the sensitive overseas investors that aging industrial towns in Britain so greatly, and so ambivalently, require. In spite of these doubts, nothing seems to have changed much in Nottingham, either in terms of the hero's standing or the town's capital inflow, but this modern negative move does indicate that there are ways of dissenting from the charm of the good outlaw. And there always were.

The earliest surviving reference to Robin Hood is distinctly unfriendly. In the late 1370s, in his massive, influential, deeply serious moral satire *Piers Plowman*, William Langland attacks many vices, especially those that he sees incapacitating the Christian church of his time. At one point he represents Sloth as a priest who has no knowledge of the Lord's Prayer but knows all too well some popular songs, including those about Robin Hood:

> "I kan [know] noght parfitly my Paternoster as the preest
>   it syngeth
> But I kan rymes of Robyn hood and Randolf Erl of Chestre"[2]

The tone of the *Piers Plowman* reference is negative, but that is because a priest is talking. There is no insistence that the "rymes" themselves are inherently bad. More specifically dismissive is a powerful statement made in the sixteenth century by Bishop Hugh Latimer, complaining that when he visited a village in the Worcester diocese one Sunday the people were not at church because it was "Robyn hoodes day."[3] He lamented this inattention to the church but went further than Langland with his critique, identifying Robin Hood as "a traytoure and a thefe." Such a hard line on Robin Hood was not uncommon among sixteenth- and seventeenth-century authorities, civic and religious, who because of their own official roles failed to see the charm of the antiauthoritarian outlaw.[4]

But when a writer's position was not so firmly committed to Christian duty or to the good of the orderly state, the popularity of Robin Hood was not a negative matter. The Scottish historian Andrew of Wyntoun was a churchman—a canon of St. Andrews—but in about 1420 in his *Orygynale Chronicle*, a history in verse focusing on Scotland, he wrote in an apparently positive way about the good outlaw and his associate:

> Litil Johun and Robert Hude
> Waythmen war commendit gud;
> In Ingilwode and Bernysdaile
> Thai oyssit al this tyme thar travail.[5]

This translates from medieval Scots as "Little John and Robert Hood were well praised (as) forest outlaws; in this period they did their deeds in Inglewood and Barnsdale." The "tyme" under which these four enigmatic lines were entered in the *Chronicle* was 1283. The writer must have known the same sort of popular rhymes that Langland refers to, and he adds the "outlaw" idea. "Robert" is the full form of the diminutive or youthful name "Robin." That Little John appears so early in the tradition is striking. Although his being mentioned first in the line may simply permit the rhyme on "Hude" and "gude," it does suggest that Robin was not automatically the leader in the earliest period. (Other evidence supports this; see pp. 17–18.) Even more surprising than the order of the names are the place-names: there is no Nottingham or Sherwood. This may indicate a Scottish perspective and may suggest that the outlaw myth is already being molded by the interests of its transmitters. Inglewood is a forest south of Carlisle, itself just south of the England-Scotland border. As is clear in several early texts, Barnsdale was in South Yorkshire, near Doncaster, much farther from Scotland, though on the road from London to Edinburgh. But there was also a Barnsdale forest in Rutland, and for centuries it was held from the king of England by members of the Scottish royal house. Thus, Wyntoun may have the right name but the wrong place in mind.[6] The date too reveals a possible Scottish interest: 1283 is the high tide of William Wallace's activities against Edward I, and Wyntoun may see the English outlaws as inherently operating against royal power in the forests, like the prime hero of Scottish independence, then and now. In its earliest appearance, the outlaw myth is already being re-created—by Langland in negative church-focused form, and by Wyntoun with a Scottish resonance.

Wyntoun does not seem to doubt—or even question—that Robin existed. Nor does another Scottish chronicler, Walter Bower, who, writing some twenty years later, was adding material to countryman John of Fordun's Latin prose history *Scotichronicon*, "the chronicle of the Scots."[7] Bower gives Robin's date as 1266 and mentions him as fighting among the "disinherited," those who, led by Simon de Montfort, Earl of Leicester, resisted Henry III; this theme returns in a nineteenth-century re-creation of the myth (see pp. 143–44). Bower is more explicit than Wyntoun in involving Robin in resistance to the authorities. Bower is also specific about Robin's criminality, calling him not a "waytheman," a "forest outlaw," but, worse, a *famosus siccarius*: this is usually translated as "famous cutthroat" because the Latin word *sica* means a knife, and *sicarius* is used of assassins and murderers. But like both Wyntoun and Langland, Bower also testifies to the hero's popularity: "The foolish people are so inordinately fond of celebrating (him) in tragedies and comedies" (26). He is more positive when he adds, "About whom also certain praiseworthy things are told" (26) and then gives an example of a Robin Hood story that he admires. For Wyntoun, the story has possible Scottish interest; for Bower, it signifies a recruitment of Robin to the church:

When once in Barnsdale, avoiding the anger of the king and the threats of the prince, he was according to his custom most de-

voutly hearing Mass and had no wish on any account to inter-
rupt the service—on a certain day, when he was hearing Mass,
having been discovered in that very secluded place in the woods
when the Mass was taking place by a certain sheriff and servant
of the king, who had very often lain in wait for him previously,
there came to him those who had found this out from their men
to suggest that he should make every effort to flee. This, on account of his reverence for the sacrament in which he was then
devoutly involved, he completely refused to do. But, the rest of
his men trembling through fear of death, Robert, trusting in the
one so great whom he worshipped, with the few who then
bravely remained with him, confronted his enemies and easily
overcame them, and enriched by the spoils he took from them
and their ransom, ever afterward singled out the servants of the
church and the Masses to be held in greater respect, bearing in
mind what is commonly said: "God harkens to him who hears
Mass frequently." (26)

Still formally named Robert Hood, the outlaw is a habitual robber, harassed by the sheriff, and down to a few men, but his courage
and religious faith save him—and ultimately help the church. Bower
has adapted the hero's biography to suit his own mythic interests and
has given a churchman's reason for admiring this "famous cutthroat."

That combination of criminality and admiration is evident in
early legal references. At Tutbury, Staffordshire, in 1439 the court records complain that

one Piers Venables, of Aston, gentleman, gadered and asembled
unto hym many misdoers . . . and, in maner of insurrection,
wente into the wodes in that contre, like as it hadde be Robyn
Hode and his meyne [band].[8]

Though this does not actually say Robin Hood himself was capable of insurrection, the suggested link with the "forest outlaw" and
the "famous cutthroat" of the chroniclers is clear. The same sense of
heroic menace seems to lurk in the earliest piece of Robin Hood poetry that survives, scribbled in a manuscript now in Lincoln Cathedral, written in the first quarter of the fifteenth century:

Robin Hood in scherewod stod
Hodud and hathud, hosut and schod
Ffour and thurti arrows he bar in his hondus.[9]

Vigorous and concentrated, this may well be the first stanza of a
song or even a chorus. It presents a figure found at the beginning of
many ballads, though not usually with his clothing so closely described; the second line means "wearing hood, hat, stockings and
shoes." Robin is in the forest, at his ease, standing still, but we know
he will very soon be in vigorous, dangerous action; nobody carries so
many arrows just for sport or pleasure.

A similar sense of mysterious, even alarming, force is embedded
in many of the popular Robin Hood proverbs. The most common is
"Many men speak of Robin Hood, who never drew his bow."[10] The
sense is that he is very popular but both unmatchable and unknow-
able: people claim his acquaintance in fantasy alone. The image of
drawing his bow refers to the fact that the longbow required years of
training to enable a man to pull it back fully and deliver a heavy arrow
at maximum power and accuracy.[11] In part a simple rebuke to boast-
fulness, the proverb also gives the outlaw a special and somewhat
threatening status—like the innately warlike forester of the Lincoln
Cathedral poetry. A similarly eerie proverb is simply "Good even,
good Robin Hood," which suggests that the speaker is being polite to
someone when he has no choice; Joseph Ritson explained the situation as "civility extorted by fear."[12]

Other proverbial uses suggest that Robin Hood has a special set
of heroic values: a "Robin Hood mile" was unusually long; "Robin
Hood's pennyworths," or "pennorths," would buy a good deal; and a
lengthy and puzzling journey was "to go around by Robin Hood's
barn." A less bold idea may be behind "Robin Hood could bear any
wind but a thaw wind."[13] A negative opinion in the voice of the
Christian moralists is "Tales of Robin Hood are good for fools," but
this Langlandian disapproval faced the overwhelming popularity of
the proverbs imputing to the hero mythic strength and mysterious
value.

Other pieces of evidence from the fifteenth century show that

Robin Hood the forest hero was popular both in the sense of being widely known and in being felt to be on the side of the people. In 1432 a clerk (who, perhaps not accidentally, worked for a sheriff) amused himself by writing in the margin of the Wiltshire parliamentary roll, as if in a column of single names, a jingle that includes the words "Robyn Hode Inne Greenwode Stode Godeman Was He."[14] Another legal record, in the King's Bench Rolls of 1441, suggests a darker side to the mythic figure: a group of laborers in Norfolk blocked the highway, threatening to murder Sir Geoffrey Harsyk and fiercely singing, "We arn Robynhodesmen, war, war, war."[15] The outlaw could even be a focus—or a mask—for real trouble: in 1497 Roger Marshall from Westbury in Staffordshire (not far from Piers Venables's Tutbury) was hauled before the powerful Star Chamber on charges of leading a "riotous assembly" to the town of Willenhall under the name of Robin Hood. Marshall and his supporters had been forbidden to visit Willenhall, as they were known to be trying to release an arrested man, so they attended, a hundred strong, in the guise of a Robin Hood assembly.[16]

Although the records do not reveal the outcome of the case, Marshall was clearly involving Robin Hood in a potentially violent attempt to outface the law. In a similar event in Edinburgh in 1561, the Robin Hood rioters emptied the Toll Booth, the city prison, and locked up the legal authorities, sheriff included.[17] Like Marshall, the Willenhall troublemaker, the Edinburgh rioters took beyond the limit of legality a special kind of game and carnival that was popular through parts of Britain at the time. Such events, known as Robin Hood plays and games, were a major and perhaps the earliest feature of the outlaw tradition. These elusive events deserve close attention as an important part of the mythic biography of Robin Hood.

Gatherings of Robin Hood

In the municipal records of Exeter for 1426–27 an entry mentions a sum of money being paid *lusoribus ludentibus lusum Robyn Hode*—that is, "for the players playing the play (or game) of Robin Hood."[18]

This is the first of many records that appear over the next two hundred years relating to what are usually called the plays and games of Robin Hood; since it is hard to distinguish the two entities, it seems better to call these events the Robin Hood play-games.[19] Until recently scholars were aware of about two hundred references to Robin Hood up to 1600; well over one hundred were to some form of a Robin Hood play-game.[20] Now these numbers are rising as the *Records of Early English Drama* project (based in Canada and known as *REED*) reports the findings of its thorough county-by-county survey of medieval English records.

Through the fifteenth and sixteenth centuries, in villages and small towns, especially in southern and western England, it was common for "Robin Hood" and a group of supporters to play a major part in celebrating the coming of summer. Records of the events suggest that a public procession would end at an elaborate base or bower where Robin would sit to supervise the entertainment. This would include dancing and various competitive sports such as wrestling, archery, and swordplay. The celebration also included feasting, and sometimes the evening was given over to a "Robin Hood Ale."[21]

The play-game Robin Hood and the bold outlaw story share a strong connection to nature. The play-game is consistently associated with the woods and forests that surrounded the villages and towns and which in many ways supplied people's everyday living, with wood for building and fires, nuts and berries for the table, grazing for their animals, and space for sports and other pleasures. The play-game procession sometimes arrived through a forest, and as Robin progressed with a company through a village or town he bore signs of his link with nature; the company carried boughs or wore naturally decorated clothing, and they sat in a green, forest-symbolizing bower.

But it is not all nature: there is also in both play-game and ballads a financial element. In fact, one reason we have the records in the first place is that Robin and his band usually gathered money for the community (for the upkeep of the roads in some instances). They did this much as modern charities do, by collecting money for badges, which were called "liveries," as if Robin was a lord with a retinue. One record, from Yeovil, suggests that Robin and his "crewe" were relatively menacing in the means of collection (as is suggested in the proverb "Good even, good Robin Hood"), but there is no sign that they actually stole money.[22] It is also clear that the money-collecting was linked with Robin's mobility—moving through the village or town to collect, or sometimes going through the forest to another place.

Mobile money-gathering and festivity in the context of nature sounds more like the outlaw hero than the civic Robin of the play-games, though the money-gathering was not in itself outside the law. But there may well have been a fuller connection between the play-games and the ballads. Alexandra Johnston's familiarity with the records leads her to argue that the "Summer Lord" is not, as David Wiles has suggested, an essentially benevolent figure whose ceremonies could get out of hand at times. She argues that Robin is essentially a "lord of misrule" figure whose events, though officially licensed, could become disorderly, even riotous.[23] Such a figure is much closer to the outlaw of the ballads than to the local charity organizer that the play-game Robin Hood has been taken to represent. As Johnston indicates, the most elaborate of the Robin Hood play-games probably included some theatrical performance. This, as part of the "misrule," seems likely to have included some version of resistance to authority.

One brief but valuable record surviving from about 1475 suggests how the villagers were entertained for their contributions. The Paston family of Norfolk was highly literary—they are famous for the number and richness of the letters they exchanged—and their family papers include a single sheet with the dialogue for what seem to be two short scenes involving Robin Hood. Indeed, the sheet might well be an *aide-memoire* for something that was previously only oral. The notion that these are scripts for play-games is strengthened by a letter of the same period in which John Paston complains that his servant William Wood has left him. Wood, says Paston, "has gone into Barnesdale," a reference to the fact that Wood used to "play Robin Hood." Paston is making a ruefully witty farewell to his actor-servant.[24]

Written in a single block, without actors' names or stage directions, the lines need interpretation. The first scene—or, more probably, play—runs like this:

> A knight promises the sheriff to take Robin Hood. He meets the outlaw and they compete at shooting, stone-throwing, throwing

"the axle-tree" (a form of caber-tossing) and at wrestling. Robin wins at shooting and at first at wrestling, but when the knight throws Robin, the hero blows his horn and the two men fight. He beats the knight, beheads him, dresses in the knight's clothing and carries the knight's head in his own hood.[25]

There are obvious connections with the ballad of "Robin Hood and Guy of Gisborne" (see pp. 15–16), and both ballad and play link the hero in the forest with the concept of natural law as he resists the incursion of the sheriff and his minions.

The second play, or scene, shows Robin under legal constraint:

Robin is in prison and some of his men come to rescue him. They see Friar Tuck attacking the Sheriff, but all of them are captured. The sheriff brings Robin out to be hanged while he is also putting the newly captured outlaws in.[26]

That is as much as the dialogue tells us; presumably the sheriff has made a tactical error, and through stagecraft and fighting, Robin and the outlaws escape, perhaps with the help of Friar Tuck. Wiles calls the play "a fragment,"[27] implying that final lines have been lost, but it is more likely that the final action is silent and traditional, like many a climactic performance in vaudeville and pantomime. As in the other scene, or play, and in many ballads, we have the sheriff as enemy, the outlaws risking and, it seems, resisting capture—and here, for the first time in the Robin Hood context, the image of a fighting friar. It is not the first time this figure has been mentioned: legal records from 1417 state that Robert Stafford, a chaplain from Lindfield in Sussex, has taken up a life of robbery under the name Friar Tuck.[28] This may already have been a mythical outlaw name, appropriate to use as an alias,[29] not necessarily linked so early to Robin Hood: a later play and ballad suggest he had a separate tradition (see pp. 32–33 and 40–41). The major point about this precious manuscript from about 1475 is that it links the bold and antiauthoritarian outlaw hero to early plays, and suggests the link between the popular robber and the spirit of the play-game: a myth of power was locally realized through a man who is a symbol both of the natural life and of resistance to oppressive authority.

The play-games have a firm location in the calendar: they are in

May, but not May Day; the Robin Hood play-games are not to be confused with the fertility symbolism of May Day and the maypole. Rather, Robin Hood's time is Whitsun, the "White Sunday" that celebrated Pentecost and the descent of the Holy Spirit. "White Sunday" was white not only in terms of holiness but also because then, as now, by mid- to late May the hedges and shrubs of rural England were densely white with the hawthorn flower, also known as May flower and whitethorn. Seeing the landscape change so quickly is still a striking, even moving, sight; the fertility linked to Robin Hood is not that of an aggressively masculine maypole but that of the more generalized force of fertile nature.

The play-games also have a geographic focus. Some newly discovered *REED* references are emerging from the North and North Midlands, areas that had seemed bereft of Robin Hood play-game activity, but the play-games still dominate in the South and the West, in long-settled communities where the rural way of life seems to have been validated by the qualities found in Robin Hood. In his outlaw role these communities may well have seen an imaginary defense against the growing mercantile power of large towns and the extending of royal authority that was a feature of the period. This may also help to explain why East Anglia, with its more developed economy based on the wool trade with continental Europe, and its lack of a heavily wooded and hilly landscape, apparently did not develop a sense of the value of the hero.

The Robin Hood who led the local play-games was primarily a figure empowered by the myth of nature and a sense of local community; his capacity to break the law seems to have been no more than a possible activity in a benign context. The Robin Hood of the ballads, however, from the start exemplifies a more direct and active form of boldness. He confronts the authorities as a central part of his meaning; this is why the outlaws are at risk. Although such confrontation may have been an element in the entertainment of the play-games, as in the play in which Robin is imprisoned by the sheriff, in the ballads it is a central feature. Though literary scholars have thought the play-games were rustic imitations of their own treasured literary texts,[30] the likelihood is that the ballads are a town-based form of the outlaw myth, a reshaped story about freedom and oppression. The story uses the forest not as a natural and readily accessible part of everyday life, to be paraded in organic celebration through the streets, but as a symbolic location for a type of freedom not available in the towns where the ballads seem to have flourished. The play-games belonged to villages and small towns, but in some larger towns of the North Midlands and the North, close to major forests, the outlaw hero seemed to symbolize something more risky than the figure who presided over rural summer celebrations. It is in the early ballads that the outlaw possibilities of the hero's mythic biography are most fully demonstrated.

Rhymes of Robin Hood

"Robin Hood in greenwood stood" was the archetypal image of the outlaw hero. In court usage the phrase—sometimes using "Barnsdale" for "greenwood"—was a maxim to illustrate stating the legally obvious, and was first recorded in the Court of Common Pleas in 1429.[31] Where the play-games celebrated the hero and the natural protection he seemed to provide, the ballads offer fairly extensive narratives, showing Robin Hood moving in and out of trouble of various kinds. They test and expose his values a good deal more than the play-games seem to have done, and they provide a fine source of material for this phase of his mythic biography. None of the elements in the early ballads conflicts with the image of Robin that comes through the outlaw references discussed earlier—the chronicle, legal, proverbial and casual realizations of his reputation. But the ballad hero is clearly more active and more insistently outside the law than the hero of the play-games, and the ballads all depict a tough and resourceful figure, with a small band, based in the forest, resisting the corrupt church and the power of the sheriff, but ultimately loyal to the king and to the Virgin Mary.

The early ballad material is rich and detailed, but not large in extent. There are three fairly long ballads, all over two hundred lines, and presenting quite complex plots: "Robin Hood and the Monk"

(1450 at the earliest), "Robin Hood and the Potter" (1500 or a little later), and "Robin Hood and Guy of Gisborne" (not recorded until about 1650, but evidently composed a good deal earlier). These three form a coherent group to establish the character of the early bandit, and they embody and elaborate the elusive Robin of the early references. These three texts allow us to establish a mythic biography for Robin, to consider its meaning in context, and then to see that it relates quite closely to the representation of the hero in the lengthy early text the *Gest of Robin Hood.* The *Gest* was in print by 1510, remained popular in the period, and became a major source for later presentations of the hero. Other ballads seem to have been around by at least the sixteenth century and are extensions of this image of a bold and nonaristocratic Robin Hood who directly resists authority.

So, first, the stories.

"Robin Hood and the Monk" starts with a celebration of early summer in the forest, and Robin desires, with St. Mary's help, to go to Mass in Nottingham. One of his men, named Much, says it is dangerous, so John goes with Robin. Along the way they shoot for money; John claims to win, but Robin says he is lying and refuses to pay him. They separate in anger.

In Nottingham Robin is recognized by a monk he has previously robbed and after a fight he is captured by the sheriff's men at St. Mary's church. (A lost page in the manuscript creates a gap here.) The outlaws in Sherwood hear of Robin's arrest, and John and Much go off to help, trusting in St. Mary. They meet the monk and his page, pretend they also have been robbed by Robin Hood, and escort the monk for his "safety." Then they kill him and the page, and take letters about Robin that the monk was carrying to the king. The king gives John his seal to command the sheriff to bring Robin Hood before him, and John returns as a royal messenger. He feasts with the sheriff, who gets drunk. John and Much tell the jailer Robin Hood has broken out, then kill the jailer and escape with Robin to Sherwood. John tells Robin he has done him a good turn for an ill, and Robin offers John the leadership of the band. John refuses, preferring to be a "felow." The king hears that Robin has escaped and praises John's loyalty to Robin. The ballad ends with a prayer to God, who is also "a crowned kyng."

"Robin Hood and the Potter" also opens with a "forest summer" stanza. Robin and his men see a potter with his cart coming toward the forest, across open ground. Some recognize him; he has never paid them a toll. John knows him as a good fighter from Wentbridge (near the Yorkshire Barnsdale) and says nobody can make him pay. Robin bets John that he can. The potter refuses to pay a toll and fights with Robin; the potter has a staff, Robin a sword and shield. The potter wins and Robin pays John. The potter agrees to give Robin his clothing and cart, and Robin goes to Nottingham in disguise. John and the others warn him to be wary of the sheriff.

In Nottingham Robin sets up outside the sheriff's house and sells the pots very cheaply. He gives the last five of them to the sheriff's wife; she is very polite to him and invites him to dinner. At dinner the men discuss a shooting match to be held that day. They go to the targets. The sheriff gives Robin a bow; he thinks it is weak, but still wins. Robin says he has a bow in his cart that Robin Hood gave him. The sheriff is excited, and Robin agrees to take him the next day to see (and capture) Robin Hood.

Early the next day Robin gives the sheriff's wife a gold ring and leads the sheriff to the forest. Robin blows his horn and the outlaws appear. They take the sheriff's horse and belongings and send him back humiliated; Robin sends a white mare to the sheriff's wife. She asks the sheriff if he has brought Robin with him, and on being told what happened says that the sheriff has paid for the pots Robin gave her. (How did she know that the potter was Robin?) Back in the forest Robin asks the potter what his pots were worth. He says two nobles (two-thirds of a pound), so Robin gives him ten pounds. They vow friendship, and the poem ends with a prayer for God to save "all good yeomanry."

"Robin Hood and Guy of Gisborne" also opens with a forest summer stanza (very much like that in "Robin Hood and the Monk" and possibly copied from it). Robin has had a bad dream about two "wight (strong) yeomen" who have attacked him. So he and John go to look for them; they shoot on the way and see a "wight yeoman" leaning against a tree, fully armed, dressed in horsehide, including head and tail. John says he will deal with him, but Robin is offended at the suggestion that he needs John's help. They argue and separate,

John going back to Barnsdale (apparently a village in the forest), which he finds the sheriff attacking; John picks up a bow, but it breaks when he pulls it. John is trapped and is taken away to be hanged.

Meanwhile, a hired killer named Guy says he is seeking Robin Hood, and Robin offers to walk with Guy in case they meet the outlaw. They compete at archery and Robin wins. They exchange names (the hero identifies himself as Robin Hood of Barnesdale) and they fight with swords. Robin stumbles, Guy hits him, and Robin prays to Mary; he then jumps up and kills Guy. He beheads him, calls him "traytour," cuts his face with a knife, then exchanges clothes with him. With Guy's defaced head on the end of Robin's bow and dressed in Guy's horsehide, Robin goes to Barnsdale and blows Guy's horn. The sheriff hears it, sees the disguised Robin and offers him (thinking it is the successful Guy) a reward. All Robin (as Guy) asks is to be permitted to execute Little John, who is tied up. The sheriff thinks he is foolish to ask no more, but agrees. Robin moves toward John, and the sheriff's men follow, but he asks them to keep back so the dying man can confess. They do as he asks. He cuts John free and gives him Guy's bow and bloodstained arrows; as the sheriff runs away toward his house in Nottingham, John shoots him through the heart. There is no final prayer.

Taken together, these stories give a remarkably consistent, overlapping, and self-supporting account of bold Robin Hood, the medieval outlaw who clearly existed well before and was crucially different from the distressed gentleman. This pattern of interlocking themes makes it credible to treat "Robin Hood and Guy of Gisborne" in this context, even though the surviving text was not written until the mid seventeenth century—as much as two hundred years after "Robin Hood and the Monk" and at a time when many changes had come over the hero and his story. While "Robin Hood and Guy of Gisborne" may have late and literary features—the opening stanza possibly borrowed from "Robin Hood and the Monk," the lack of a final forest celebration and a final prayer—the language, the detail, and many of the attitudes have persuaded scholars that this is a much older story. Primary pieces of evidence are its similarity to the simpler story told in the play of about 1475 (see pp. 10–11) and the fact that the three ballads all represent the forest outlaw in much the same way—a way not found so fully or vividly elsewhere.

They all have a powerful natural forest opening; "Robin Hood and the Monk" is the classic, with what Gray calls a "fine lyrical introduction":[32]

> In summer, when the shaws [groves] be sheen,
> And leaves be large and long,
> It is ful merry in fair forest
> To hear the foules [birds'] song,
>
> To see the deer draw to the dale
> And leave the hilles hee [high]
> And shadow them in the leaves green
> Under the greenwood tree.[33]

The forest exists on its own, rich with trees, birds, and animals, and there is a strong sense of the lush beauty of summer. The deer find shelter in the forest like the men who themselves are likely to be preyed on. A sense of unity between the outlaws and their natural setting continues as the ballad speaks of the sun and the birds, and then John states, "This is a merry morning." In "Robin Hood and the Potter" Robin stands on the edge of the summer forest and sees the potter coming; in "Robin Hood and Guy of Gisborne" Robin and John plunge into the "merry greenwood" in search of the threatening yeomen. The opening statement realizes harmony between the outlaws and nature, but the story then unsettles that harmony in the outlaw's encounter with authority outside the forest. Except in "Robin Hood and Guy of Gisborne," the story finally returns to order and to the forest setting.

The first incident of disharmony in these works is dissension between Robin and John. The two men argue and separate, into danger. They cannot contain their competitiveness, and it is Robin who is at fault: denying the bet in "Robin Hood and the Monk," insisting that John does not take precedence over him in fighting in "Robin Hood and Guy of Gisborne." Although no argument occurs in "Robin Hood and the Potter," a trace of tension nonetheless exists as John, who knows that this potter is a fierce fighter, sets Robin up for a bout with him and a bet—but the resultant hostility of the other ballads is avoided. The general sense that Robin is not automatically a leader is underscored in "Robin Hood and the Monk" because after John has rescued Robin (and for his efforts he should surely have a place in the title of this ballad) he mentions the original struggle. He refuses the leadership Robin offers, but Robin's position is obviously negotiable, not an automatic status as has become the case in later periods. A parallel to this democratic reading of Robin's position is the fact that in "Robin Hood and the Potter" the brawny potter simply defeats him. Robin is almost always the best archer, but he is never represented as the supreme fighter with a sword or even a staff. Kelly de Vriess has pointed out that in the early ballads archery is not a prime method of fighting; it is rather a sport for self-assertion, while Dean Hoffman has argued that archery has thematic meaning as a symbol of popular justice.[34]

Both the arguments with John and the unsuccessful fighting indicate that Robin in the early ballads is represented as being in some way vulnerable, even fallible. Although he remains leader, this is not by birth or right; it is more like a consensual position. And his success—as well as Little John's safety—depends on the continued loyalty of the outlaw band. The tensions and securities that surround Robin are those of a cooperative group, not those of a hierarchical structure and a single dominant hero. Though the hero himself undergoes changes through time, especially social ones, these mutual and democratic values remain an important and lasting element in the outlaw myth.

The enemy in each story is the sheriff and his agents—in "Robin Hood and the Monk," the monk who has Robin arrested and the jailer; in "Robin Hood and Guy of Gisborne," a hired killer as well as the sheriff's other men who capture John; in "Robin Hood and the Potter," the sheriff himself. These enemies can be treated roughly by the outlaws: the sheriff loses two supporters in "Robin Hood and the Monk" (three including the monk's boy) and two in "Robin Hood and Guy of Gisborne," before being killed himself. In the less aggressive, more humorous "Robin Hood and the Potter" he is not harmed but is seriously humiliated.

It is very much a man's world, with little place for women. Robin has a special devotion to the Virgin Mary; it is to St. Mary's Notting-

ham that he goes to Mass in "Robin Hood and the Monk," and a
prayer to her seems to save him in "Robin Hood and Guy of Gisborne." His encounter with the sheriff's wife in "Robin Hood and the
Potter" is unusual, as a unique relationship with a woman before
Marian enters the story but also being at a raised social level. She
thanks Robin in very polite terms, saying "Gereamarsey" (the medieval French for "Thank you very much") as if he were a real gentleman and even addresses him as "sir" (143). His gifts of a gold ring and
a white horse are those of a lord to an admired lady; it may be suggested at the end of the ballad that she knew him, and liked him, all
the time. This momentary social rise in Robin's role above that of
yeoman seems inconsistent, but may simply be invoked by the presence of a female character of some social standing; she introduces the
tone of romance in linguistic terms, if not amatory ones.

The yeoman outlaws defeat their enemies comprehensively, but
skill and courage play a surprisingly small part: in different ballads
Robin and John are both taken by the sheriff and by superior numbers, Robin is on the point of defeat by Guy, and he is certainly infe-
rior to the potter. The outlaws' major weapon is cunning: the persua-
siveness and disguise of John in "Robin Hood and the Monk," the
disguise and coolness of Robin while pretending to be a potter, and
again disguise and deceptive action in "Robin Hood and Guy of Gisborne." These are features of the international hero known as the
Trickster, better known in contexts such as Native American story
than classic literature. The Trickster outwits enemies and uses their
strength and folly against themselves, as in the case of the sheriff gal-
loping off with Robin to the forest, or the king's writ allowing Little
John, of all people, inside the jail.[35]

Outwitting the king, shaming the sheriff, impersonating Guy,
being socially mobile and irrepressible—all of these hallmarks of
Robin Hood are elements of the Trickster narrative. The Trickster's
witty and spirited behavior is shown to be a means of frustrating, even
defeating, the powerful. This feature recurs in popular Robin Hood
stories such as the prose "Life" pamphlets of the eighteenth and nineteenth centuries and the films of the twentieth century. Particularly
important in the early texts, and found throughout the Robin Hood
tradition in many forms, is the motif of infiltration: John becomes a

sheriff's agent by assuming the monk's role; the sheriff thinks the quasi-potter is a valuable informant; Robin offers himself as John's executioner. Deep in these ballads is an inherently antiauthoritarian idea that the powerful depend for their power on the consent and activity of ordinary people, and so ordinary people could assume those roles in a spirit of resistance, whether serious, playfully deceptive, or both at once.

The three early ballads raise a puzzle about the hero's location. "Robin Hood and the Monk" is evidently set outside and inside Nottingham, and once names the forest as Sherwood. But though the potter visits the same town, the forest is never named as Sherwood and curiously Little John knew this potter from Wentbridge, a town adjacent to the Yorkshire Barnsdale and too far away for a potter to travel to the Nottingham market. (The northern edge of Sherwood is at least forty miles away.) More obviously a topographical compromise is "Robin Hood and Guy of Gisborne": it starts in Barnsdale, and Robin gives that as part of his identity. But at the end the sheriff runs for safety toward his house in Nottingham, an unlikely sixty miles away. That one of the sheriff's men is named William a Trent, presumably after the river on which Nottingham stands, further suggests that this is a hybrid story, combining two forests if not two ballads.

Recurring themes of the outlaw world include the negative impact of money—John and Robin fight over it, Guy wants to kill for it, the monk mourns for his lost hundred marks. Other thematic motifs are strength in bow-drawing—both John and Robin have trouble with "weak gear"—and the value of feasting—to celebrate in the forest, to pretend friendship in the town. Contrary to modern assumptions, only in the later-recorded "Robin Hood and Guy of Gisborne" does Robin wear green. Likewise, there is no suggestion that Robin has more than a few men with him—whereas the sheriff in "Robin Hood and Guy of Gisborne" employs seven-score men to attack Barnsdale. Similar absences are Marian herself and any idea of a Saxon-Norman distinction between the outlaws and their enemies.

Another surprising feature of these texts is that there is no explanation of how Robin and the others came to be in the forest. They are, just like the deer, a part of this natural world, at ease in the forest, not hoping always to leave it to resume their lives. The outlaws are elemental forces, part of the forest, one of the dangers that those who impose laws from afar must face. Also, the famously oppressive forest laws play no part in the plot: unlike many modern versions, there is no hint of the sheriff or the foresters pursuing men for killing deer. Presumably the outlaws killed the king's deer, but nobody mentions this as a crime in the early ballads, not even the king in "Robin Hood and the Monk." The mythic meaning of Robin and the other outlaws here is quite general, not tied to events or actions: they simply embody the spirit of freedom, eluding the grasp of the agents of law. The outlaws, like the opening "forest summer" stanzas, have a natural and utopian value for ordinary people that is summed up compactly in the last stanza of "Robin Hood and the Potter":

> Thus parted Robin, the sheriff and the potter,
> Underneath the greenwood tree;
> God have mercy on Robin Hood's soul
> And save all good yeomanry.[36]

The abiding value of the outlaw is linked with the enduring natural value of the greenwood tree and those ordinary people whom Robin, at this stage, directly represents and through the processes of fiction imaginatively protects. Fitting well as it does with the multiple early references to the mythic identity of Robin Hood, the ballad image of a heroic, vulnerable, yet always triumphant man of the people provides an interesting comparison with the major medieval realization of the hero, the lengthy ballad-epic *A Gest of Robyn Hode.*

A Proud Outlaw

Plays, games, references, songs, rare ballads—all the manifestations of the early Robin Hood are in some way marginal and casual, and have many features of the world of oral communication. The chroniclers' references say the hero's story is on people's lips. The ballads, which lack the refrains that indicate singing, seem intended to be spoken, chanted, or perhaps even shouted to entertain a popular audience. That all seems very appropriate for an outlaw hero who embodies the spirit of a carnival and bears the values of the natural world. But the early ballads are recorded in a literary context, written in anthologies of other material, some of it serious and moral, not entertaining or potentially antiauthoritarian. This apparent move of the outlaw material toward respectability makes it less surprising to find the Robin Hood story as one of the earliest and most popular of the materials that find their way into print. The *Gest of Robin Hood* is a prominent and substantial piece of early English printed literature—1824 lines of well-organized poetry. Some of its early printed versions have survived only in fragments, but it is clear that four editions had become available by 1530. The poem was reprinted several times later in that century.

Appearing in this form gives Robin Hood considerable weight. The title of the *Gest* itself gives the hero status: it has the connotations of the Latin *res gestae*, the "things done" by a true hero. (The word does not mean either "jest" or "guest," as unwary students have sometimes thought.) The work is to some degree a biography of Robin Hood, but not in a fully planned way; there is no early account of his birth or upbringing, no explanatory prelude to his appearing as an outlaw in the forest. In addition, the story of his death seems distinctly tacked on. As a whole, however, the work is a substantial saga-like set of adventures that gives the sense that the deeds of an important hero are being chronicled. Unlike the elusive, damaged, and hard-to-read manuscripts, this is a solid, printed book: the *Gest* is the encyclopedia of the medieval Robin Hood, and it had a major influence on later re-creators of the myth, right through to twentieth-century films. The story is full and in many ways familiar.

Robin Hood and his men are in Barnsdale; before having dinner Robin wants, by custom, to meet a stranger who can pay for it. He also practices the custom of hearing Mass three times before dinner, and loves Our Lady most of all. John asks for general advice, and Robin tells them to favor farmers and yeomen, as well as knights or squires who are friendly, but to attack bishops and archbishops and to watch out for the sheriff of Nottingham.

John, Much, and Scarlet go up to the highway and meet a poor knight. He owes money to St. Mary's Abbey, in York, and unless he pays it he will lose his land. Robin feeds him, lends him the money (on the surety of the Virgin Mary), and the outlaws reequip the knight. With John as squire he goes to York, frustrates the greedy clerics, and gets his land back; he then goes home to save for Robin's repayment. After a period he sets off to return the money, but is detained when he tries to help a yeoman who is being attacked.

Meanwhile, the sheriff has seen John shooting and asks the knight if he can have John as his "man." The knight agrees. One day John is not given dinner by the sheriff, so John fights with his cook. Then they make friends and leave for the forest, taking with them the sheriff's food and tableware and more than £300. John then decides on more revenge and goes back to tell the sheriff he has seen a wonderful hart (stag). The sheriff goes with him and is ambushed: Robin is "the mayster-herte." Humiliated, the sheriff eats his own feast and promises to be friendly to the outlaws.

Robin waits again for dinner; he and his comrades wonder where the knight has gone with the money. John and the others go up to the highway and this time meet two monks, with fifty men and many packhorses. The monks are from St. Mary's, in York, and have £800 with them (though they lie and say it is only twenty marks, about £7). Robin claims that Mary has returned the money with interest. The knight arrives and returns the £400 to Robin, but he gives it back.

The sheriff then declares an archery contest, which Robin wins (apparently not in disguise), but afterward the sheriff ambushes the outlaws. Little John is hurt and they take refuge in the knight's castle. The sheriff besieges the castle, but then goes to tell the king, who promises to go to Nottingham. The sheriff ambushes the knight; his wife tells Robin. The outlaws enter Nottingham, kill the sheriff because he has broken his oath of friendship to them, and rescue the knight.

The king (Edward, without any number) goes to Nottingham but cannot lay hands on Robin. A forester advises the king to go into the forest in disguise as an abbot, and Robin will find him. This happens. The king-abbot says he has £40; because he tells the truth, Robin takes only half. The king-abbot shows Robin the royal seal and says the king invites him to Nottingham to dine. Because of his love for the king, Robin invites the king-abbot to dine. They eat and enjoy games. One is "pluck-buffet," a shooting competition in which the winner hits the loser. The king-abbot hits Robin powerfully, and

Robin recognizes him. The king dresses in green and they go in procession to Nottingham.

Robin agrees to serve the king and goes to court. But he quickly spends all his money and after a year, one day sees young men shooting arrows. He asks the king for permission to return to Barnsdale; he claims he wants to worship at the chapel he built for Mary Magdalene. He leaves, the outlaws welcome him, and he does not return. Twenty-two years later he is ill and goes to Kirklees, where his relative is the prioress. She and her lover, Sir Roger, kill him there.

The poem ends with a prayer for mercy for Robin's soul:

For he was a gode outlawe
And dyde pore men moch god.[37]

The *Gest* presents to a large degree the same sort of hero as the early ballads, basically because it appears to have been constructed from them—though not from any that have survived. The *Gest* was in print about 1500—not long after "Robin Hood and the Monk" was written down and at about the same time as "Robin Hood and the Potter." Its author seems to have compiled the text from a set of ballads of about the same length and complexity as those stories, and covering similar topics. Although the *Gest* does not use any of the surviving early ballads, it clearly is based on similar kinds of stories—indicating, as we might well expect, that many of the "rymes of Robin Hood" have been lost, or perhaps were never written down.

The *Gest* apparently includes a ballad about "Little John and the Sheriff," going from the moment when the sheriff takes John as his servant to the sheriff's ultimate humiliation (very much like the end of "Robin Hood and the Potter"). The work also includes a story about "Robin Hood Robbing the Monks"—similar perhaps to the robbery mentioned in "Robin Hood and the Monk" which leads to the monk's revenge on Robin in Nottingham. This story has been neatly fitted in by paralleling the monks' money with that lent to the knight, a character who does not relate to the early ballads. Another familiar sequence, which could be called "The Archery Tournament," concerns the sheriff's deceitful attempt to catch the outlaws. Finally there may well have been a separate ballad about "Robin Hood and the King," developing in action the admiring thoughts about the outlaws that the king expresses at the end of "Robin Hood and the Monk." Other late medieval ballads with this structure are called "King and Subject" ballads, in which the king in disguise meets a member of the public, of a fairly low class. They come into conflict in some way, but it is resolved, mutual respect is exchanged, and they resume their former social roles.

Not only are these elements of the *Gest* familiar. Equally recognizable and popular are the values embodied in them and the image of Robin and his men that emerges. The outlaws are well known; John, Scarlet, and Much are the constant supporters, though others—such as Gilbert of the White Hand, who shoots well in an archery contest—occasionally appear. Among the outlaws, the values of loyalty, cunning, and wit are still as important as, and more evident than, fighting and endurance. Security remains in numbers (they carry John to safety after he is wounded in the ambush); disguise and infiltration are once more used to good effect (John acts as the sheriff's servant); archery is a means of display, not combat, and real fighting is with swords. In addition, the corrupt church is exposed and opposed but Mary is worshipped; the sheriff's authority and personal treachery are confronted and outwitted; and the king is revered.

Elements of the early ballads that do not clearly appear here include the danger of dissent within the band. A brief indication of it occurs as, after Robin gives him orders, John goes up to the road "Half in tray and tene" (842)—that is, "half in anger and annoyance"—but there is no explanation or consequence. The powerful "forest summer" openings of the early ballads are not found, presumably because they have been trimmed off in the compiling process. Nevertheless many references throughout allude to the greenwood and to the sense of security in the forest and its communal feasts, so the well-established natural element of the outlaw myth seems to be maintained, if not as vividly re-created as elsewhere.

The bulk of the *Gest* can be seen as consistent with the thrust of the early ballads and the early references: Robin is a man of the people, as if naturally found in the forest, always bold, always free, with a trickster-like wit, martial skills, and a reliable, small group of supporters. The established church and the policing systems of the town and extended royal power are their enemies, and the outlaws consistently elude and frustrate those forces, profit from them, and enjoy the forest life in constant summer and plenty. A characteristic forest feast is bread, ale, and venison, a vision of simple but ample communal good cheer. It is a male world where the good outlaw enjoys life without any of the problems of everyday existence.

Yet the *Gest* adds to this world, and the scene in which the outlaws feast the knight shows this sharply. After the familiar bread, ale, and venison, there is another stanza with a quite different tone:

> Swans and fessauntes they had full gode,
> And foules of the ryvere [riverbank];
> There fayled [lacked] none so litell a birde
> That ever was bred on bryre [branch].
>
> (129–32)

The forest meal has suddenly become a feast fit for a lord, with swan, pheasant, and the tiny birds that were elaborately cooked and mightily savored by the powerful.

The sudden rise in gastronomic level at the feast has a parallel in the narrative. An element in the *Gest* that certainly seems different from the earlier tradition—and indeed from almost all its later versions as well—is Robin's encounter with the knight. Although Robin is evidently popular with the common people and certainly opposes their enemies, the early ballads include no instance of his helping anyone who is not part of his band. The *Gest* does end with the rather vague statement "He did pore men moch god" ("he greatly helped the poor," 1824), but this is not made evident in the text. Later ballads give instances—rescuing young men from execution, giving clothing to the poor, helping widows in various ways—but nothing from the earliest period illustrates this noble outlaw behavior. The *Gest,* however, shows clear charity to the knight—a social class that Robin has not otherwise been involved with in the early ballads, either as friend or enemy. As a result of this charity, Robin later is able to take refuge in the knight's castle, and Robin rescues him from Nottingham at the request of his lady, just as if Robin himself were a chivalrous knight and not a forest outlaw. This social rise seems to mesh with another feature of the *Gest* not found in the ballads: namely, the rather formal opening, which realizes Robin's authority in an unusual way. Instead of having a "forest summer" opening, followed by action, the *Gest* begins by establishing Robin as:

> . . . a prude outlaw,
> Whyles he walked on grounde;
> So curteyse an outlawe as he was one
> Was nevere non founde.
>
> (5–8)

The words "prude" and "curteyse" seem to construct Robin as a more lordly figure than the usual yeoman, though he does not remain at this level.

Another Robin-elevating sequence occurs before the outlaws take to the highway and meet the knight. John, more like a steward than the tough near-equal of the other ballads, urges Robin to dine, and then asks for his guidance on how his men should behave. Robin, in turn, gives a formal, lord-like set of instructions. John acknowledges his own role as a follower:

> "This worde shalbe holde [kept]," sayde Lytell Johnn,
> "And this lesson we shal lere [learn]"
>
> (61–62)

In hearing Mass before dinner, in having a habit of requiring a visitor before dinner, and in dictating a code of behavior for his followers, the "prude" and "curteyse" Robin of the opening of the *Gest* is quite unlike the earlier, lower-level amiable forest ruffian. He has suddenly taken on elements of a higher status, which in the period would inevitably be compared with King Arthur, especially with regard to waiting for an adventure before eating. This is how many of the Arthurian hero-adventures begin, including ones as famous as the *Quest for the Holy Grail* and *Sir Gawain and the Green Knight*.

While his men go off to do the hard work, Robin waits on his own, in a "lodge" (113): this means a forest hut, but it is a French word and implies a hut used by gentlemen when hunting. Robin is also lordly to the knight, once he has proved his truth and explained his misery. Robin feasts him elaborately and provides money; he and his men also reequip the knight and send him off in proper form to restore his fortunes. The sequence seems not from a popular ballad so much as a chivalric romance, where a worthy hero, somehow displaced from his knightly honor, is helped back to noble status by a friendly fairy or a generous lord; outlaws could hardly be expected to have stores of chivalric goods like those they bestow on the knight.

It seems especially striking that this story comes first in the *Gest*; its unusual presence cannot be explained away by suggesting that the compiler ran short of real ballad material and so added something from a romance. The newly elevated material is given precedence; it sets the opening tone. This Robin is a "proud outlaw," not simply the honest and sometimes battling yeoman of the early ballads, the chronicle, and proverbial references, or indeed the local hero of the somewhat differently oriented play-games.

It is very likely that the form of the *Gest* has something to do with this innovative and inherently socially elevated material. There is no manuscript of the *Gest*, and though the ballads that it is based on may well have been known as early as the fourteenth century, there is no sign from its language that it is so old.[38] The probability is that, like Malory's *Morte D'Arthur* (1470–71, printed in 1485), the *Gest* was one of the encyclopedic collections of material that catered to the growing number of English readers in the fifteenth century. They were a different audience from that for the less literary ballads, and their social status and concerns were the same as those served by early printing: the literary audience had grown too great for scribes to handle, so printing was profitable. An interesting and credible argument to explain the combination of semi-aristocratic and popular elements in the *Gest* has been offered by Ohlgren, who sees strong elements of mercantile ideology in the poem, and suggests that it was composed for an audience of urban merchants.[39]

The topics of early printing tended to be almost entirely religious, moral/educational, or chivalric. Caxton did print *Reynard the Fox*, but it was a translation from French and was in any case a satire on lordly behavior, far from the yeoman world of the outlaws. People bought books to help them live imaginatively in the worlds of worship, self-improvement or chivalry. Books were expensive items, much treasured. It appears that the first concern of the *Gest* compiler has been to pitch his hero at a new social and literary level: the story of Robin's involvement with the knight helps to justify the rather grand title of *Gest* and establishes Robin as a proud hero deserving a heroic saga, with a tragic heroic death. It is notable that Pynson's edition uses as an initial illustration a woodcut showing an archer on a horse (figure 1); it is in fact the same as that used for the knight's yeoman in *The Canterbury Tales*, who is riding because he is on pilgrimage. This is a characteristic early printer's economy, but it also has meaning. Scholars have assumed that this figure is Robin Hood, even though he never rides a horse in the early materials (see p. 80). It is conceivable that Pynson is illustrating the knight, the major figure of the first part of the story: he does ride back to forest, carrying bows as a gift to Robin Hood, so the illustration could fit him. But whether it is the knight—perhaps unlikely—or a dubious mounted version of Robin, the illustration fits with and is itself part of the initial social elevation of the yeoman outlaw.

Another new element that seems to elevate the hero is his death at the end of the poem. The early ballads are single adventures, not sagas in which time passes, so they have no need to foresee an end for the hero. And yet this element of the *Gest* also may pick up an existing theme. Walter Bower wrote that the common people loved "comedies and tragedies" about Robin Hood, and it is hard to imagine what could be a Robin Hood tragedy other than the story of his death;[40] killing the sheriff or Guy of Gisborne could hardly be seen in a tragic light. It is also true that the well-known pattern of the international mythic hero, whether it be King Arthur, Siegfried, or even Jesus Christ, normally includes his betrayal by a close friend or relative and his mysterious passing from the world.[41] Yet the tragic death of the hero, while probably an element of the story from very early times, is in some way never a central part of it. The "Robin Hood's Death" ballad appears in separate form only in a late eighteenth century print, and was never very popular; the "Robin Hood's Garland" publications, gathering together popular ballads, rarely include it. In the same spirit, the only modern film that has shown the hero's death, *Robin and Marian* (1976), is the only one to have lost money at the box office (see p. 164). Unlike the deaths of King Arthur and most other major heroes, the tragic death of Robin Hood is not the necessary climax of the story, and indeed it seems to contradict the sense of vitality and free action that is inherent to the outlaw's myth.

FIG. I. Robin Hood in Pynson's edition of the *Gest*. *By permission of the Syndics of Cambridge University Library.*

Just as the death has limited impact in the tradition as a whole, so the somewhat gentrified opening to the *Gest* has a surprisingly limited overall effect in the poem. Though the compiler has evidently worked to raise the tone of the outlaw's myth and his social level, the tradition of the outlaw seems in some way to operate against that social promotion. Overall, the *Gest* does not seem a first stage in gentrification in any substantial way; rather, the weight of the early ballad material and the strength of the image of the bold yeoman outlaw seem to contradict, even disable, the social elevation with which the *Gest* begins.

Though Robin is initially called "prude," he does not retain this adjective. Where it is used elsewhere in the poem, it refers only to the sheriff, and is his recurring description.[42] Robin's own repeating adjective is simply "good." And in the same way, Robin's goodness, not pride, seems to embrace the knight himself: he first appears as a poor figure, whose only value resides in his fidelity to Mary and his ability to speak the truth—yeoman values in the early ballads. When he goes to confront the monks in York, secretly rich as he is, he acts just as Robin does in "Robin Hood and the Potter" or when disguised in Guy's costume: the knight behaves like the infiltrator who has secret power, and triumphs over the oppressors. Then on his way back to Robin, the knight and his men intervene on behalf of an oppressed yeoman, another quasi-Robin Hood activity. Finally the knight is rescued from the sheriff in Nottingham (as is Robin in "Robin Hood and the Monk"), and the sheriff is killed in retribution, as he is in both "Robin Hood and Guy of Gisborne" and the popular and fairly early ballad "Robin Hood Rescues Three Young Men."

In this way the knight, while retaining his status, is absorbed into the Robin Hood framework rather than initiating a real thematic or generic variation. The strength, it seems, of bold Robin Hood resists the *Gest* compiler's initial move toward some form of gentrification. The later history of the tradition supports this notion that the knight's story, though it starts the *Gest*, has very limited impact. Though seventeenth-century ballad writers mined the *Gest* for material, notably the archery contest and Robin's encounters with the sheriff and the king,[43] the story of the knight was never picked up by any successor until the nineteenth century, when Sir Richard Lee was woven into the narrative expansion of the novels—and in Tennyson's *The Foresters*—and then always in a secondary way, often as Marian's father.

So in spite of its different format, the *Gest*'s concept of Robin Hood's identity and meaning is not ultimately significantly different from the thrust of the other early material. The *Gest* still centrally celebrates Robin as a yeoman, a free spirit of the forest, directly loyal to St. Mary and the king, an enemy to any authority, religious or secular, who is not of true value. Indeed the last extensive sequence of the story in itself rejects gentrification: the king takes Robin with him to court, but Robin finds it a miserable experience and returns to the natural liberty of the forest. Gray's sense that the *Gest* is "full of various kinds of comedy and irony," which for him includes the quasi-Arthurian opening, is another way in which the poem resists any elements of gentrification that have been included.[44]

But if the world of the *Gest* is not ultimately different from that of the ballads, the character of the hero is still changed to some degree. He has greater authority, in that he is not really challenged by John, and he does not get into personal danger. He also seems to have lost much of the trickster element, which Little John seems to have picked up; though Robin strongly appreciates wit and carnival behavior, he does not initiate it. The Robin of the *Gest* seems perhaps a little older, a little more mature than the headstrong hero of the early ballads, but he is identifiably the same powerful, compelling hero of the people.

The antiauthoritarian Robin of the ballads and the actively dramatic Robin of the play-games come together in two texts that William Copland added to his edition of the *Gest*, published in about 1560. They are mentioned on the title page as "verye proper to be played in Maye Games,"[45] and this may well be the play that was entered in the Stationers' Register in 1560 as "the play of Robyn Hoode." But this is really two plays, or scenes (not unlike the c. 1475 manuscript in this double structure). The first tells the story of Robin Hood and the potter in much simplified form; here Robin smashes the pots, abuses the potter's boy, and then fights the potter, in a scene that apparently ends the play. This is usually taken as a simplified version of the rather complex ballad, but literary scholars' assumption that the plays are decadent versions of the ballads is highly doubtful (see p. 12). This play could simply be based on a "Potter" version of one of the "Robin meets his match" stories and, just as the c. 1475 play precedes a ballad in "Robin Hood and Guy of Gisborne," so this too may be an old play from which "Robin Hood and the Potter" was elaborated. The other play—hardly more than a scene—also relates to a ballad, usually called "Robin Hood and the Curtal Friar." The play tells how Robin has been beaten by a strong friar and asks his men to help him. Little John agrees, but before this can happen the friar arrives. He and Robin fight briefly; Robin blows his horn and his men appear, so the friar whistles and his men—with dogs' names—leap onto the stage. A major battle follows, which ends with peace being made. Robin not only offers the friar "both golde and fee," as is customary in the "fellowship" end to a "Robin meets his match" ballad, but also a woman. The play ends vividly as the friar dismisses the outlaws:

Go home, ye knaves, and lay crabbes in the fyre,
For my ladye and I wil daunce in the myre
For veri pure joye.[46]

The friar's final dominance suggests this is not simply a "Robin meets his match" story, but that a hero of a separate tradition has been incorporated into the Robin Hood tradition. Independent reference to him as an outlaw was made in 1417 (see p. 11), and in the c. 1475 play he seems to be separate from Robin's band. This process of incorporation clearly happened with the pinder of Wakefield in a ballad and a play (see pp. 42 and 49–51), and the play-game tradition includes other links between Robin and the friar.[47] Copland's linking of the plays and the *Gest* indicates that the major poem had not supplanted the other elements of the early tradition, and this widespread multifocal vitality continues in the myth.

Garlands for Robin Hood

Although bold Robin Hood is in existence by the fourteenth century, and clearly lives on in the early sixteenth century in the *Gest*, this is by no means the end of his career. A substantial number of ballads survive in print from the next two centuries. One common medium is the broadside, a single ballad printed on one side of a sheet of paper,[48] often with the name of a tune that will suit it, and almost always with a woodcut illustration. Broadsides were for singing as much as, or more than, for reading. Robin is represented in modern dress, either that of a stalwart foot soldier carrying a pike, though attended by bowmen (figure 2), or as a more cavalier-like figure, bearing a bow and admired by all (figure 3). The broadside was a popular way of disseminating songs, about everything from contemporary politics and current events to heroic tales and even the absurd—battles, great storms, whales washed up, women giving birth to rabbits. Several collectors, including Samuel Pepys, gathered copies, and more than thirty Robin Hood ballads have survived among them. Curiously, none of them is the same as the three early ballads, though one,

FIG. 2. The seventeenth-century yeoman: woodcut for "Robin Hood's Delight." *By permission of the Bodleian Library, University of Oxford, Wood 401, 41v.*

"Robin Hood and the Butcher," is a version of "Robin Hood and the Potter," simply with a different trade.

Ballads also survived from the later seventeenth century on in "garlands," collections of twelve or more ballads printed and bound as small books, sometimes with a brief introduction about this bold and honorable hero. The earliest to survive, from 1663, was a new edition of an earlier one of uncertain date—probably not much earlier—and its title page shows figures in rather theatrical poses inside an honorific garland itself (figure 4). The form must have been popular: another edition was printed in 1670, which is also roughly the date when someone who knew the outlaw tradition well put together the "Forresters" manuscript, named after its first ballad, "Robin Hood and the Forresters" (a variant of "Robin Hood's Progress to Nottingham"). It provides different versions of a number of ballads that survive elsewhere in broadside form, and, with a neat contents page (figure 5), may well have been meant as copy for a garland that was never published.[49] Along with many broadside ballads, several garlands, and

FIG. 3. The seventeenth-century gentleman: woodcut for "Robin Hood and Queen Katherine." *By permission of the Bodleian Library, University of Oxford, Wood 401, 21v.*

"Lives of Robin Hood," the manuscript represents significant interest in developing and disseminating the outlaw tradition in the Restoration.[50]

Most of these ballads in some way realize the bold Robin Hood of the earliest texts—sometimes a little diluted, often in those post-Reformation days more hostile to the Catholic Church than to the sheriff, sometimes less violent and with much more stress on the sport of archery. But Robin is still a man of the people, free, brave, and trickster-like, and he stands up for a natural law outside the formal structures of legal constraints.

Some of these later ballads offer types of bandit action familiar from the first three ballads and the *Gest*. In "Robin Hood and the

FIG. 4. Frontispiece for the 1663 Robin Hood garland. *By permission of the Bodleian Library, University of Oxford, Wood 79.*

Bishop" and "Robin Hood and the Bishop of Hereford" the outlaws treat important church figures with the same contempt and claim the same cash reward that they did in the *Gest*—and with a clearer sense of carnival. Robin escapes the warlike bishop in the first of those ballads by exchanging clothes with an old widow he has previously helped, and at the end he and his men humiliate the bishop thoroughly, just as they did the monks or the sheriff before. They give him the traditional carnival humiliation of being reversed on his horse:

> Then Robin Hood took the Bishop by the hand,
> And bound him fast to a tree,
> And made him sing a mass, God wot,
> To him and his yeomandree.

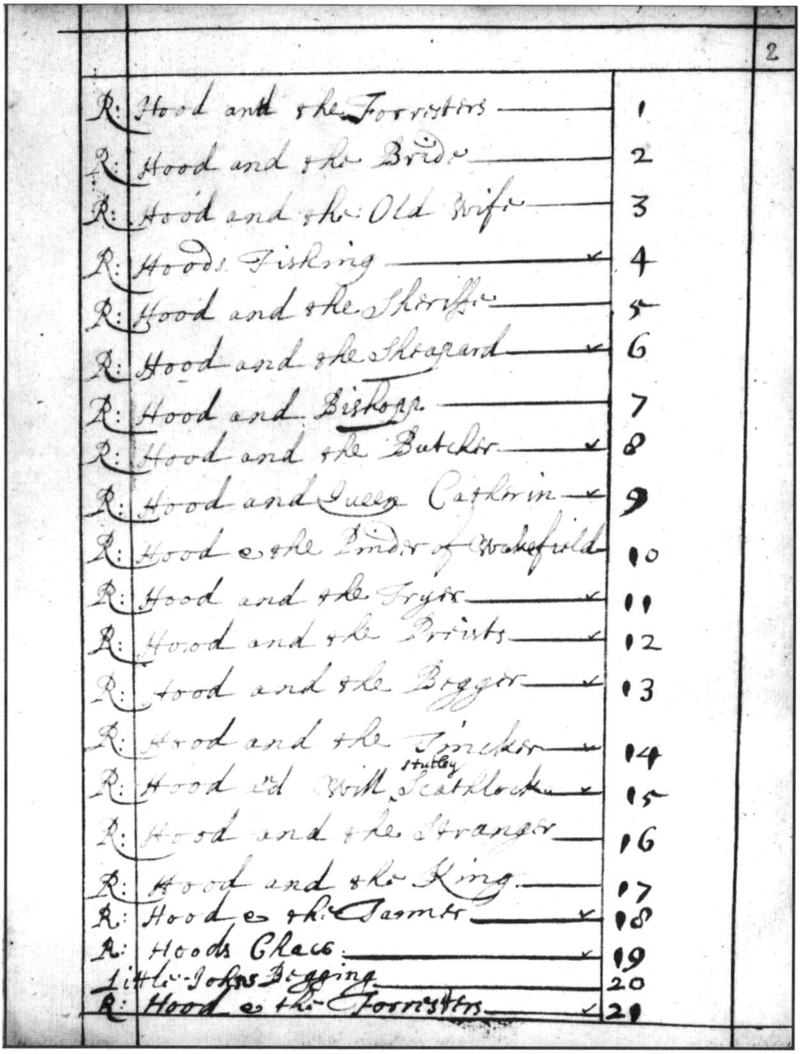
2

R: Hood and the Forresters — 1
R: Hood and the Bride — 2
R: Hood and the Old Wife — 3
R: Hoods Fishing — 4
R: Hood and the Sheriffe — 5
R: Hood and the Sheapard — 6
R: Hood and Bishopp — 7
R: Hood and the Butcher — 8
R: Hood and Queen Cathrin — 9
R: Hood & the Pindar of Wakefield — 10
R: Hood and the Fryer — 11
R: Hood and the Preists — 12
R: Hood and the Begger — 13
R: Hood and the Tincker — 14
R: Hood and Will Scatlock (Stutley) — 15
R: Hood and the Stranger — 16
R: Hood and the King — 17
R: Hood & the Farmer — 18
R: Hoods Chace — 19
Little Johns Begging — 20
R: Hood & the Forresters — 21

FIG. 5. Contents page in the "Forresters" manuscript, c. 1670. *By permission of the British Library, Additional Ms. 71158.*

And then they brought him through the wood,
And set him on his dapple-grey,
And gave the tail within his hand,
And bade him for Robin pray.[51]

From the Bishop of Hereford they merely take money, and Little John does the same with three false pilgrims in "Little John's Begging": the impostors pretend to be lame from their labors in the service of religion, but actually carry a lot of money and prove to be able to run fast when Little John "heals" them with some lusty blows—and takes the £603 they carry.

A daring rescue, like that of the knight in the *Gest* or of Little John in "Robin Hood and Guy of Gisborne," appears in the very popular ballad best called "Robin Hood Rescues Three Young Men":[52] a widow laments that her sons have been seized for breach of the forest laws, and will be hanged by the sheriff. Robin goes to town (usually Nottingham in the many versions that survive), changes clothes with an old man, and offers himself to the sheriff as executioner—a familiar kind of infiltration. On the scaffold, he blows his horn, his men arrive, and the rescue is made. The outlaws are in unforgiving mood:

> They took the gallows from the slack [town common],
> They set it in the glen,
> They hangd the proud sheriff on that,
> Released their own three men.[53]

A radically different version of Robin's boldness appears in the ballad called in the broadsides "The Noble Fisherman" or "Robin Hood's Preferment" but best titled, as in the Forresters manuscript, "Robin Hood's Fishing." Robin declares himself tired of the forest and interested in a change. As fishermen earn more money than outlaws, he goes to Whitby, on the northeast coast, and takes to sea. He catches no fish, however, and the men revile him. But when a French ship tries to capture the boat, Robin shoots down the steersman and his replacement, then leaps aboard with a sword and takes the vessel as a prize. The change of profession may well indicate that this is a later story, as may the sense of charity with which Robin finally divides his prize money, but the ballad is not as strange as it has seemed to many. Child thought it "may strike us as infantile,"[54] and Dobson and Taylor found it "a bizarre metamorphosis,"[55] but in the past soldiers routinely fought on shipboard as there were no big guns to sink the enemy. Both of the famous earlier outlaws who may have influenced the Robin Hood story, Fulk Fitz Warren and Eustace of Boulogne (especially the latter), fought at sea as well as in forests.[56]

Life as a nautical archer is certainly an extension, if perhaps a bizarre one, of Robin's career, but the context of two seventeenth-century archery ballads is much more familiar. "Robin Hood and the Golden Arrow" retells the story of the sheriff's tournament in the *Gest* with a simpler conclusion: instead of an ambush and bitter fighting, this ends with the outlaws back in camp, having been successful. But they suddenly realize that because they were in disguise, the sheriff will not know who won and, in their view, will not be sufficiently humiliated. So they fire an arrow into Nottingham Castle to tell him of their honor and his shame, a strangely anticlimactic ending that suggests a rather less bold Robin than before. In "Robin Hood and Queen Katherine" he is well-known as the finest archer, though the fact that they win the tournament at court, shooting for the queen against the king's party, makes this ballad something of a social rise (or perhaps a comedown) for the toughly independent outlaw of the early ballads.

Consistent as these broadsides more or less are with the early figure, another set of seventeenth-century ballads seem quite different in form; these ballads are basically "prequels," telling how the group of outlaws came together. The most striking of these both in theme and level of violence is "Robin Hood's Progress to Nottingham," which gives an account of how Robin came to be an outlaw in the first place. As a "tall young man"[57] ("tall" means big and strong, rather than high), Robin is on his way to Nottingham when he meets fifteen foresters. He tells them he is going to a shooting match, and they are scornful of "a boy so young." So Robin bets one of them twenty marks he can hit a deer at "a hundred rod," more than five hundred yards away. They accept the bet and he kills the deer, but they refuse to pay him and threaten to beat him. So:

> Robin Hood he took up his noble bow
> And his arrows all amain [strongly]
> And Robin Hood laughd, and begun to smile
> As hee went over the plain.
>
> (43–46)

Robin shoots at his opponent to stop him in his tracks, and taunts him:

"You said I was no archer," said Robin Hood
"But say so now again."

(55–56)

With this mocking heroic laughter he shoots dead fourteen of the foresters, leaving alive the one "that did this quarrel first begin" (51). Then, without fuss, "he sent another arrow / That split his head in twain" (57–58). The people of Nottingham rush out, trying to arrest Robin; he does not kill them, but "Some lost legs, and some lost arms / And some did lose their blood" (67–68). Robin escapes to the "merry green wood"—apparently for the first time as an outlaw.

Fiercer than any of the early ballads, even "Robin Hood and Guy of Gisborne," this has a bloodthirsty relish that in tone links it with the violent but sometimes heroic deeds of criminals reported in various versions of the eighteenth-century *Newgate Calendar,* where Robin and other highwaymen often appeared. This ballad survives from the early seventeenth century and is very popular: it frequently begins the garlands, as if to explain his outlaw status. The story was clearly known in the sixteenth century, as it is referred to in the prose "Sloane" life of Robin Hood written in manuscript form in about 1600. But there is no suggestion that this savage ballad is ancient. Rather, it testifies to the urge to explain how Robin became an outlaw—a similar story is told of William Wallace—and indicates how popular the bold image of Robin was well after he had become an aristocrat in other contexts.

Other "prequel" ballads tell how particular outlaws joined the group, and these have long remained popular, appearing in modern film and television versions. The best known and most faithfully preserved to the present is "Robin Hood and Little John," telling the story of how they meet on a bridge and fight; Robin loses, and then they become firm friends. The ballad survives from the 1680s, but a ballad with this title was registered in 1624 and is probably the same one. In fact, the ballad may well be even older, and might have provided part of the action for the play with this name that was recorded in 1594 but has not survived in print.

Not much earlier in survival, but clearly medieval in some sense is the Friar Tuck story, called in its earliest version "Robin Hood and the Curtal Friar." Friars were religious men devoted to wandering the country, preaching and spreading the Christian word. They were, as Chaucer and Langland tell us, famously corrupt—but they were also in contact with the people, not rich and powerful like monks, so it is not surprising that this religious man is a member of the outlaw band. This ballad presents the fighting friar of the early plays (see pp. 11 and 32–33). "Curtal" means wearing a short, or curtailed, gown, easy to walk in, and this is also the meaning of "Tuck." It has nothing to do with the modern British and Australian word "tuck" or "tucker," meaning food, as many think because of the modern friar's greediness, popularized by Sir Walter Scott in *Ivanhoe*.

As in "Robin Hood and the Potter" an outlaw—Will, in this case—has heard of a good fighter, and Robin is set up to meet him. He and the friar encounter at a river, and Robin gets wet again, as in the exchange with Little John, but this time through their contest in carrying each other across. That is where the film version ends, with friendship and food. In the ballad (as in the play of c. 1560), however, a major fight occurs between the outlaw band and the friar and now his fierce hunting dogs, who answer the friar's whistle as Robin's men do his horn. Finally they declare a truce and the friar joins the band, so shaping an elaborated version of the "Robin meets his match" pattern. It is a powerful ballad, with a somewhat magical feeling, through the ritualistic tone of the ford-crossing and the fighting animals. These mythic traces, in addition to the compelling image of a fighting churchman, may have perpetuated the popularity of this story, right to the present.

Other ballads deal in somewhat different ways with how the band was increased. Two seventeenth-century broadsides tell how Will Scarlet and Maid Marian joined Robin's band, but both of them depend, in different ways, on the concept of Robin as a distressed gentleman (see pp. 73–75 and 78–80). Other ballads indicate how Robin forms friendships or alliances with people who do not join his band, or who may be occasional members. In these simple "Robin meets his match" ballads he is normally on his own, in the forest or on a road, and meets a stranger. They fight, and Robin does not win; he usually calls it a draw, but sometimes loses. But he takes this well, and the two become friends, even to the extent of the stranger joining the band.

This seems to be the only way that people can join Robin's band; it is both a statement of the leader's own limitations and a process of initiation. It proves, as with John and Robin in the earlier ballads, that a kind of equality is the basis of the band's coherence.

An early example is "Robin Hood and the Pinder of Wakefield." Robin, John, and Will are often together, and popular songs celebrated this trio;[58] here they pass through a cornfield outside Wakefield, in Yorkshire. The pinder, whose job is to protect the crops by rounding up stray animals and warning off trespassers—he is a small-scale sheriff— appears and threatens them. They fight, three against one, and the pinder holds his own. Robin stops the fight, praises the pinder, and says:

> "O wilt thou forsake the pinder his craft
> And go to the greenwood with me?
> Thou shalt have a livery twice in the year;
> One green, the other brown."[59]

The lack of rhyme probably indicates some antiquity—this is certainly a sixteenth-century ballad. As elsewhere, Robin's band is conceived of like a trade or craft guild, with liveries (that is, uniforms), but here they are natural: like the leaves they will turn green and brown at different times of the year. The pinder says his response depends on his master's treatment of him; if he treats him badly:

> "I'le take my benbowe [bent bow] in my hand
> And come to the grenwode to thee."
>
> (49–50)

The pinder, like the friar, is a figure with a separate tradition, with his own "Life" surviving from 1632, and here he is accreted, as folklorists say, to the Robin Hood tradition. The reverse happens in the play of about 1592, *George a Greene* (see pp. 49–51), in which Robin becomes something like a second in command or even stooge for the pinder, known there as George a Greene.

Robin fights many similar "meets his match" battles in separate ballads—with a tanner, a tinker, a shepherd, a ranger, a beggar. Perhaps because of their simplicity, these ballads were all highly popular, appearing in garlands right up to the nineteenth century, and they went, often via the garland format, into the children's prose narratives of the mid to late nineteenth century. Howard Pyle, a young American artist, used them as a basis for his own splendid illustrations for an influential 1883 version. The "Robin meets his match" motif has remained popular to the present. Like the car chase in modern films, physical drama seems a central part of the Robin Hood tradition, a marker of his boldness and his capacity, whether in fight or feast, to operate on the same level as the ordinary people who made him their hero. Arguing with his colleagues, defeating the sheriff, rebuking the monks, facing up to the king, defending natural values—all with a lively wit and a rigorous sense of right—the early bold Robin Hood is a man and a myth of powerful and widespread appeal across a wide range of popular cultural forms.

The tradition has, to the present day, not forgotten that figure, and at times he survives almost unchanged. But other elements in the hero's mythic biography overlap with the bold yeoman and sometimes obscure his simple, blunt, lively, ancient value. The first of these is the gentrified figure of Robert, Earl of Huntington.

CHAPTER II

Robert, Earl of Huntingdon

Toward a Lord

Bold Robin Hood of the early ballads and plays had no origin. He stood in the greenwood, discovered as an outlaw; there was never any interest in how that had happened, what else he had done, or what he might become again if his outlawry was lifted. Robin Hood the distressed gentleman is different: he has fallen from aristocratic grace, and that fall is explained or even demonstrated. He aspires to return to noble rank, and that is the usual end of the story. In the *Gest* the yeoman Robin comes to hate the court to which the king has invited him, and he returns to his apparently natural state as outlaw in the forest, but in the gentrified texts his stay in the forest is temporary. Anthony Munday's *The Downfall of Robert, Earle of Huntington* (1598) expresses in its title the unnatural, fallen, and temporary nature of forest life for this new version of the hero.

Robin the distressed aristocrat is a creation of the sixteenth century, and the impact has survived to the present, when, with dubious names such as Sir Robin of Loxley, or Earl Huntingdon, the outlaw in the age of Hollywood usually has some noble lineage on display in his name. But the development of Munday's full-blown mistreated earl was not immediate or simple. Some elements of gentrification can be found in the *Gest*, but after initially presenting Robin as a rustic King Arthur, friendly to knights, the poem moves back into the familiar field of the bold yeoman. The first suggestion that the outlaw might be of originally elevated social status is implied by the Scottish historian John Major. A scholar on the international scale, teaching at Paris and publishing in Europe in Latin, in 1521 Major produced his *Historia Majoris Britanniae*, "The History of Great Britain"—though he would no doubt have also been aware that his title also meant "Major's History of Britain."

He speaks of

> those most famous robbers Robert Hood, an Englishman, and Little John, who lay in wait in the woods, but spoiled of their goods only those that were wealthy.[1]

The first statement seems like a translation of Wyntoun's "waythemen were commendit gud," but the second comment clearly gives them a moral standing as redistributors of money. Apparently with Bower's comment that they were "cutthroats" in mind, Major goes on:

> They took the life of no man, unless he either attacked them or offered resistance in defence of his property. Robert supported by his plundering one hundred bowmen, ready fighters every one, with whom four hundred of the strongest would not dare to engage in combat. (27)

Beginning with an exculpation of violence as self-defense (less than convincing, as they also killed those who defended themselves well), this goes on to define a new kind of Robin Hood, leader of a hundred men, not just one of a few forest robbers. Bower had thought of Robin with a band of men, but most deserted him in trouble; Major has in mind an effective war leader, the outlaw equivalent of a feudal lord. He redates the hero to the late twelfth century, for no clear reason, but with what was to be later, and to the present, great impact.

He goes on to note the hero's popularity, as did Wyntoun and Bower: "The feats of this Robert are told in song all over Britain" (27), but he seems more interested in continuing with his moral elevation of the outlaw hero:

He would allow no woman to suffer injustice, nor would he spoil the poor, but rather enriched them from the plunder taken from the abbots. The robberies of this man I condemn, but of all robbers he was the humanest and the chief. (27)

The first clause is reminiscent of King Arthur—serving and saving women was part of the oath of the Round Table—and the second is the earliest statement of the "rob the rich to give to the poor" motif. At the end of the *Gest* it was said he "dyde pore men moch god" (1824), and it would seem from this and the quasi-Arthurian touch that Major knew the *Gest*. But Robin here is a much nobler figure, and Major's Latin word for "chief" is *dux*—leader, general, or, as it became, "duke."

A massive tome, written in Latin, Major's history was not widely known—though it is clear that Robin Hood was of interest among the elevated before Major wrote. Edward Hall's chronicle, published in English in 1548, reports that in 1510 King Henry VIII, no less, played Robin:

His grace, therles of Essex, Wilshire, and other noble menne, to the nombre of twelve, came sodainly in a mornyng, into the Quenes Chambere, al appareled in shorte cotes, of Kentishe Kendal, with hodes on their heddes and hosen of the same, every one of them, his bowes and arowes, and a sword and a bucklar, like out lawes, or Robyn Hodes men, whereof the Quene, the Ladies, and al other there, were abashed aswell for the straunge sight, and also for their sodain commyng, and after certain daunces and pastime made, thei departed.[2]

If a king could play a Robin Hood game, then the outlaw's social rise was a distinct possibility. Someone who did read Major carefully—in fact repeated much of what he said—was the English-language chronicler Richard Grafton. In his *Chronicle at Large* (1569), Grafton summarized Major's account and then struck out on his own, claiming the authority of an "olde and auncient Pamphlet"— just what a source-conscious Renaissance historian would like to have, or invent. This, Grafton says, gave two origins for Robin's nobility: one was that he "discended of a noble parentage"; the other, that he "beyng of a base stocke and lineage, was for his manhoode and chivalry advaunced to the noble dignite of an Erle."[3]

Both accounts make Robin noble. The doubt is whether birth or achievements lay behind his status—a recognition, even explanation, of the now double social character of the hero, both lord and yeoman. Having offered an account of how Robin became noble, Grafton, unlike Major, gives a reason for the fall of this earl of uncertain origin:

> He so prodigally exceeded in charge and expences, that he fell into great debt, by reason wherof, so many sutes and actions were commenced against him, whereunto he answered not, that by order of lawe he was outlawed. (28)

Right through to modern fiction, overspending has been a characteristic but inherently tolerable vice of a young nobleman. It suggests generosity, spirit, a lack of mean-minded penny-counting; it explains being outlawed in a way at least semi-acceptable. But Grafton continues about the outlaw's aggressiveness:

> . . . and then for a lewde shift, as his last refuge, gathered together a companye of Roysters and Cutters, and practised robberyes and spoylyng of the kynges subjects, and occupied and frequented the Forestes or wilde Countries. (28)

Earl though he may be, as an outlaw he is a criminal; he has the substantial company of men envisaged by Major, and he is by no means a passive exile in the forest. The idea of Robin's earldom does not obscure the notion of a violent and troublesome outlaw. As with Robin's enigmatic social origins, Grafton offers a double figure, gentlemanly and violent at the same time.

Grafton's Robin Hood finally gains heroic status in tragedy: he is betrayed to death (using the *Gest* as a source). That seems to resolve the conflict of gentlemanly and social bandit behavior in this figure who is being reclaimed, with some difficulty, for respectable society from his violent yeoman status in the earlier texts. From Major's suggestions of moral and social nobility in the outlaw, Grafton has developed a fairly full picture of a distressed gentleman. This was to have great influence, though it was not the only view. The historian Raphael Holinshed, so influential on Shakespeare, merely gives in his *History of Scotland* a brief summary of what Wyntoun and Bower had to say (through his immediate source Hector Boece, another Scot), without anything as interesting as Bower's example or any element of gentrification. He, like Boece, accepts Bower's dating of the outlaw to the time of Simon de Montfort, about 1263:

> In these daies (as the translator of Hector Boece hath written) that notable and most famous outlaw Robin Hood lived, with his fellow little John, of whom are manie fables and merie jests devised and soong amongst the vulgar people. But Iohn Major writeth that they lived (as he dooth gesse) in the daies of King Richard the first king of English 1198.[4]

Grafton's innovative account became especially widely known through his rival as a chronicler, archivist, and collector of historical and legendary data, John Stow. Among his many works was the *Annales of England* (1592), which mentions Robin Hood and Little John as "renowmed theeves" who were known for "dispoyling and robbing the goods of the rich" and recognizes Grafton's sense of their violence but attempts to justify it: "They killed none but such as would invade them, or by resistance for their owne defence." He also amplifies the notion of Robin's moral standing:

> Hee suffered no woman to bee oppressed, violated, or otherwise molested: poore men's goodes hee spared, abundantly releeving them with that, which by thefte hee gote from Abbeyes and the houses of riche Carles.[5]

Sharing as he does Major's date—he gives the year as 1189—Stow concludes by quoting Major's view that Robin was a "Prince" and "the most gentle Theefe."

Stow's account was to inspire the most important gentrification of Robin Hood, by the dramatist Anthony Munday. But just as the historians and chroniclers veered about, seeking to ennoble the hard-handed outlaw, some late sixteenth-century playwrights made several unsuccessful attempts to incorporate into their plays the energy of bold Robin Hood in a respectable and unalarming way.

Dramatizing Gentrification

Seven plays dealing to a greater or lesser degree with Robin Hood appeared on the London stage around the end of the sixteenth century. Two have been lost: *Robin Hood and Little John* was entered as a publication in the Stationers' Register in 1594 and *Robin Hood's Pennorths* in 1600–1601. They may well have been written and produced earlier; plays were usually published some time, even years, after they had been performed. Both titles relate to ballads, and are presumably extended versions of ballad-related plays such as the two printed by William Copland at the end of his c. 1560 edition of the *Gest*. Perhaps *Robin Hood and Little John* started with the fight on the bridge, beloved of modern cinema (though that ballad only survives from nearly a century later). The title of the other play suggests the action of "Robin Hood and the Potter" in which the hero sells his pots so cheaply that his "pennyworths" have special value. That play, however, might well have been based on the "Robin Hood and the Butcher" version of that story, much better known at the time, as is indicated by the number of surviving broadsides.[6] But barring a lucky discovery, we will never know what was in those plays; it is perhaps no accident that the two plays with titles that sound ballad-related— that is, inherently popular—are the two that did not survive. Those that did are in some way gentrified and in one way or another control the vigor of the social bandit to make his role more respectable.

George a Greene is a play of only 1381 lines and is difficult to date exactly; not printed until 1599, it was played as early as 1588–89. It has been attributed to Richard Greene, but the simplicity of the style makes that seem uncertain, even unlikely.[7] The play honors the bold pinder of Wakefield, named George, who leads his townspeople in resisting the rebellion of the Earl of Kendall against King Edward (unnumbered, as in the *Gest*). Robin Hood plays a secondary role: he is not mentioned until line 944, and it is Marian, angry because the fame of George and his love Bettris have outstripped that of Robin and herself, who insists he go to Wakefield to deal with this rival. So Robin, Scarlet, and Much, plus Marian (Little John is not in the play), head off in a reenactment of the ballad "Robin Hood and the Pinder of Wakefield," but they are soon tamed by the pinder and become his supporters. George takes

Robin with him on a tour of the North, where George and the king—not Robin—defeat the rebellious shoemakers of Bradford. George then, with lordly generosity, invites the outlaw to dine:

> Here, Robin, sit thou here; for thou art the best man
> At the boord this day.[8]

This is all in honor of George a Greene and Wakefield; yet the play also deals in a displaced way with the twin themes of nobility and the resistance to authority characteristic of Robin Hood the bold yeoman. The Earl of Kendall, through his very name, must be associated with the outlaw who wears Kendall green as often as green cloth from Lincoln. The earl has raised rebellion in the North, as did the historical rebel Robin of Redesdale in Yorkshire in 1469; he will, he claims, "relieve the poore" (18), an idea by this time associated with the gentrified Robin Hood. The earl also is strongly supported by the king of Scotland, an area much involved with Robin Hood himself in the chronicles and general literary references, and which also staged Robin Hood processions and play-games.[9] This Northern resistance of a boldly incursive kind is defeated by a Northern loyalist in George. But the resemblance between the earl's rising and the old yeoman's antiauthoritarianism is much more specific than that—in a deliberate reworking of "Robin Hood and the Pinder of Wakefield," Lord Kendall and two associates walk through a cornfield into Wakefield and are stopped and defeated by the pinder.

Robin's mythic biography has, it appears, split in two in this play: the idea of a rebellious earl, clearly stated in Grafton, has been displaced onto a ghostly earl in green, to be defeated by the trusty, patriotic townsman George. And the bold Robin Hood of the ballads is also brought under firm control: when they fight, George wins his battle against the first two outlaws, and Robin asks him to stop. Later on George insists on making Robin swear allegiance to the king and participate in attacking his enemies:

> Robin, here's a carouse to good King Edwardes selfe;
> And they that love him not, I would we had
> The basting of them a little.
>
> (1081–2)

The play appears to know the two contradictory aspects of Robin's developing personality, both bold yeoman and displaced earl, but handles them both with caution. Robin Hood here is neither fully gentrified nor really bold, without either the dissenting vigor of the ballads or the nobility yet to come.

Another play of the same period uses the traditional material, but again in a strikingly displaced way. George Peele's *Edward I* was performed in 1590–91 and published in 1593; here Robin appears as a character played by a character. Lluellen (correctly Llewelyn), the last independent prince of Wales, is hounded by the invading King Edward I; Shapiro notes that Peele is, on the evidence of this play, both "imperialist and xenophobic."[10] Lluellen decides for entertainment to play a Robin Hood game, with his cousin Rice (Rhys) as Little John, his lover Nel (or Eleanor) as Marian, and "Frier David" as Tuck. The impetus is clearly a traditional play-game, but, just as this is a literary play, so the tradition is given a printed source. Lluellen says:

> Weele get the next daie from Brecknocke the booke of Robin Hood, the Frier he shal instruct us in his cause and weele even here fair and well, since the king hath put us in the discarding cardes . . . and wander like irregulers up and down the wildernesse, ile be master of misrule, ile be Robin Hood.[11]

Peele imposes the game of Robin Hood on a definitely dangerous rebel as part of his theatrical and also political emasculation, but the game grows dramatically within the play in scenes 7 and 8. King Edward comes to visit (like his unnumbered namesake in the *Gest*) and then, with his supporter Mortimer (disguised as a potter, showing more knowledge of the early ballads), fights a "meets his match" duel with Robin and Little John—that is, the Prince of Wales and his cousin. This scene ends inconclusively: the king wins, Mortimer loses, and the characters troop off the stage to end the Robin Hood play-game. But the identification of Lluellen and the outlaw is not forgotten: he is later called "our thrise renowmed Lluellen Prince of Wales and Robin Hood of the great mountain" (1843–44), and references to him as Robin recur through the rest of the play. This indicates that, as in *George a Greene*, a sense of dangerous rebellion about the figure justifies his displacement and repression.

In these two plays the idea that Robin Hood might be noble is apparently known but kept at a distance: the equal knowledge that he has antiauthoritarian, even rebellious, possibilities is also encoded in the text, in order to be controlled. The popularity of Robin Hood, in games, ballads, proverbs, and place-names, is no doubt why these writers are eager to incorporate his vigor into their plays. But the plays also include a disturbing, ill-fitting, disruptive element about the hero, part-lord and part-yeoman, that is not resolved.

These plays are marked with the strain that incited sixteenth-century society—by no means only religiously purist Catholics or Puritans—to repress Robin Hood activities. In 1528 the Lord Warden of the Cinque Ports banned Robin Hood games in Kent and Sussex towns under his control; in 1545 Bishop Garner is recorded as having banned Robin Hood plays and other secular entertainment. The Scottish Parliament banned Robin Hood games in 1555; action was taken against Robin Hood activities in Edinburgh in 1561 and in 1579; Robin Hood processions were banned in Aberdeen in 1575.[12] David Wiles sums up: "Elizabethan authorities, unlike their medieval predecessors, were determined to prevent any institutional expression of egalitarian sentiment."[13]

Yet however much increasingly centralized and increasingly repressive powers sought to contain a lively antiauthoritarian figure such as Robin Hood, he remained popular on a wide basis in ballads and songs.[14] Dramatists eager for popular themes in the play-hungry 1590s were not likely to avoid such rich material completely in spite of the difficulty of handling it without offense to the authorities. Such conflicts could be resolved by reshaping the myth: a new treatment created a compromise between the new nobility and the outlaw challenge of the now multiform hero, and so introduced a highly influential element to his mythic biography.

The Noble Earl on Stage

Anthony Munday was a versatile writer, producing prose as well as verse drama, and was involved on behalf of the government as an informer, or probably a spy, against Catholics. Like a number of writers and intellectuals of the period, he was also a close acquaintance of John Stow, and it is probable that his two plays on Robin Hood, *The Downfall of Robert, Earle of Huntington* and *The Death of Robert, Earle of Huntington*, take their immediate origin from Stow's compilation of the remarks by Major and Grafton in his *Annales of England* (1592), together with other elements.[15] The records indicate that Henry Chettle played some part in the writing of the second play, and perhaps the reworking of the first, but Munday was the essential creator of this important new stage in the outlaw biography.[16] He developed the idea that Robin was a noble exile in the time of King Richard I and Prince John and provided the narrative to make this a full-length story, gathering material from a range of sources. Crucially, he excluded any sense of social challenge through outlawry, where Peele and the author of *George a Greene* had referred in a distanced way to the awkward combination of nobility and a bold yeoman.

Inspired by Major's redating of the hero to the end of the twelfth century, this relocation of Robin Hood's resistance to authority to the time of bad Prince John has the remarkable effect of reversing his political tendency. As a bold yeoman, fighting fiercely against the sheriff and the abbeys, the early Robin Hood is a dangerous social bandit: although his ultimate loyalty to the king and the Virgin Mary gives him an overarching respect for order, he still expresses a good deal of rebellious feeling. But when, as in Munday, his enemies are only the corrupt and the dishonest, the enemies of an loyal lord, he is nothing less than an upholder of true order, aristocratic, religious, and royal. What were for some the disconcertingly radical elements in the Robin Hood tradition were substantially eased by this major relocation of the hero in time, class, and moral authority.

Munday's Robin is no longer opposed to local power and its injustices. His enemies are the Prior of York and Sir Doncaster; the names come from the *Gest*, but now the prior is Earl Robert's malicious uncle, and Sir Doncaster is a priest in the *Downfall* and a knight in the *Death* (one of the inconsistencies in the somewhat underfinished plays). A third enemy is Warman, Earl Robert's treacherous steward, whom the prior rewards for his treason by making him sheriff of Nottingham. The villainous forces that drive Robin into exile are not oppressive agents of the law, but people personally treacherous to the hero; this is an individualized drama for the landed gentry, not a yeoman's struggle for popular liberty.

Even evil forces are personalized, depoliticized. Prince John is Robin's enemy, but only because he loves Marian, or Matilda as she is known before she enters the forest. John is hot-tempered, killing a man needlessly early on; he does try to seize his brother's throne, but the play makes Richard's regent, the Bishop of Ely, a worse villain. John himself eventually chooses exile when his brother's army returns from crusade. He wanders into the forest, dressed in green, taking the name "Woodnet." This is probably a deliberately rustic pastoral name: "woodnit" or "woodnet" is recorded in the *English Dialect Dictionary* as a southwestern version of "woodnut," the hazel. In the second play, John becomes a worse but still personalized villain; after Robin dies in the first act, as prince and then king he lustfully pursues Matilda throughout the play, to her eventual death by suicide.

But if Robin's opposition to evil is personal, not political, that does not mean the play is without social meaning. Rather than a heartwarming series of Robin's outlaw adventures, the action of the *Downfall* is filled with lengthy scenes in which aristocrats and their royal leaders battle for control of England. John and his barons fight against Ely the regent, then against the returning Richard and his army. Some confusions occur—the Earl of Leicester initially appears with John and then returns from crusade with Richard—and there are some outlaw interrelations—Prince John is furious with Baron Fitzwater, Matilda's father, for not supporting him, and drives him too into the forest, where they eventually meet again as exiles. Much of the play reads like a rehash of Shakespeare's *King John* (completed in the 1590s, possibly as recently as 1596). The gentrification of Robin Hood here causes the inclusion of a great deal of aristocratic business with little real impact by or on the hero, though he is eventually restored by Richard, and starts the second play at court.

In the absence of his bold yeoman persona, Robin is less than active and dramatic. The first scene is a feast at which Earl Robert learns he has been betrayed; instead of seizing his sword in bold style, he discusses matters with John and Marian, and then addresses his enemies more like a melancholic contemporary than a bold rebellious spirit:

You are a sort of fawning sycophants,
That while the sunshine of my greatnesse dur'd
Reveld out all day for your delights,
And now yee see the blacke night of my woe
Oreshade the beautie of my smiling good,
You to my griefe adde griefe, and are agreed
With that false Prior, to reprive my joyes
From execution of all happinesse.[17]

And so they leave for the forest; John, who has been demoted so-cially as Robin has ascended, goes off to pack his bags like a faithful steward.

In the forest Robin has a limited role to play as an active outlaw. The only ballad used to any extent is "Robin Hood Rescuing Three Young Men": news comes that Warman, Robin's faithless steward and now Sheriff of Nottingham, is to hang Scarlet and Scathlock, the sons of Widow Scarlet. Robin and his men rescue them as in the ballad: Robin, dressed "like an old man" (950), offers to execute them be-cause they killed his son. But he himself is not physically involved; he simply blows his horn, and the other outlaws arrive to effect a rescue. The friar, absent in the ballad version, is comically prominent when he, "making as if he helpt the Sheriffe, knockes downe his men, cry-ing 'Keepe the kings peace'" (990–91).

Earl Robert is joined by Scathlock and Scarlet (who have for seven years been outlaws in Barnsdale), but there are no more en-counters with the law, just the establishment of a forest code called the Articles of Sherwood, an elaborate version of Robin's commands to John in the beginning of the *Gest*. The foresters consent to a num-ber of stipulations. They agree to call Earl Robert "Robin" and Lady Matilda "Maid Marian." Robin and Marian swear to be chaste and "by true labour, lustfull thoughts expell" (1343). They all agree that passersby shall feast with Robin (no mention is made of robbing them to pay for it). Then the Articles detail the moralizations of the outlaw trade that are central to gentrification, climaxed by:

Lit. John Fiftly, you never shall the poore man wrong,
       Nor spare a priest, a usurer or a clarke.
Much Nor a faire wench, meete we her in the darke.

Lit. John Lastly, you shall defend with all your power,
        Maids, widows, orphants, and distressed men.
All All these wee vowe to keepe, as we are men.

(1354–59)

Lost is the class edge of the *Gest*, in which only those knights and squires who would be friendly were to be helped, and in which the sheriff was to be carefully observed. The emphasis here is on charity, that euphemizing instrument of hierarchy, and there is no indication where the oppressions that afflict the wretched might come from. Only priests, usurers, and clerks (the last meaning lawyers) are identified as the enemy, an encouraging analysis for the wealthy landowners who supported the players and who were usually living in mansions in the country that before the Reformation had belonged to the conveniently scapegoated Catholic clergy. (Munday himself was writing for a troupe called "The Admiral's Men.") Under such auspices, the agenda for outlaws was heartwarming but vague, with none of the ballads' toughness in verse or action—though Much's remark may reflect that aggression, suggesting that the "faire wench" will not be "spared" in a decidedly sexist sense. But such brusque elements are few, and apart from the rescue of the widow's sons we do not actually see Earl Robert or his men in any bandit-like action. It is true that Prince John says that:

All the wilds
Are full of outlawes that in Kendall greene
Followe the outlawed Earle of Huntingdon

(2073–74)

but this action does not occur in the play, and it sounds more like *George a Greene's* image of noble rebellion than the pastoral picnicking of Munday's Robin Hood.

Immediately after the charitable agenda is sworn—the attenuated remains of the bold yeoman tradition—Robin dedicates himself to a life of pastoral pleasure: true gentlemanly behavior is what the play essentially realizes. First he celebrates hunting:

Then wend ye to the Grenewod merrily,
And let the light roes bootless from yee runne

Marian and I, as soveraignes of your toyles,
Will wait, within our bower, your bent bowes spoiles.

(1360–63)

The Robin of the *Gest* waited alone while the other outlaws went hunting wealthy travelers—something of a rise in his position from the early ballads. Now he is elevated further to a "soveraigne," waiting with his queen to be provided with the outcome of others' efforts. This noble pastoral position, developed from the "bower" of the play-game, is celebrated in elaborate pastoral poetry, as Robin interprets their forest surroundings to Marian as a natural court, full of ecological splendor:

For the soul-ravishing delicious sound
Of instrumental musique, we have found
The winged quiristers, with divers notes,
Sent from their quaint recording prettie throats,
On every braunch that compasseth our bower,
Without commaund, contenting us each hower.
For Arras hangings, and rich Tapestrie,
We have sweete natures best imbrothery.
For thy steele glasse, wherin thou wontst to looke,
Thy christiall eyes, gaze in a christiall brooke.
At court, a flower or two did decke thy head:
Now with whole garlands is it circled.
For what in wealth we had, we have in flowers,
And what wee loose in halles, we finde in bowers.

(1368–81)

The early ballads celebrated no less vividly, if more briefly, the richness of summer in terms of birdsong, leaves, and flowers, and here the same theme is celebrated in elevated language. But pastoral is always only a visit—Marie Antoinette merely played at dairymaid—and here there is a constant reminder that the forest provides just a charming reflex of the cultural realities of the court. This is, the poetry reminds us, Robin enjoying his "downfall." It is not, as it will often be in the nineteenth century, a statement that life *au naturel* is actually much better than the harassments of ordinary urban society. Just as the play does not give an active role to Robin himself—no doubt because his bold yeoman activities would seem too rebellious—so the values of the forest world are also glimpsed at a safe distance.

Munday both recognizes and reduces the bold actions of the yeoman outlaw, and in the same way he represents and also sidelines the comic trickster tradition. With some imagination, he makes the creator of the play the poet Skelton, who was known in the period both as a comedian, initiator of many jokes and pranks, and also as tutor to the young Henry VIII and author of some highly learned poems. A preface shows that Skelton has written and directed the play—he explains this at the beginning to Sir John Eltham, a bureaucrat at Henry's court who goes on to play Little John; Skelton himself is the friar. That Munday is using Skelton as a way of controlling his material is suggested when he introduces the hero to the audience as "oure Earle Robert, or your Robin Hoode" (88). This becomes clear in a return to the frame story late in the play when Sir John Eltham complains at the lack of familiar material:

> Me thinks I see no jeasts of Robin Hoode,
> No merry morices of Frier Tuck
> No pleasant skippings up and downe the wodde
>
> (2210–12)

and Skelton replies that he has royal authority for this version:

> His Majestie himselfe survaid the plat
> And bad me boldly write it, it was good
>
> (2219–20)

The action and style of the text consistently reveal the way in which Munday, drawing leads from others, has reworked the nature of the tradition and the hero in this crucial and very influential new gentrified stage in the mythic biography of Robin Hood.

A Lady for a Lord

Munday's Robin does not, as in the *Gest*, sit alone as a sovereign in a bower. In this play, for the first time, there is an extended role for Marian, and any analysis of the hero's mythic biography must from now on usually include an assessment of his partner and her significance. As *George a Greene* and *Edward I* make clear, by this time Robin was assumed to have a female partner and her name is Marian. Like much else, she derives from the play-game tradition. As early as 1509 her name is mentioned in the Kingston Robin Hood play-game,[18] and in at least some contexts she, Robin, John, and the friar seem to form a basic quartet for a dance—perhaps a village parallel for those pillars of the national state, queen and king, general and bishop. Where her name came from before that is hard to say, but the likeliest suggestion is that once Robin has, for the purposes of a dance or procession, a female companion, then the name Marian falls into place because of the well-known medieval French *pastourelle* songs about the two lovers Robin and Marion. Helen Cooper notes that they "appear in dozens of lyrics from the early thirteenth century onwards."[19]

Whatever her origin, the first time a role of substance for a lady emerges in the outlaw myth is when its hero has become a lord, and so needs a lady, both as part of his gracious style of living and to provide the continuation of his landed line. In undertaking a major play about the gentrified hero, Munday apparently realized that he needed a countess for his earl; he used the name Marian from the popular tradition for that role. In the first part of the play she is the daughter of Lord Lacy; his brother, her uncle, is the man Prince John kills early on. But at line 781 she enters as Matilda and is now the daughter of Baron Fitzwater, who remains faithful to King Richard and so is exiled to the forest by Prince John (the role that Robin himself is to adopt in many later versions). It appears that Munday started off by making up Marian's role as he went along, but then acquired a useful source in Michael Drayton's poem *Matilda the Faire and Chaste Daughter of Lord R. Fitzwater*, which appeared in 1594. This is a tragic story of a beautiful young woman pursued by the vile desires of King John, eventually to her death, and it provides most of the material for the second play, the *Death*. It has of course nothing to do with Robin Hood, but is set in Munday's period, and before him Major's, with a shared villain, though Drayton's John is worse than Munday's starts off being. Neatly enough, Munday makes both Robert and Matilda change their names in the forest to Robin and Marian, and he apparently never went back to correct the early references to the non-exiled Marian.

But Marian's role is nothing more than Earl Robert's consort; she is not even, as often happens later, kidnapped or imprisoned, and has little of the assisting spirit that sometimes activates Marian in later versions. There is however, the first instance of a very striking feature that recurs: the false Marian. Prince John's love of Marian is not the only passion at the start of the play: Queen Eleanor, mother to John and Richard, is attracted to the Earl of Huntington and plans to disguise herself as Marian to elope with the hero. She presents the idea to Marian as female solidarity against John:

> Marian, thou shalt go with him clad in my attire,
> And for a shift, I'le put thy garments on,
> It is not mee, my sonne John doth desire;
> But Marian it is thee he doteth on.
>
> (398–401)

Marian is not fooled and plans to warn Robin; the queen is very excited, and no doubt some vulgar stage business accompanied the line

> My roabe is loose, and it will soone be off
>
> (412)

but she is also vicious; if Robin refuses her then:

> Of treason capitall I will accuse him
> For traiterous forcing me out of the court,
> And guerdon his disdaine with guiltie death,
> That of a Princes love so lightly weighes.
>
> (426–29)

When they meet, Robin rejects the queen as

> . . . foule Marian, fair though thou be nam'd,
> For thy bewitching eyes have raised storms
> That have my name and noblesse ever sham'd
>
> (601–3)

and when she reveals herself he speaks directly:

> Hence, sorceresse, thy beauty I defie.
>
> (616)

It is striking that as a noble, beautiful, loved woman enters the outlaw tradition, the play realizes her opposite, a sexually aggressive, deceptive, dangerous harridan. The lovely woman, it seems, calls up her other, the witch—a concept used twice in the scene. This pattern of a witch-like "false Marian" recurs with surprising—depressing—regularity, right into modern films, and indicates a strong undercurrent of male gender anxiety in the tradition.

With Marian as his lady, Robin is both a lord and, in an undemonstrative way, a lover; he does not, however, survive to be husband and father. Most of the international heroes identified in the seminal study by Lord Raglan[20] had no heirs, and even when Robin has become a lord and regains his lands, his story goes no further. In Munday's *Death* (as in the *Gest* and Grafton), he dies at the hands of his enemies, but here it is in a sonorous and rather ill-managed fashion. The prior plans to poison the king; Robin, offstage, and for no explained reason, drinks the potion instead, and staggers onstage to die, but not before Sir Doncaster has a lengthy trial and punishment: aristocratic politics upstage Robin to the end. Having started like a muffed draft of the end of *Hamlet*, the death scene moves into pastoral elegy with a simple but theatrically effective dirge:

> Weepe, weepe, ye wod-men waile,
> Youre handes with sorrow wring:
> Your master Robin Hood lies deade,
> Therefore sigh as you sing.[21]

The end of the outlaw was the least influential aspect of the play, as few versions later included a death scene. But the rest of Munday's work has had a major impact on the tradition. The crucial thing about the double play is that it establishes a new narrative, realizing what has become a classic sequence for the gentrified outlaw: his banishment, his forest adventures, his encounter with the returned king, the outcome of the story—here tragic, but elsewhere happy. Modern Robin Hood texts often follow that structure, from children's retellings to Hollywood spectaculars, and Munday, this largely forgotten and somewhat clumsy playwright, should receive the credit for imagining a new biography for Robin Hood.

Munday also introduced the title Huntington, but where it came from is not clear. David Bevington has argued that the Elizabethan Puritan Earl was the source,[22] yet no connection seems

evident. Through Stow, Munday may have known that the title was
in the 1190s connected with Barnsdale, but it was the Rutland
Barnsdale, and the earls were members of the Scottish royal house.
Perhaps the reason for the name was simply the association with
hunting, a lordly sport that was being much more heavily stressed
in gentrification than before.[23] Whatever its origins, the name, like
the gentrified narrative structure outlined by Munday, has survived
the centuries.

The success of the Earl Robert plays is indicated partly by their
being restaged at court,[24] but especially by two dramatic responses
to them. One was *Looke About You*, subtitled "a plesaunt commod-
dye," but better described as a ludicrous disguise farce in an aristocratic context. In this Robin is merely a young aristocrat, never an
outlaw, who helps Richard I woo Lady Marian Faukenbridge; on
one occasion he appears cross-dressed, with the memorable stage direction: "Enter Robin Hood in the Lady Faukenbridge's gowne,
night attire on his head."[25] A mixture of medieval comedy of manners with clumsy farce, the play does nothing for Robin Hood's biography or the outlaw tradition, except to show how easy it is in
gentrification for the antiauthoritarian aspect of the hero to disappear altogether.

But he could be even more anonymous: while the Admiral's Men
were doing good business with Robin Hood plays, the Lord Cham-
berlain's men's star writer, William Shakespeare, responded with *As
You Like It*. The play is also about gentry exiled in the forest, but it is
consciously superior in many ways: these are continental aristocrats,
not simple English historical figures, and the play's cross-dressers are
involved in elegant romance, not nighttime farce. A deliberate, even
cheeky, reference to Robin Hood occurs in the first scene, when the
duke and his men are said to live in the forest "like Old Robin Hood
of England" (I.i.116). The source is *Rosalynde*, Thomas Lodge's up-
market Renaissance version of the robust fourteenth-century disinherited outlaw text *Gamelyn*, though Shakespeare apparently also
knew *Gamelyn* and had at least seen Munday's play.[26] The context
suggests that *As You Like It* is deliberately a non-Robin Hood play, a
negative response to the emergence of the theatrical and gentrified
version of the outlaw hero.

Lord Robert's Origin

From the vantage point of fully realized gentrification in Munday's work it is possible to speculate just where the new identity for the outlaw came from. Earl Robert is changed in many ways from Robin the bold yeoman, but the crucial innovation is Major's redating of the myth. By placing the outlaw in the 1190s he enables the hero's spirited resistance to become not a challenge to oppressive authority but a brave blow for true authority: the ennobled outlaw resists only the law of a bad ruler. Whatever history may say about Richard I's absenteeism and King John's shrewd management, the image held by Tudor historians from Major to Stow was that King John was a thorough wastrel; to locate an outlaw then was implicitly to justify his extralegal actions. But a model for such an idea already existed. Fulk Fitz Warren was a historical baron who did rebel against John and was outlawed as a result. His deeds have been preserved in an Anglo-Norman prose text of the early fourteenth century; an English version has been lost.[27] Major probably had this figure in mind as he reshaped Robin's biography in date, morals, and, implicitly, social status. It is possible that Langland's puzzling association of Robin Hood and Randolph, Earl of Chester (found in *Piers Plowman* and the Forresters manuscript, as well as a little-known song, "By Landsdale, mery Landsdale," published in 1609),[28] could link back to Fulk, as Randolph was a powerful figure who befriended him in his difficulties with King John.

It is also notable that two names of obscure origin in Munday's *Downfall* may derive from Fulk's story—Lacy, the first name for Marian's father, is an enemy of Fulk's patron, and Prince John's pastoral pseudonym Woodnet may be partly inspired by Baldwin de Hodenet, a friend of Fulk's. The English version of the original Anglo-Norman Fulk story existed in the sixteenth century: the antiquarian John Leland saw it and made some notes.[29] Munday, perhaps through John Stow, may well have known this poem and taken some ideas from it for his construction of a noble outlaw.

Fulk, like many outlaws, resembled Robin Hood in several ways, including using disguises, ambushing and robbing, and fighting at sea. These actions may have filtered into the general mythic development of the yeoman outlaw, but Fulk's story is less likely to have been widely known and influential in these detailed ways than the similar stories about William Wallace. Wyntoun located Robin Hood in the 1280s, the time of Wallace, and a number of Scottish writers see the two heroes as being similar.[30] But the links may be closer than analogy. The full poem about Wallace, composed about 1476, was available by 1488—when of the surviving texts only "Robin Hood and the Monk" had any chance of being complete.[31] The resemblance between Robin Hood and William Wallace is striking: both are provoked to outlawry by legal violence, both go disguised as a potter, both command substantial numbers of well-disciplined men. Wallace also married a woman called Matilda (as did Fulk; it was a common medieval noblewoman's name, though Wallace's wife had the unladylike nickname "Broadfoot"). There is also the matter of Robin Hood's following: Major, Grafton, a number of the later ballads, and, even in one reference, Munday all envisage Robin Hood as the leader of a significant band, an outlaw of substance on the national scene, just like Wallace. In the transition from small-time yeoman defender of local rights to major threat to national law and order, Robin appears to be in part remodeled in the form of Wallace. In Scotland, especially Edinburgh, around the year 1500 a clear connection was made between these heroes, and a more lordly, warlike version of Robin Hood may have been exported back to England.[32]

If Wallace suggested the idea of a substantial outlaw, and provided—or at least shared—much of the detailed activities, and Fulk provided the date and the usually happy outcome, these were no more than fragmentary inputs until Munday wielded his influence. In an enduringly influential act, Munday redesigned Robin Hood's biography as earl, exile, nature-admiring gentleman, innate leader of a large band of social inferiors, and practicer of noble charities. Through his many virtues but especially his fidelity to established authority, the hero earns his reinstatement to the aristocracy. That pattern has resounded through modern Robin Hood culture, but it was by no means the only form of gentrification in the Renaissance. In fact, it did not gain real authority until it was transmitted in 1795 by Joseph Ritson, the hero-reconstructing Munday of his day. In

Munday's own time, although his voice was strong, it was only one of many.

Pastoral Lordship

Working between the 1580s and the 1630s, William Warner, Michael Drayton, and Ben Jonson were all aware of the bold yeoman tradition and the new ideas of gentrification, but they mollified the outlaw's disruptive potential by associating him with topographic and pastoral themes, merging the outlaw hero into the landscape rather than the aristocracy. In his semi-mythical verse chronicle *Albions England,* first published in 1589 and frequently reprinted, Warner recognizes the older Robin Hood tradition when in book V "a simple Northerne man" talks about the old days of village feasts:

> At Paske [Easter] begun our Morrise, and ere Pentecost
> our May
> Tho [Then] Robin hood, Litell John, Frier Tucke and
> Marion deftly play[33]

Later Warner acknowledges the post-Grafton gentrified account. A hermit is talking with Thomas, Earl of Lancaster, who has lost his earldom, and who will eventually lose his life, in resisting Edward II. After offering a few sage moralisms, the hermit says something rather complicated:

> But you, perhaps, expect I should of novelties intreate.
> I haue no tales of Robin Hood, though mal-content was hee
> In better dayes, first Richards days, and liu'd in woods as we
> A Tymon of the world: but not deuoutly was he so,
> And therefore praise I not the man
>
> (132)

The phrase "tales of Robin Hood" suggests mere comedy, as in the proverb "Tales of Robin Hood are good for fools." But Robin also has a reputation as a "mal-content"—a conservative way of interpreting someone who stood up for his and others' rights. He is located, following Grafton, in the time of King Richard, but his rebel spirit is

attenuated through classicism, not history. He is a "Tymon"—that is,
a severe critic of others—but as his views were not religiously based,
he cannot be praised here; by implication, he is praised by many others elsewhere. In this passage Warner presents different Robin
Hoods—the entertainer, the protester, even the critic of normal society—and he expresses both an interest in the outlaw and a distinct
nervousness about the force that gathers about this name.

But Grafton's 1569 *Chronicle* enables Warner to read Robin's personality in a coherent and acceptable way; there is more to say:

> . . . for from him did groe
> Words worth the note, a word or twain of him ere hence we go
> A Countie [earl] was, that with a troope of Yeomandry did rome
> Braue Archers and deliuer [nimble] men, since nor before so
> good
> Those took from rich to giue the poore, and manned [served]
> *Robin-Hood*
> He fed them well, and lodg'd them safe in pleasant caues and
> bowers
> Oft saying to his merry men, what iuster life than ours?
>
> (132)

This is a classic statement of the gentrified hero, in terms of date,
title, and activities. It expresses, for the first preserved time, the rich-
poor motif in just the way it has survived, uses the concept of being
"merry," makes Robin the definite leader of a substantial body of men,
and yet suggests that their forest life was enjoyed with pastoral delight.
This well-focused account, which Munday no doubt knew, recognizes
the central motifs of gentrification as it has permeated later outlaw texts.

But, curiously, Warner does not leave it there; first he makes
Robin moralize some more:

> Here use we Talents that abroad the Churles abuse or hide
>
> (132)

and then, to prove the hypocrisy of those abusive churls, Robin tells
a vulgar story, found in Giovanni Boccaccio's *Decameron*, about a prioress (always in some way Robin's enemy). She jumps out of bed to
chide a noisy novice, but the novice points out that the headgear the
prioress has snatched up is in fact a canon's hosiery. Having arrived at

this "novelty," in spite of his initial disavowal of them, Warner signs off Robin Hood with a benignly peaceful statement: "Then happie we (quoth *Robin-Hood*) in merry Sherwood dwell" (133).

The malcontent, the hater of society, backed not by a few yeomen but by a formidable "troope of Yeomandry," has through the idea of the charitable earl been transmuted into a cheerful forester telling a vulgar anti-clerical joke—albeit one with a literary heritage. Robin is reborn as a much more comfortable fellow to live with from the view-point of protestant conservatism, no longer a yeoman rogue but a ro-guish gentleman.

But Warner, like Munday, was not the only one to rework Robin Hood in the period. Michael Drayton, a fine and underappreciated poet, not only contributed the Matilda story to Munday's play but also compiled *Poly-Olbion*, a poetical gazetteer of Britain. The work relates the myths and legends of each area and so constructs something like a national topographical mythology, while also shaping the mythic figures who symbolize each region as cultural versions of the landowners for whom Drayton and most contemporary poets worked.

The Robin Hood material comes in the Nottingham section, song 26, one of the additions in the 1622 edition. (The first appeared in 1612.) The nymph of Sherwood sings the fame of "lustie *Robin Hood*, who long time like a King / Within her compasse liv'd."[34] What the marginal note calls "Robin Hoods story" follows. First, as with Warner, there is the idea of "novelties":

> The merry pranks he playd, would aske an age to tell
> And the adventures strange that Robin Hood befell,
> When Mansfield many a time for Robin hath been layd
> How he hath cosned [tricked] them, that him would have
>   betrayd
>
> (305–8)

Then the story reviews the adventures of the ballads:

> And to the end of time, the Tales shall ne'er be done
> Of *Scarlock*, *George a Greene*, and *Much* the Millers sonne,
> Of *Tuck*, the merry Frier, which many a Sermon made
> In praise of *Robin Hood*, his Out-lawes and their Trade.
>
> (313–16)

With his characteristic fluent weightiness Drayton goes into detail on their equipment, horn-blowing, archery ("they had the very perfect craft," 329), hunting skills, and finally their redistributive robbery:

> From wealthy Abbots chests, and Churles abundant store,
> What ofte times he tooke, he shar'd amongst the poore:
> No lordly Bishop came in lusty *Robins* way,
> To him before he went, but for his Passe must pay:
> The Widdow in distresse he graciously relieved,
> And remedied the wrongs of many a Virgin griev'd
>
> (345–50)

This, compared with Warner and Munday, is strongly ballad-oriented: it sounds as if Drayton knows the *Gest* and "Robin Hood and the Bishop" (though it is not preserved from as early as 1622, the first surviving text being dated to c. 1650). Presumably he also had heard of the other outlaws generally—though no surviving ballad names the pinder of Wakefield as George a Greene, and the play may well be his source here. It is noticeable that Drayton's bold Robin does not fight any sheriffs, and his only secular enemies are the rich "Churles" that gentry disliked as much as outlaws did. (No rich churl is robbed in the ballads; Drayton may be thinking of Chaucer's "The Summoner's Tale.") However, he has not located Robin in King Richard's days, and has not made him any sort of aristocrat; so far the hero is not at all gentrified, just a little updated to the post-Reformation and anti-rebellion period.

But the topic of being kind to "Widdows" and "many a Virgin griev'd" leads Drayton on, and up in tone:

> He from the husbands bed no married woman wan,
> But to his mistris deare, his loved *Marian*
> Was ever constant knowne, which whersoere shee came
> Was soveraigne of the Woods, chief Lady of the Game:
> Her Clothes tuck'd to the knee, and daintie braided haire
> With Bow and Quiver arm'd, shee wandred here and there,
> Amongst the Forrests wild; Diana never knew
> Such pleasures, nor such *Harts* as *Mariana* slew.
>
> (351–58)

Robin may be a trickster robber of priests, but Marian is a "soveraigne," and she is referentially linked to aristocratic life through her love of elaborate hunting and to classical myth as a version of Diana. The elevated poetry itself expresses a form of gentrification, and Robin is honored through his lover—as indeed was the Robin of the French *pastourelle*, a fact likely known to the learned and leisured Drayton, who apparently never undertook any activity other than writing for his patrons.

Drayton, it seems, was able to appreciate and to pass on the robust, even dissenting, force of the bold yeoman Robin Hood simply because he could write so well that the potentially dangerous impact of a robber could be contained within whispers of classicism and mythicizing. Drayton did not need to change the story and to limit the ballad action—or not much, at least—because his Robin Hood kept fine company in Drayton the poet and his goddess-like Marian. Drayton's limited gentrification, a matter of style rather than narrative, is both less extreme than Munday's and more difficult to imitate, because it is so delicately poised in tone. But there was one writer capable of such work, who clearly had read Drayton and was inspired to write about the hero in the same form of acculturated gentrification. But, sadly for readers and playgoers, especially those interested in Robin Hood, Ben Jonson never finished *The Sad Shepherd*.

His inspiration seems to have been the illustration for Drayton's East Midland section, which shows not only a nymph on a hill as the spirit of Nottingham and Sherwood but also a naked nymph bathing in the Trent as it flows through the Vale of Belvoir (figure 6). The area was famous not only for its beauty but also for being the home of the Earls of Rutland at Belvoir Castle, then as now—though today they are dukes. Julie Sanders has argued that Jonson's interest in the area led him to a Robin Hood theme.[35] He had already written a lost masque called "The May Lord" for an aristocratic cast including the countess; this has some links with *The Sad Shepherd* and may well have been its basis.[36] As might be expected, Jonson deploys his classical learning and indicates in language and some characters' names a debt to Spenser's *The Faerie Queene*[37] but also, unnoticed by most commentators, draws on earlier Robin Hood material.[38] He was clearly familiar with Munday's work—mostly for Scarlet and Scathlock as hunting foresters and

Robin and Marian as forest lovers, and drew on the *Gest*—for Robin's feasting habits and a distressed genteel visitor (the knight in the *Gest* equates to Aeglamour, the sad shepherd himself).

In Jonson's play, as in Drayton's poem, Robin is not officially gentrified. Nowhere is he called an earl; indeed, it is not clear that he is an exile. He appears to be living happily in the forest with his band of men and Marian. The poetic tone is that of gentry culture, with Jonson's characteristic mix of deep learning, lyrically powerful writing, and a gift for creating sudden switches of emotion; this forest-loving Robin's poetic world is a long way from the simple, direct communication of the ballads. But the work is unfinished. Two of five acts are complete, along with the "Argument" and five scenes of a third. "Reuben the Reconciler," a hermit (like the wise voice of *Albions England*), was to draw together everything in the five acts. This was, it appears, to have a happy pastoral ending, following Drayton rather than Munday.

The basic plot is that Robin Hood has invited the shepherds of the Vale of Belvoir to the forest for a feast. But these are no dog-training, straw-chewing shepherds: they are pastoral gentry, and the young man Aeglamour (the name is from *The Faerie Queene*) has lost his love Earine. The nymph has apparently drowned in the Trent—Jonson's skillful, perhaps even playful, interpretation of the *Poly-Olbion* illustration. Highly emotive speeches, sighs, and breast-beating flow from this event, much as political rhetoric spouted from the quarrelling aristocrats in *The Downfall*. Meanwhile, Robin has his problems, and they too have some parallel in Munday. Jonson has taken the trouble to provide local settings, and Robin's enemy is the Witch of Papplewick, a Sherwood village. She wishes "to abuse Robin Hood and perplex his guests,"[39] so another false Marian appears: the witch assumes Marian's identity, spreads general confusion, and vilifies Robin. This makes him very nervous and he is in turn hostile to the real Marian. The tension of these scenes expresses the gender anxiety that the formerly all-male saga has developed because a woman has arrived. As Lois Potter comments:

> The relationship of witch to heroine can be read in both directions: the witch can tell the "truth" about the heroine or can represent the atypically successful female figure as she is *perceived* by an unsympathetic society.[40]

FIG. 6. Sherwood and the Trent in Michael Drayton's *Poly-Olbion*, 1622

The witch's threat is, strikingly, in balanced opposition to (as if called up by) the delightful and sexually aware relation between Robin and the real Marian. She, as in Drayton, is a serious and successful hunter who here leads the food-providing process that in Munday was consigned to the lower-class outlaws. Robin is a genially passive figure, except during his struggle with the witch, and is delighted when Marian returns from the chase:

> *Rob.* My Marian and my Mistris.
> *Mar.* My lov'd Robin.
> *Mellifleur.* The Moone's at full, the happy paire are met.
> *Mar.* How hath this morning paid me, for my rising!
>) First, with my sports; but most with meeting you!
> I did not half so well reward my hounds,
> As she hath me today: although I gave them
> All the sweet morsels, Calle, Tongue, Eares and
> Dowcets!
> *Rob.* What? And the inch-pin?
> *Mar.* Yes.
> *Rob.* Your sports then pleas'd you?
> *Mar.* You are a wanton.
> *Rob.* One I doe confesse,
> I wanted till you came. But now I have you,
> I'le grow to your embraces, till two soules
> Distilled into kisses, thorough your lips
> Do make one spirit of love.
> *Mar.* O Robin! Robin!
>
> (1.6.1–13)

Marian's technical language makes her a real hunter, not a lady onlooker, but Robin gains the upper hand as her lover through punning about the "inch-pin"—part of the entrails of a deer but also a pin or peg an inch thick, and so, suggestively, the penis. Not until the late twentieth century will Robin and Marian become lovers in so erotic a way, as Jonson makes poetically good the promise in his Prologue to write a truly English pastoral.

Most people think the play remained unfinished because Jonson died, but the unfinished nature of the work could stem from the fact that, in this gentrified world, there is remarkably little for Robin to do and inventing enough action is not easy. Robin does not even appear in the title. Without the activities of the yeoman outlaw, both comic and redistributive, Jonson is left with the hero as little more than a good host and a fine lover; in the absence of outlaw activity, the witch has to take over as the source of dramatic tension. Jonson may simply have decided that the play, like this inactive Robin, had nowhere to go, and abandoned both. The lack of action and resolution in *The Sad Shepherd* indicates, at least symbolically, that gentrifying Robin has cut him off from the dynamic core of the outlaw story. What he has gained in social status and conservative acceptability he has largely lost in terms of the power to command attention through exciting stories. The first moves in gentrification, it seems, have weakened the hero seriously: Lord Robin dies in Munday, but in Jonson he just fades out. He also makes a distinctly muted appearance in popular literature of the seventeenth century.

Gentrified Broadsides

While Robin was being promoted by the gentrifiers, the bold yeoman was not forgotten, especially in the broadside ballads of the seventeenth century. It is a testimony to the multiple levels of social culture and to the continuing strength of its most popular forms that the Robin of these texts is largely the Robin of the social bandit and yeoman tradition. His resistance may be a little diluted and more anti-church than anti-law, but he is still a handful for the authorities. It is striking how few ballads are in any way gentrified, and when they are, how ungenteel they are in comparison with Munday's Earl Robert.

The most popular gentrified ballad, and the most influential, especially on the nineteenth-century novel, is one that has as many titles as any nobleman. Child prints it as "Robin Hood Newly Reviv'd," a title found in the earliest surviving broadside, dated to about 1673. However, Joseph Ritson, in his 1795 edition, thought its action suited the title "Robin Hood and the Stranger," the name of a tune that was mentioned in the broadsides as appropriate for other ballads but which had not survived as a title for a printed ballad itself. He thought it had been "foolishly altered" to "Newly Reviv'd" (though a

publisher's sales instinct is a more likely motive than folly).[41] A de-
rivative of it is known as "The Bold Pedlar and Robin Hood,"[42] while
Knight and Ohlgren have given it the title "Robin Hood and Will
Scarlet" to match the other "prequel" ballads.

The ballad tells how Will Scarlet joined the outlaw band, but it
also opens a new window onto Robin Hood's biography. It begins as
if predicting this raised social status, by addressing "gentlemen all"[43]
and then tells how Robin, strolling in the forest, sees a well-dressed
young man—his stockings are scarlet. The stranger shoots a deer;
Robin offers him a place as a yeoman, but he is both angry and rude
in return. They aim arrows at each other, but agree to fight with
swords as less dangerous:

> The stranger he drew out a good broad sword,
> And hit Robin on the crown,
> That from every haire of bold Robins head
> The blood ran trickling down.
>
> (58–61)

They agree on a pause, during which the stranger says he is
named "Young Gamwell" and explains:

> "For killing of my own fathers steward
> I am forc'd to this English wood,
> And for to seek an uncle of mine;
> Some call him Robin Hood."
>
> (70–73)

His father had a steward, and so they are gentry. Robin, as his
uncle, must have had much the same social status; the gentrified outlaw hero himself is revealed in this apparently simple "Robin meets his
match" recruiting ballad. Robin is delighted; John appears and they
all became friends and travel together. This ballad also helps to explain
the popular songs of the "Robin Hood, Scarlet, and John" style.

The origin of the Gamwell family name may be a little easier to
explain than Huntington but is still not a simple process. A robust
poem (Shakespeare's ultimate source for *As You Like It*) survives from
the fourteenth century, having been written about 1360. The poem,
called *Gamelyn*, tells of a youngest brother of three whose inheritance

is stolen by an elder brother; Gamelyn is forced into exile and meets some outlaws. Their unnamed "king" (who may be an anonymous Robin Hood) is soon reprieved and goes home, and Gamwell replaces him as leader of the band. With the outlaws' help he seizes his rights, by breaking the judge's neck and hanging the jury and his brother, who is the sheriff. He is not a robbing or adventurous outlaw and he is not long in the forest at all, but this story has become associated with the Robin Hood myth and has provided a higher-class attachment for Robin when it was felt to be needed.[44]

An early connection between *Gamelyn* and Robin is suggested by a short song-like poem, which had been written by the mid fourteenth century, at least a century before any of the Robin Hood texts. The poem is called "Robyn and Gandelyn," and its action seems curiously like the first half of "Robin Hood Newly Reviv'd." Robyn and Gandelyn are "stronge thevys"[45] and go hunting in the forest. Suddenly Robyn is killed by an arrow shot by a "lytyl boy" called Wrennok of Donne. Gandelyn and Wrennock exchange shots, and Gandelyn wins:

> Gandelyn bent his goode bowe,
> And set ther in a flo [arrow];
> He schet [shot] throw his grene certyl,
> His herte he clef [cleft] on to.
>
> "Now schal thu never yelpe [boast], Wrennock,
> At ale ne at wyn
> That thou has slawe [slain] goode Robyn,
> And his knave [man] Gandelyn."

(64–71)

Although the name is not explicitly Robin Hood, and Robyn dies, it sounds as if this potent little poem has been swept up in the whole mix of songs and stories about the outlaw and may have inspired the idea of a fierce conflict. The hostility between Robin and Will is the strongest in all the "Robin meets his match" ballads, and the names Gandelyn and Gamwell are, in the context of oral transmission, quite close; in "The Bold Pedlar and Robin Hood" the stranger has become "Gamblegold." Stories with a gentrification theme may have drawn on "Robyn and Gandelyn" as well as on

Gamelyn for material. Furthermore, Wrennock of Dunne, Robyn's killer, is a name borne by one of Fulk Fitz Warren's Welsh enemies in that noble outlaw saga of the days of King John, the story that may be a basis for Munday's gentrification of the hero.

Another striking and somewhat gentrified feature of "Robin Hood Newly Reviv'd" is that it promises more, ending with the words:

> If you will any more of bold Robin Hood
> In his second part it will be.
>
> (100–101)

This second part, in some broadsides actually attached to "Robin Hood Newly Reviv'd," is "Robin Hood and the Prince of Aragon," a decidedly exotic affair, described by Child as "a pseudo-chivalric romance."[46] Loosely based on Arthurian adventure, this ballad presents Robin, his nephew Will, and John strolling through the forest and meeting "a beautiful damsel."[47] (Such a figure is a clear sign that this is romance, not an outlaw text.) They hear from her that the Prince of Aragon has besieged London, and unless someone defeats him and his two giant companions he will abduct the beautiful princess. Off to the rescue go our heroes; Robin beheads the "Tyrant Turk, the infidel" (stanza 36a) while John and Will make short work of the giants. Robin begs pardon for his men and receives it; the princess, who was promised to the victor, must choose one of these three. She selects Will; and then his father, the Earl of Maxfield, steps forward. This improbable piece of popular gentrification ends with the jigging rhythms and banal sentiments typical of the seventeenth-century commercial ballad:

> But lord! what imbracing and kissing was there,
> When all these friends were met!
> They are gone to the wedding, and so to bedding,
> And so I bid you good night.
>
> (stanza 58)

The ballad makes nothing of Robin's relation to the earl; they must be either brothers or brothers-in-law, but the ballad does not relate to the central material of the bold outlaw tradition found in so many contemporary ballads.

Nor does another ballad that links Robin with the Gamwell family and higher modes of life and literature. From its title on, there is a banal richness about "Robin Hood's Birth, Breeding, Valour and Marriage." The earliest existing text is dated at 1681–84, and it opens clearly in the gentrified line. Robin is the nephew of "Gamwel, of Great Gamwel Hall,"[48] who welcomes him and his mother to a grand Christmas feast—an unusual time of year for a Robin Hood ballad. Although Robin's father was a "forester" and presumably not of gentry family himself, his son is acknowledged at his mother's social level: Squire Gamwell gives Little John to Robin as a "page" (88)—the servant-like role John often plays in gentrification. Robin goes hunting in Sherwood, which is apparently near Gamwell Hall, meets a large band of yeomen and, most striking of all, Clorinda, "the queen of the shepherds" (106), a name and a figure straight from pastoral. She is beautiful:

> Her eyebrows were black, ay and so was her hair,
> And her skin was as smooth as glass
>
> (123–24)

But she also has talents. Robin invites her to a bower, and on the way:

> . . . as we were going towards the green bower
> Two hundred good bucks we espy'd;
> She chose out the fattest that was in the herd
> And she shot him through side and side.
>
> (125–28)

Part pastoral princess, part huntress, Clorinda clearly belongs to the gentrified tradition of Drayton and Jonson rather than Munday,[49] but the story also has a cheerful demotic element. Robin's feast has a humble appeal rather than the lavishness of a truly courtly feast:

> . . . there was hot venison and warden [pear] pies cold,
> Cream-clouted [clotted] with honey-combs plenty
>
> (137–38)

In the bower, Robin asks for Clorinda's hand in marriage and "after a pause" (149) she agrees. Off they go to marry at Tutbury feast, scene of a major festival (curiously, the place where Piers Venables operated like Robin Hood; see p. 6). On the way they meet eight yeomen who try to rob Robin of the stag that Clorinda has killed (reminiscent of "Robin Hood's Progress to Nottingham"). John and Robin kill five, and both the narrator and Clorinda respond with naive delight:

> For I saw them fighting, and fidld the while,
> And Clorinda sung, "Hey derry down!
> The bumpkins are beaten, put up thy sword Bob,
> And now let's dance into the town."
>
> (177–80)

This low-level gentrification, a mixture of social and sexual fantasy of a somewhat boyish kind, ends with local reference to Tutbury people and a hope that Robin and Clorinda will have many children. The hero celebrated here has little contact with the usual, more elusive, more austere forest outlaw, or with the equally elusive noble earl or genteel forester, though Phillips has read the festive spirit as a celebration of the restoration of King Charles II.[50] With its bouncy but wordy style the ballad is evidently a lively piece of professional hackwork, and indicates that, by the late seventeenth century at least, the idea that Robin was of gentry birth had penetrated to some degree the popular tradition. This tradition could itself dictate what sort of adventures he and his new noble lady might enjoy.

From a similarly late period comes the one clearly gentrified ballad, "Robin Hood and Maid Marian." It survives only in one version and is not a garland ballad; this apparent unpopularity in itself suggests the essentially ungentrified—as well as masculine—nature of the broadside Robin Hood and of audience expectations of him. In this one case, he has a lady who:

> Did live in the North, of excellent worth,
> For she was a gallant dame.
>
> For favour and face, and beauty most rare,
> Queen Helen shee did excell;
> For Marian then was praisd of all men
> That did in the country dwell.[51]

She meets "The Earl of Huntington, nobly born," though unexplainedly he goes "by the name of Robin Hood" (14 and 17). Combining clumsy poetry with sugary feeling, the poem celebrates their love, as "with kisses sweet their red lips meet" (18). But also without explanation they must part, "fortune bering these lovers a spight" (22), and Robin takes to the "merry green wood" (24).

Marian acts:

Perplexed and vexed, and troubled in mind,
Shee drest herself like a page,
And ranged the wood to find Robin Hood
The bravest of men in that age.

With quiver and bow, sword, buckler, and all,
Thus armed was Marian most bold,
Still wandering about to find Robin out
Whose person was better than gold.

(30–37)

She then finds him. The Robin Hood ballad knows what to do when two armed people meet in the forest: they have a fierce battle. Robin asks for quarter but does not invite the opponent to join his band; instead, Marian recognizes his voice and they fall into each other's arms. It is striking how well she has fought:

They drew out their swords, and to cutting they went,
At least an hour or more,
That the blood ran apace from bold Robin's face
And Marian was wounded sore.

(42–45)

Marian does as well as Will did against Robin; she is much better with a sword than the cross-dressers Viola and Rosalind in Shakespeare's comedies.[52]

All ends with celebration, but there is a continuing quasi-masculine role for Marian as she fills Will's part in the threesome led by Robin and completed by John. All also ends rather simply and yeoman-like: although this is the only ballad to name Robin as the Earl of Huntington, and Marian is clearly a spirited lady, there is no thought of restoration to their lands, nor any sense that in the forest they have suffered a downfall:

In sollid content together they livd,
With all their yeoman gay;

They livd by their hands, without any lands,
And so they did many a day.

(82–85)

No truly gentrified figure had no care for lands, nor did much with his—or her—hands. In the end, the yeoman ballad seems to have claimed this initially highly gentrified hero and heroine.

In fact, none of the ballads that approach gentrification give it much respect: a good index is how rarely Robin rides a horse. He and his men, like all serious archers, fight on foot. The knight in the *Gest* does, and the king does, both as king and quasi-abbot; abbots and monks ride, and are supported by riders, as signs of both their sloth and their pride. In the enigmatic Pynson illustration for the *Gest* (see p. 30) Robin rides, but this seems exceptional. Even when he, John, and Will defeat the Prince of Aragon and his giants, they walk into battle. When the queen summons him from Sherwood to London in "Robin Hood and Queen Katherine," there is no suggestion that he rides there, nor, even more strangely, when King Henry chases him around the country in "Robin Hood's Chase" does Robin ever apparently mount a horse. He does with the fair Clorinda in "Robin Hood's Birth, Breeding, Valour and Marriage" but this is unusual. In "Robin Hood and the Bishop" it hardly counts when he is arrested as an old woman and taken off on a horse by the sheriff, nor does the odd event in "Robin Hood and the Potter" when he in generous—almost lordly—mode gives a fine white horse to the sheriff's wife. (Where did it come from?) Although a few late ballad versions let him ride (such as "Robin Hood and the Butcher" and "Robin Hood and Queen Katherine," both in Child's B version) and a few broadsides show Robin wearing spurs (see figure 3), the essential medieval difference between ordinary people and the gentry is fairly rigidly observed.

One major text strongly related to the ballad does present a fully gentrified Robin, however. Martin Parker, a professional writer of popular poetry, produced in 1632 "A True Tale of Robin Hood," which is, like the *Gest,* a ballad epic—120 ballad stanzas about Earl Robert. The hero falls as a result of his rash generosity (from Grafton) and a hostile abbot (drawing on Munday rather than the *Gest*), takes to the forest, robs rich travelers, helps the poor, attacks the clergy (and, with post-Reformation fervor, occasionally castrates clergymen), and angers the king—events which, while consistent with the gentrified chroniclers, also draw on the ballad hero's activities.

The style is vigorous and a much better pastiche of the original than most seventeenth-century efforts:

> The abbot of St Maries then,
> Who him undid before,
> Was riding with two hundred men,
> And gold and silver store.

> But Robbin Hood upon him set
> With his courageous sparkes,
> And all the coyne perforce did get,
> Which was two hundred markes.

> He bound the abbot to a tree,
> And woud not let him passe
> Before that to his men and he
> His lordship had sayd masse.[53]

The image of the hero is that of a war leader, a Wallace rather than a fugitive outlaw; he successfully fights several major encounters, against the abbot's five hundred men, the Bishop of Ely (from Munday) and his thousand-horse contingent—though Robin and his men are, again, never said to be mounted. But when King Richard returns, this martial figure seeks a truce—behaving now like an outlawed earl— but he is betrayed by "th'crewell clergie" (274) and "some lords" who see the king's wish to make peace as a dangerous precedent (326–28). In the crisis, many of Robin's men leave him. They also did this in Bower, but Parker is unlikely to have known this source; the model seems to be hostilities and treacheries that preceded civil war. In the same spirit, the king's pardon arrives too late because Robin has been treacherously killed, not by the prioress, his relative, but by a "faithless fryer"; the prioress, as in Grafton, arranges his tombstone and epitaph.

This is in basis a gentrified story, but it is still quite close to the ballads. It does not introduce Marian and eschews both the poetic pastoral of Warner and Drayton (Jonson's *The Sad Shepherd* was probably not yet known) and, to its benefit, avoids the political maneuverings of Munday. Once more the world of the ballad has restrained gentrification to little more than a noble name for the hero, some aggrandizement in his following, and, here as in Munday, some sense of Robin's place in history. It is also a place in the present, because Parker ends with a striking conclusion saying that outlaws like this could not survive in the modern period:

> We that live in these latter dayes
> Of civill government,
> If neede be, have a hundred wayes
> Such outlawes to prevent.

> In those dayes men more barbarous were,
> And lived lesse in awe;
> Now, God be thanked! people feare
> More to ofend the law.

> (433–40)

The passage makes clear what is implicit in sixteenth-century legislation against Robin Hood play-games and what made the bold yeoman of the seventeenth-century broadsides so popular among those "less in awe" than Parker. The idea that Robin Hood could threaten public order was not unfamiliar in Parker's period. In a letter from 1605 Robert Cecil, a powerful aristocrat, called Guy Fawkes's colleagues in the Gunpowder Plot "Robin Hoods."[54] Sir Edward Coke, the conservative legal expert, identified Robin Hood with "roberdesmen"—that is, robbers[55]—and even King Charles I's slighting reference to Robin Hood songs has political significance: he autocratically told the parliamentary messengers that if he sent one as a message, they could do nothing about the insult.[56] Parker sought to defuse such criticism with the gentrification and the historicizing of the outlaw tradition, but its dangerous possibilities could still rankle.

One of the most startling pieces of Robin's mythic biography is a short play that was performed in Nottingham on the coronation day of the restored King Charles II in 1661. The whole purpose of *Robin Hood and His Crew of Souldiers* is to brand the outlaw hero a disgraceful rebel against the law and against what was once more the king's peace, and to dramatize the rebel's submission to the new royal order. As the outlaws are resting, they hear a great shout acclaiming the king's coronation; a royal messenger arrives to demand submission. For the only time in the whole outlaw tradition, they do not resist: they speak angrily, but when the messenger outlines at length the king's virtues, Robin is at once converted:

> I am quite another man; thaw'd into conscience of my Crime and Duty; melted into loyalty and respect to vertue.[57]

The outlaws dance and sing in honor of the king; the bold and rebellious yeomen submit, without a blow struck, to the ultimate forces of noble authority. The play epitomizes the undercurrent of conflict throughout this period, between the dual personalities of Robin Hood, both bold resister of authority and a mildly errant member of the ruling class. The complaisant Robin of this play is not really a new figure; rather, from a royalist viewpoint in the tense atmosphere of the civil war, the only imaginable behavior of a noble person consists of not resisting authority. Such a code precludes even the licensed dissent of the distressed gentleman, and so any form of outlawry must be suppressed.

A Real Lord Robin

Robin Hood the distressed gentleman flourishes in genres with higher-level connections than the ballad-based yeoman outlaw, but in addition to appearing in full-length play, pastoral, masque, and serious poetry, he appears in a genre deeply involved with lords and their stories—genealogy and biography. Only in recent decades has the history of ordinary people become a thriving form; in the past, history was always the deeds of great people, usually men, and the rise of a Robin Hood historicity in the Renaissance became closely linked with the gentrification of the hero. A lord's life is associated with places he might have owned, signified through tombs and epitaphs, the physical traces of a great man; it is not located less individualistically in the caves and wells, butts and leaps that were the topographical remembrance of a mythic or folkloric hero.

The first trace of a historicist response to the hero is remarkably early and remarkably well-connected. John Leland was antiquary to

Henry VIII and in his *Itinerary of Britain* (an account of a journey made by 1540, but not published until the eighteenth century)[58] he associated Barnsdale with Robin. Leland's source was presumably the *Gest* and the early chroniclers. In his notes he shows an interest in Kirklees as the burial place of this outlaw, whom he also refers to as "nobilis"; the word can mean noble in moral or class terms, or both.[59] This account was developed by Grafton, and he added the information that a gravestone in Kirklees bore the outlaw's name. The gravestone and the various things written on it have been the focus of much of the early historicism, being a tangible token of the dead noble individual, an early version of the photographed corpse in the *Sun*. The gravestone is mentioned again in the first "Life" of the hero.

By about 1600, with Robin Hood firmly established as a lord by Grafton and Stow and realized on the Elizabethan stage as an earl, he had earned the right to a proper biography; the "Sloane Life," a manuscript surviving in the British Library, gives a full account of the hero's life and death, mostly based on ballads, but adding the long-lasting information (from an unknown source) that the outlaw was born in Locksley. The historicity is very close to the texts; indeed, Dobson and Taylor suggest that the Locksley birthplace itself comes from a lost ballad.[60] But the tangible fact of the gravestone attracted increased attention: it was described by William Camden in the fifth edition of his *Britannia* in 1607, and it was drawn by Nathaniel Johnston, a Yorkshire doctor, in 1669[61] (figure 7). This stone—which presumably existed—recorded three names, Robard Hude, William Goldburgh, and Thomas. Neither of the other names appear in the tradition, and though some historically minded twentieth-century fiction writers have inserted William into the outlaw saga, the likelihood is that the name on the Kirklees slab is a coincidence. There were plenty of Hoods in Yorkshire, and the gravestone itself may have given rise to the Kirklees story, which first appears in the *Gest*. But historicity is a mobile force, and before Johnston drew the stone, another version of the epitaph was already in circulation. At the end of Martin Parker's *A True Tale of Robin Hood*, of 1632, the Kirklees story is told, his grave described, and an epitaph given:

Robert Earle of Huntington
Lies under this little stone.
No archer was like him so good:
His wildnesse named him Robbin Hood.
Ful thirteene years, and something more,
These northerne parts he vexed sore.
Such out-lawes as he and his men
May England never know agen.[62]

This can hardly be ancient: Robin was not made an earl until Grafton published in 1569. The verse has the slightly clumsy jog-trot of Parker's other work, and there seems no need to look further for a source. But the influence was great. Thomas Gale, a respectable scholar and Dean of York, recorded among his papers an epitaph allegedly found on the grave. It gave Robin's death as 24 Kalends of December 1247. This is a joke. The Romans did count dates from the first, the Kalends, but not that far into the month, and while it would seem the date is meant to be Christmas day, Gale's date represents bad Roman counting. The Romans worked inclusively, with twenty five days from the first to Christmas day, and Gale is bound to have known that. That scholarly tease is repeated in the epitaph; it is a comically fake old-fashioned version of Parker's effort:

Hear underneath this laitl stean
Laid Robert earl of Huntington
Nea arcir ver as hei sae geud
An pipl kauld im robin heud
Sick utlaws as hi an his men
Vil England nivr si agen.[63]

All that remained for the fetishistic lord was genealogical elaboration, and this was provided by William Stukeley, the enthusiastic archivist from Stamford who, among other things, argued that Stamford had a university in the ninth century B.C., supervised by the same King Bladud who discovered the hot springs at Bath. Inventing something for Robin Hood must have seemed light work, and, as Holt describes, he inserted a few people into contemporary lists of peers and produced a "fictitious family of fitz Ooth, with Robert fitz Ooth

FIG. 7. Nathaniel Johnston's drawing of the grave of Robard Hude and others, 1669

'commonly called Robin Hood, pretended Earl of Huntington' in the third generation."[64] This ludicrous family tree (figure 8) traced Robin Hood back to Norman lords who came over with William, an idea that has coexisted surprisingly well with Sir Walter Scott's equally fictitious piece of origination that he was a Saxon freedom fighter. Both are equally improbable and equally tendentious—as is all of this early sequence of historicism.

Fabrication of a gravestone was as easy as inventing a genealogy: at some stage in the eighteenth century the grave that Johnston sketched was forgotten (or perhaps broken up for souvenirs), and the verse that started with Parker was carved onto a slab lying on a hill above the road, a longbow shot from the gatehouse of the old Kirklees Abbey (figure 9). The mystique of the site, now shrouded in gloomy pines, has been intensified by the Armitage family's long-standing insistence on privacy, extending so far as sheriff-like legal action against outlaw-enthusiasts who might intrude.[65]

The grave, the verse, and the idea of an emotive lordly monument

The Pedigree of Robin Hood, Earl of Huntingdon.

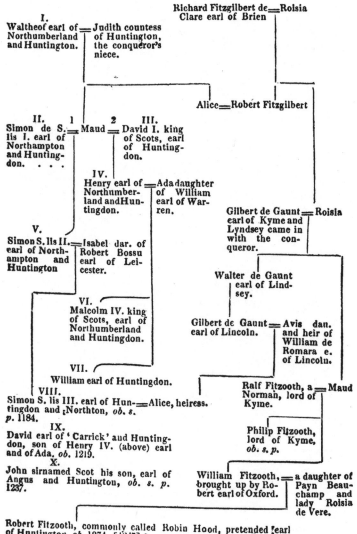

Richard Fitzgilbert de══Roisia
Clare earl of Brien

I.
Waltheof earl of ══ Judith countess
Northumberland   of Huntington,
and Huntington.   the conqueror's
                   niece.

Alice══Robert Fitzgilbert

II.   1   2   **III.**
Simon de S. ══ Maud ══ David I. king
lis I. earl of   of Scots, earl
Northampton   of Hunting-
and Hunting-   don.
don. . . .

IV.
Henry earl of ══Ada daughter
Northumber-   of William
land and Hun-   earl of War-
tingdon.   ren.

Gilbert de Gaunt ══ Roisia
earl of Kyme and
Lyndsey came in
with the con-
queror.

V.
Simon S. lis II.══Isabel dar. of
earl of North-   Robert Bossu
ampton and   earl of Lei-
Huntington   cester.

Walter de Gaunt
earl of Lind-
sey.

VI.
Malcolm IV. king
of Scots, earl of
Northumberland
and Huntingdon.

Gilbert de Gaunt══Avis dau.
earl of Lincoln. and heir of
                  William de
                  Romara e.
                  of Lincoln.

VII.
William earl of Huntingdon.

VIII.
Simon S. lis III. earl of Hun-══Alice, heiress.
tingdon and Northton, ob. s.
p. 1184.

Ralf Fitzooth, a══Maud
Norman, lord of
Kyme.

IX.
David earl of 'Carrick' and Huntingdon, son of Henry IV. (above) earl
and of Ada. ob. 1219.

Philip Fitzooth,
lord of Kyme,
ob. s. p.

X.
John sirnamed Scot his son, earl of
Angus and Huntington, ob. s. p.
1237.

William Fitzooth,══a daughter of
brought up by Ro- Payn Beau-
bert earl of Oxford. champ and
                    lady Roisia
                    de Vere.

Robert Fitzooth, commonly called Robin Hood, pretended earl
of Huntington, ob. 1274 [1247].*

* Stukeley's *Palæographia Britannica*, No. II. p. 115.

FIG. 8. William Stukeley's genealogy of Robin Hood, 1746

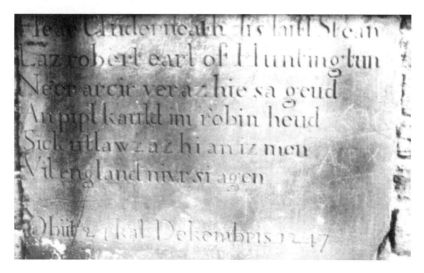

FIG. 9. Epitaph carved on the "grave of Robin Hood" at Kirklees

are all fictions clad in the apparent legitimacy of history, and all have a tale to tell about the desires of the audience to nail down the outlaw and his individualized noble identity. But fictions can be reversed, and Roger Dodsworth, a major seventeenth-century antiquarian, had a quite different account. He suggested that "Robert Locksley, born in Bradfield parish, in Hallamshire, wounded his stepfather to death at plough, fled into the woods."[66] The name may suggest that Dodsworth knew a source used by the "Sloane Life," or he may just be playing games: he refers to Little John's grave (which as he says is very long, and still to be seen at Hathersage in Derbyshire), but then seems to tease the Munday tradition, saying skeptically that Little John was said to have been "an earl Huntington."

If Dodsworth's suggestion indicates confusing variety—or at least imaginative play—among historicist inventors, other commentators have been calmer. Thomas Percy thought the Parker epitaph was "suspicious," as "the most ancient poems on Robin Hood make no mention of his earldom."[67] This view earned abuse from Joseph Ritson later on, but it seems to Percy's credit now that he was sensibly skeptical, as was Sir Samuel Armitage, who in the mid eighteenth century had men dig under the gravestone and discovered that nothing was there.[68]

The early chroniclers, who spoke about a bandit, had no interest in title or tomb: Grafton is the first clearly gentrifying author who introduces both and moves toward a life of the hero, so that the "Sloane Life" author, with material drawn from the ballads and the *Gest*, shapes a biography and so gives literary status to a lordly figure. The inventions and fancies that gather around the grave and the epitaph reveal how historicity is involved with power—and not the power of a person who resists wrongful oppression, but primarily the power of someone who has established status, who owns both land and individual identity. But just what that identity might be was something that would haunt future historicists.

A Gentleman on the Eighteenth-Century Stage

While some elements of a gentrified biography were being compiled, the fictional hero flourished, especially after the royal restoration in 1660. Drawing the sting of the hero's capacity for resistance certainly seems to have helped his popularity in the market: the first surviving garland comes from 1663, apparently a new edition of a slightly earlier one that has been lost. Another appears in 1670, at about the same time an intelligent scholar-scribe was gathering together the Forresters manuscript, which looks very much like a better garland that never reached print.[69] Printed "Lives" of the hero appear regularly as well, usually short and usually gentrified;[70] it is clear that broadside printing was very active in this period and into the eighteenth century.

What is less clear is whether a tradition of Robin Hood theater continued. When the theaters were closed by the Puritans in 1642, the tradition was broken that was established by Munday and continued, if erratically, in *Looke About You* and his own somewhat servile *Metropolis Coronata* of 1616, in which Earl Robert rises from his grave to celebrate the Master Drapers' Guild.[71] The wide-ranging prohibitions of Robin Hood play-games of the sixteenth century were strengthened by increasing Puritanism in the seventeenth century, and the play-games die out in local records. A couple of late instances are in conservative rural areas near Oxford, at Woodstock in 1628 and Burford in 1630, and as Alexandra Johnston suggests, they may have been nostalgic revivals.[72] In those instances, as in the Restoration flood of material, Robin is beginning to mean something new: he is becoming consciously a figure of the past, whose value is in part that of a distant and possibly better period. The bold yeoman operated in an unspecified here and now; Earl Robert, while clearly set in the past, was, like Shakespeare's historical figures, primarily a medium for contemporary concerns. From the Restoration on, the Robin Hood tradition acquired that mixture of quaintness, mystery, and lost simplicity that has been for recent centuries the charm of the medieval. This is seen in a limited way in the lightweight musical versions of a vaguely gentrified version of the story that found their way onto the eighteenth-century stage.

Robin Hood: An Opera is the grand title of a 1730 re-creation of the outlaw hero, but it played at "Lee and Harper's Great Theatrical Booth in Bartholomew Fair"—not so distant in level from the village-green activities of earlier centuries.[73] It is a slight affair, with many songs: Matilda, sister to another unnumbered King Edward, is sought by the king's favorite, the Earl of Pembroke, so he has his rival the Earl of Huntingdon exiled. Theatrical and film versions have always loved a triangular romance plot, and Robin's role as a serious, if preoccupied, lover is a new biographic element that will persevere.

In spite of borrowing King Edward from the ballad tradition,[74] there is no bandit activity here apart from robbing a miserable Puritan called Prim. The opera is filled out with entertaining pieces of theatrical business, including a comic outlaw band much like Bottom's friends in *A Midsummer Night's Dream* and a love subplot between Darnel (the Little John role) and Marina (Matilda's friend). The bandit possibility is sensationally remembered—and presumably parodied—when Will and his friends plan to gang-rape Matilda and Marina, but the opera veers off into harmless, even ludicrous, comedy. Darnel has an affair with the pinder's wife, which involves his hiding under the bed in the guise of Towzer, the dog; the kindly but myopic pinder gives him some scraps.

Sad though it may be that Mel Brooks never read this script before planning *Robin Hood: Men in Tights*, it is of fairly limited importance. What it does show is how the hero was reinterpreted through a lengthy interregnum—as a gentleman presiding over a chaotic world that somehow comes out well and as the figurehead of a tradition that is in a new medium and in the context of gentrification jettisoning much of its old narrative groping for new material.

In 1751 another version appeared: Moses Mendez, a busy theatrical professional, wrote *Robin Hood: A New Musical Entertainment*,[75] which Joseph Ritson in 1795 called a "ballad farce," perhaps a little dismissively.[76] Mendez varied his work from its predecessor by making Robin not an earl, just on the run from the sheriff. But the gentrified strain is still clear: in this version Marian is Clarinda, presumably borrowed from "Robin Hood's Birth, Breeding, Valour and Marriage," except that the plot is based on "Robin Hood and Alan a Dale," and Robin helps Clarinda avoid marriage to the fop Glitter, favorite of her father, Graspall, and espouse the noble Leander. Robin manages much of this by masquerading as Sir Humphrey Wealthy, another possible suitor. But if the play in these ways looks backward toward Restoration comedy in rather shallow satire, Mendez in this well-organized piece also has some sense of the outlaw, again via Shakespeare, as a mythical forest lord. As Robin finally links the hands of Clarinda and Leander, the reference to Theseus, and indeed Oberon, is clear:

> See how along the East the purple Morn
> Drives the young Hours, and dims pale *Cynthia's* Horn;
> To-day you both a Forest-Chear must prove,
> At Night we'll leave you to the Sweets of Love.
>
> (p. 23)

These two inherently gentrified theatrical pieces, which helped keep the story of Robin Hood alive in the theater, were drawing on the continuing popularity of the basically ungentrified Robin Hood in the ballads. Garlands and broadsides continued to be printed throughout the century, and, presumably because of the political element lurking in them, grew more popular in the increasingly reformist mood that existed toward the century's end; at least eleven garlands and five "Lives of Robin Hood" appeared in the last twenty years of the century.[77] But these two theatrical pieces also exhibit the characteristic weakness of the gentrified texts: by setting aside the socially disruptive activities of the social bandit, they are hard put to find interesting narrative material. Because Earl Robert and bold Robin Hood are basically separate,

with different generic contexts and different narrative material, the nobility of the one has never been made dynamic by the vigor of the other.

The gentrified drift away from the bandit went even further in
the 1784 comic opera *Robin Hood, or Sherwood Forest*, with music by
William Shield and book by the prolific Irish writer Lawrence Mc-
Nally, who was also active as an English agent against the United
Irishmen.[78] Pastoral is the basic mode, with Marian's role played by
another Clorinda. The text claims to have used "the ballads of Robin
Hood" as a source, as well as "The Nut-Brown Maid" and "The Hermit of the Dale" (p. 3), but there is clearly little interest in bandit action and not much more of the gentrified tradition. One of the villains is Baron Fitzherbert, who, disguised as Friar Tuck (identified as
a Catholic, a hint of McNally's pro-English Irish politics), tries to per-
suade Robin's bowmen to defect while the bishop of Hereford (another Catholic) is attacking the forest with five hundred men. While
this bizarre version of outlaw action is going on, there are other dangers, more contemporary in mode: Clorinda says, "It is rumoured
that the French have threatened an invasion" (p. 27), and she later
persuades Robin to be loyal to the king "because he has been insulted
by an enemy." Robin agrees, saying, "I will join my country" (p. 40).
Various complications intervene, involving resisting the bishop and
sorting the good characters into amatory duets, but the whole show
ends patriotically in much the same way as *Robin Hood and his Crew
of Souldiers,* uniting Robin's physical force with the interests of
monarch and state. Finally all the outlaws agree:

> Strains of liberty we'll sing
> To our country, Queen and King.

While Thomas Evans's 1777 collection (see p. 95) appears to have
made McNally aware of the ballads, there is little sign that they are
used for more than a few names. This situation clearly changes in the
last of the eighteenth-century outlaw operas, John O'Keeffe's 1795
production of *Merry Sherwood, or Harlequin Forester.*[79] Highly fash-
ionable in its use of the Harlequin pattern, in which an opening sequence undergoes a magical transformation under Harlequin's wand,
this also derives entire sequences from the ballads, probably the new
Ritson edition of 1795 (see pp. 95–98). At the beginning a tanner sings

a song that includes a stanza from "Robin Hood and the Tanner"; the next song is by one of the damsels from "Robin Hood and the Prince of Aragon." The story involves a strand about an aged knight, which comes from "Robin Hood and Alan a Dale," though it was also a theme of the 1751 comic opera.

This "operatical pantomime" was very popular: it was the Covent Garden Christmas show for 1795, taking receipts second only to "The Provok'd Husband" in that period, and its published *Airs* went into at least seven editions quickly. Marian's father is the sheriff, and he wants her to marry Squire Arthur O'Bradley (a name from folk song, sometimes used for the tanner). In the Harlequin tradition there are scenes of high action and magic, including a box that somehow encloses Squire Arthur. But the pantomime also includes ballad action such as Robin's fights with the pinder of Wakefield and the Prince of Aragon, the rescue of Will, Alan a Dale's wedding, and Robin Hood at sea. The stage has its own inventions: Robin is killed by Squire Arthur's men but revived by "the Witch of Nottingham Well," and the whole ends triumphantly with "Clouds with Angels supporting Wreaths" and a "Grand Dance of Archers."

Although there is some relation to the gentrified comic operas of the eighteenth century in the "old husband" plot, Robin himself is not in any way gentrified; the ballad materials and the distressed earl still seem separate. The vigor of this piece comes largely from new theatrical forces in the harlequinade tradition, but it still draws on the strength of the yeoman ballads. The source here was presumably Joseph Ritson's 1795 collection, though Evans's second edition of 1784 could equally have been a stimulus over a longer period.

Although O'Keeffe's version has real performance vigor, it had no lasting impact. In the same year, the crucial step had been taken to dissipate the long-standing separation between the two strands of the tradition and the mythic biography, the social bandit and the distressed gentleman. In his influential anthology, Joseph Ritson created a structure in which the acceptably gentleman-like concept of a distressed aristocrat can be combined with the energetic, memorable stories of the social bandit. At the end of the eighteenth century, Robin Hood became a new man, and one who is still with us.

CHAPTER III

Robin Hood Esquire

Transmitting an Outlaw

Robin Hood is still so well known because both his persona and his meaning were changed so much in the crucial reconstruction of the outlaw hero that occurred in the late eighteenth and early nineteenth centuries. Major changes emerged in what the hero might stand for, what values he might bear, and what oppressions he might resist—and so how his story should unfold. In this remarkable period, in so many ways the noisy cradle of modernity, the Robin Hood tradition was radically reshaped, and as a result has survived powerfully. Had the hero remained simply either a robust or genteel forester, restricted to local power struggles around Sherwood Forest or to boyish festivity before his final reestablishment as a lord, he would have probably faded from public memory along with Sir Guy of Warwick, Sir Beves of Southampton, Thomas of Ercildoune, and Herne the Hunter, medieval heroes who did not struggle free of the setting amber of antiquity. Robin, as ever, escaped to illuminate another day, another part of the sociocultural forest, with his multiple, contradictory and essentially volatile set of values.

By the late eighteenth century there was clear continuity and clear change in the Robin Hood tradition. The garlands were still appearing, and the largely separate gentrified tradition had continued, in an attenuated way, in the ballad operas. Literary gentry themselves found Robin Hood of limited interest, however. Though Thomas Percy's famous folio manuscript contained eight Robin Hood ballads, when he came to publish his *Reliques of English Poetry* in 1765[1] he printed only one. Most had been badly damaged where the pages of the manuscript had been torn, but even the selected one, which was complete, was edited to seem less unacceptable to genteel ears: the major change to "Robin Hood and Guy of Gisborne" was that instead of Little John shooting the sheriff through the heart, his arrow "shott him into the back-syde."[2]

Percy's selective archaism was succeeded by a more wide-ranging, less class-specific interest in past culture, which Marilyn Butler has called "popular antiquarianism,"[3] and which passed down a much fuller account of the outlaw. In 1777 Thomas Evans published *Old Ballads, Historical and Narrative*,[4] which deliberately added popular material to the distinctly gentrified approach found in Percy and in an anthology edited in 1790 by George Ellis.[5] Evans printed everything he could find, without prosodic improvements. He offers twenty-seven ballads in a coherent order, starting as many garlands do with the two "biographic" ballads "Robin Hood's Birth, Breeding, Valour and Marriage" and "Robin Hood's Progress to Nottingham." The anthology continues through the adventures to Robin's death and epitaph in the form in which they appear at the end of "Robin Hood and the Valiant Knight." As elsewhere in the anthology, broadsides are the basis; the only ones missing are "Robin Hood and Maid Marian," which has been preserved in only one copy, and "Robin Hood's Death," which is covered by "Robin Hood and the Valiant Knight." The early manuscript ballads and the *Gest* do not appear, nor does Parker's "True Tale." Though Evans left "Robin Hood and Guy of Gisborne" to Percy, this is a most impressive collection—a major garland, as it were, given a weighty and prestigious presentation.

Evans's role as a transmitter of the Robin Hood materials has been mostly overlooked as the first of the outlaw anthologizers. Joseph Ritson was more scholarly, and by far the more influential. Ritson was a famous and largely self-taught scholar, learned, aggressive, and radical—a vegetarian when that was most uncommon, and an *aficionado* of the French revolution who, even in timid England, addressed people as "Citizen." Passionate for veracity, he mocked Percy's habit of tinkering with texts to make them tasteful and was tireless in traveling to see manuscripts or in writing to people to pursue information; yet his collection is by no means simply an act of faith with a politically resistant past.

The multiple title proclaims the anthology's positions: its first element is *Robin Hood: A Collection of All the Ancient Poems, Songs and Ballads Now Extant Relative to the Celebrated English Outlaw.* Imposing as it is, this nevertheless sounds as if Ritson were just adding the manuscript poems, the *Gest,* and a few other elusive broadsides to what Evans had already offered to the public. Those functions would in themselves have been very useful; in fact, the full range of material became a major source for and influence on later rewriters of the tradition, especially as Ritson provided in his notes a thorough survey, with long quotations, of how previous authors had presented the hero. But the most important thing Ritson did is signaled by his additional subtitle *(To Which are Prefixed Historical Anecdotes of His Life)*: Ritson created a "literary life" of Robin Hood. This was the new age of biography; Hawkins on Johnson and Johnson himself on the major poets had created the genre that now seems so familiar, and this in effect is what Ritson was doing. He said he intended "to retrieve all the historical or poetical remains" of Robin Hood.[6] The figure who had been indelibly but fleetingly associated with proverbs, places, songs, and stories was now enshrined in a solid volume of life and deeds. A myth had become biography.

But Ritson did more than reprint the texts and create a life: in juxtaposing the stories and the life in one book, he brought together the yeoman and the lord and so potentially resolved the damaging split between robust narrative and noble but inactive presence. Ritson outlined a hero who was undeniably gentrified but also memorable, exciting, bold, and adventurous. The impact of Ritson's book as a single entity embracing both gentrified life and bold deeds was a major stage in the long development and variation of the outlaw hero, and the combination was the springboard for the dynamic performance of Robin Hood in the nineteenth century.

Ritson's long introduction—over a hundred pages in the first edition (abbreviated in later ones)—opens with the brisk, authoritative-seeming "Life of Robin Hood." It combines the gentrified tradition with more recent flourishes: Robin was born Earl of Huntington at Locksley in 1160, so encapsulating the gentrified tradition from Major to Munday, and following the "Sloane Life" closely. Ritson then casts his net wider, reprinting Stukeley's ludicrous genealogy deriving the surname Hood from the invented Norman Fitz Ooth. Next, simply accepting fiction as fact, Ritson assembles from the texts any data that relate to the character of the hero: where he was found, Barnsdale and Sherwood, and with whom—the other outlaws, and Marian. Robin can shoot a bow accurately for two miles, and with similarly improbable confidence Ritson dismisses Percy's well-founded doubts as to whether the early Robin Hood was indeed an aristocrat (1:xlvii–viii). But Ritson himself mixes up the pseudo-historical data—chronicle statements, alleged tombs and epitaphs—with textual mentions such as the king's accusation in the *Gest* that Robin has poached deer in Plumpton Park, or even Robin's role in a text as bizarre and unreliable as *Looke About You.*

It is curious that Percy, the conservative would-be courtier, sees the lower-class medieval yeoman clearly enough, and feels the direct power of "Robin Hood and Guy of Gisborne," while Ritson, so radical in so many ways, is in biographical terms an insistent conservative gentrifier. There are two ways of comprehending Ritson's apparent self-contradiction. The most complete explanation, and one that has received scant attention from scholars, is Bertrand Bronson's claim that Ritson offers an "express declaration of skepticism"[7] about the whole gentrified-life idea and simply states that he is passing on these accounts for readers to believe or not. This puts fairly heavy stress on Ritson's statement about his approach in his preface when discussing the "materials collected for 'the life' of this celebrated character" (1:i):

> Desirous to omit nothing that he could find upon the subject, he has everywhere faithfully vouched and exhibited his authorities, such as they are: it would, therefore, seem altogether uncandid or unjust to make him responsible for the want of authenticity of such of them as may appear liable to that imputation. (1:ii)

This sounds more like a routine disclaimer than a serious rejection of the following pages, as Bronson saw it; Ritson seems to have a commitment to the earl's life he expounds so fully and influentially.

The second way of explaining the anthology's apparent inconsistency on Earl Robin is to recognize the nature of Ritson's radicalism. As he makes clear in his famous description of Robin Hood, his real hatred is for the medieval church and oppressive kings, not for lords; the outlaw was a man who:

> in a barbarous age and under a complicated tyranny, displayed a spirit of freedom and independence which has endeared him to the common people, whose cause he maintained (for all opposition to tyranny is the cause of the people), and, in spite of the malicious endeavours of pitiful monks, by whom history was consecrated to the crimes and follies of titled ruffians and sainted idiots, to suppress all record of his patriotic exertions and virtuous acts, will render his name immortal. (1:xi–xii)

It is tyranny and its lackeys Ritson hates, not lordship itself; like many other dedicated radicals, past and present, he sees no contradiction in the cause of the people being led by someone from another class. Indeed, he seems (also like many modern radicals) to be gratified by this noble, in both senses, support. That inherently complex, if not contradictory, position, espousing radicalism but still admiring a lord, is what permits Ritson to bring together in book form the previously separate strands of the Robin Hood tradition and to combine the previously opposed elements of his biography, bold yeoman and passively genteel earl. The succeeding tradition as a whole has drawn enormously on this new and crucial combination: in film and story the lord can be a trickster, and the bold outlaw can have the justification of noble blood.

Romantic Yeoman

Ritson's anthology made no immediate impact on the tradition; no developments occurred until after the Napoleonic war, as if the hero were more relevant to the politics of postwar reorganization than to the heroic simplicities of military propaganda. However, Ritson's own aggressive and radical personality may well have in part restrained the hero's development. In his 1810 third edition of his father Thomas's *Old Ballads* of 1777, Robert Evans says Ritson's acknowledged scholarship was "disgraced by the petulance and impiety that pervade the biographic memoirs and notes,"[8] and his Jacobinism cannot have attracted many to his view of the hero.

References to Robin Hood from the period of the war with France suggest that there is a knowledge of the ballads, probably from Ritson, possibly from Evans, and that the outlaw is part of the literary landscape, but not a particularly dynamic one. Wordsworth begins "Rob Roy's Grave," written in 1806, with a reference to Robin before moving to his real topic:

> A famous man is Robin Hood,
> The English ballad singer's joy!
> And Scotland has a thief as good . . .[9]

Scott, in *The Lady of the Lake* (1810), speaks of:

> Bold Robin Hood and all his band—
> Friar Tuck with quarter-staff and cowl,
> Old Scathelocke with his surly scowl
> Maid Marion, fair as ivory bone,
> Scarlet and Mutch and Little John[10]

The presence of Marian, Scarlet, and Scathelock suggests that Scott has drawn on Ritson's "Notes and Illustrations" with their wealth of material, especially from Munday, in whose work these three appear. (The spelling of "Scathelocke" is Ritson's own.) But their purpose in the text is to watch as "The Douglas" wins the archery tournament.

Other authors found the outlaw hero less than interesting. Robert Southey in 1804 was thinking of an English epic; he was drawn toward the topic of King Arthur, and then said, "I am afraid there cannot be another found for an English poem except Robin Hood, and that lowers the key too much."[11] Equally negative is the treatment by Elizabeth Villa-Real Gooch, a successful popular author, who in 1804 published a novel with an outlaw-sounding title, *Sherwood Forest; or*

Northern Adventures. She says in the dedication that she was born in the area, but the opening chapters describe the forest without mentioning outlaws, dealing only in terms of its aristocratic owners. The only reference to Robin Hood comes at the beginning of chapter 2, where the ancient Sherwood House, now occupied by a fugitive from Scottish clan warfare, is alleged by the locals to have been one of Robin's hiding places.[12]

In a nonliterary context Robin Hood was also imagined as a past benchmark from which people could move forward in the present. In 1811 the Luddites of the North Midlands used as the address on their threatening letters "Ned Ludd's Office, Sherwood Forest"; a letter to the Prime Minister was signed "General C. Ludd, at Shirewood Camp"; and a Luddite song begins:

> Chant no more your old rhymes about bold Robin Hood,
> His feats I but little admire.
> I will sing the achievements of General Ludd
> Now the hero of Nottinghamshire.[13]

Not everybody in the area was forgetting Robin Hood: as Lois Potter has shown,[14] Robert Milhouse, Spencer T. Hall, and William and Mary Howitt were serious local writers who used the outlaw material as a totem of value, not irrelevance, but their work was not produced until after the crucial developments in the tradition that occurred in and shortly after the year 1818.

The year 1818–19 is the most important single period in Robin Hood's whole mythic biography. Three major writers were then at work on the tradition in ways that would reshape it and generate crucial elements of the modern Robin Hood—all unaware of each other's work and writing in essentially different genres. Between them John Keats (with help from John Hamilton Reynolds and Leigh Hunt), Sir Walter Scott, and Thomas Love Peacock reconstructed both the mythic biography of Robin Hood and the outlaw tradition itself. In various ways they brought together the noble status and inherent dignity of the gentrified outlaw with the vigor and dynamic meaning of the old social bandit, and they did this not simply in terms of narrative, but also, and preeminently, in terms of values. The noble bandit now came to symbolize values central to the nineteenth and even twentieth centuries—especially ideals of national identity, masculine vigor, and natural value. The potency of the Robin Hood tradition to the present depends to a large degree on this striking period of reformation.

Why it happened then remains something of a mystery. General explanations can be given: the war was over and internal political tensions, the kind that the Robin Hood myth has always related to in one way or another, were high. The strains of industrial development, an unevenly developing capital economy, and the new forces of urban growth all combined with pressures for an enlarged right to vote. A specific trigger may have been the 1817 trial of William Hone. On trial for blasphemy—part of the political tension and repression of the era—he defended himself by referring to the ancient rights of the English to resist oppression, represented in their traditions and literature.[15] In discussing the new outlaw literature of this period, Nicholas Roe indicates that the first published example of this "greenwood" writing (though it does not specifically mention Robin Hood) was Leigh Hunt's collection of poems *Foliage*, with its combination of a valued natural past and contemporary political unease.[16]

Other activity did not wait until the publication of *Foliage*, early in 1818. On the no doubt cold morning of Tuesday, February 3, 1818, in still rural Hampstead, John Keats received a letter from his friend John Hamilton Reynolds, containing two sonnets. The mood is Romantic:

> The trees in Sherwood forest are old and good,—
> The grass beneath them now is dimly green;
> Are they deserted all? Is no young mien,
> With loose slung bugle, met within in the wood?
> No arrow found,—foil'd of its antler'd food,—
> Stuck in the oak's rude side?—Is there nought seen,
> To mark the revelries which there have been,
> In the sweet days of merry Robin Hood?
> Go there with summer, and with evening,—go
> In the soft shadow, like some wandering man,—
> And thou shalt far amid the Forest know
> The archer-men in green, with belt and bow
> Feasting on pheasant, river fowl, and swan,
> With Robin at their head, and Marian.[17]

Reynolds imagines a nostalgic visit to the outlaw world and shows familiarity with the early ballads; his forest feast is directly from the *Gest* (129–30). The overt point of the sonnet's octave is to ask if the woods are in fact "deserted all" because of passing time, and if there is now any sign to "mark" the "revelries" of "the sweet days of merry Robin Hood." The sestet votes for the value of nostalgia to create its own experience: if you "go there with summer, and with evening" then "thou shalt far amid the Forest know / The archer-men in green" at their feast.

It is a classic Romantic moment, an emotion of forest delight— not outlawry or justified violence—recollected in tranquility. This sonnet speaks from a sensitized distance, as if looking at a fine lake or mountain, but the second sonnet closes the focus and, for the first time in the tradition, creates an affective, one-to-one rapport between the reader and the outlaw figures:

> With coat of Lincoln green, and mantle too,
> And horn of ivory mouth and buckle bright,
> And arrows wing'd with peacock-feathers bright,—
> And trusty bow, well gathered of the yew,—
> Stands Robin Hood:—and near, with eyes of blue
> Shining through dusk hair, like the stars of the night,
> And habited in pretty forest plight,
> His greenwood beauty sits, young as the dew.
> Oh, gentle tressed girl! Maid Marian!
> Are thine eyes bent upon the gallant game
> That stray in the merry Sherwood? Thy sweet fame
> Can never, never die. And thou, high man,
> Would we might pledge thee with thy silver can
> Of Rhenish, in the woods of Nottingham.
>
> (125–26)

Robin Hood is well-armed but now in a theatrically attractive way, not with the heavy weaponry of the medieval outlaw; he bears "horn of ivory mouth and buckle bright, / And arrows wing'd with peacock feathers bright." There "stands Robin Hood"—Reynolds has clearly read the early ballads. But he also knows the gentrified texts containing Marian, and he responds to them strongly, personally:

> . . . and near, with eyes of blue
> Shining through dusk hair, like the stars of the night,

And habited in pretty forest plight,
His greenwood beauty sits, young as the dew.

This could be taken ambiguously: there is enough male gazing at males in the nineteenth-century Robin Hood novel for "his green-wood beauty" to suggest Robin's own looks, but here that is only a subliminal suggestion of homoerotic feeling; the word "near" assigns, a little elusively, such admirable beauty to the "gentle tressed girl," Maid Marian.

Her fame, the sestet tells us, "can never, never die" and so, in another type of exclusive male bonding, recognizing and sharing her quality, we imaginatively drink with Robin. The sonnet presents a new way of seeing the hero in terms both biographic and mythic. Before this, Robin has been a village celebrant, a proverbial mystery, a figure of social boldness, an admirable lord, a topographical symbol, an emblem of natural forces, even an antiquarian fantasy, but he has never been a living and breathing, sensually realized, identity with whom we can empathize. Reynolds has made Robin Hood a character in his own right, when previously he has always been a figure who primarily means something. Romantic poetry, like the novel, is above all a means of realizing the sentient self, in characters, narrative voice, and self-identifying readers.

Keats, whose Romanticism is less direct, mediated as it is through metaphor and idealism, was at first negative. The poem he wrote to Reynolds the same day begins with the word "No."[18] At first his negative is because that time is past:

No! those days are gone away,
And their hours are old and gray,
Under the down-trodden pall
Of the leaves of many years.

(2–5)

But Keats is intrigued, as any Romantic poet would be, by such an engaging vista, and he reworks his negative to review in detail all the things he claims not to hear—an intellectually stronger and more tension-filled rejection than made in Reynolds's first sonnet:

There is no mid-forest laugh,
Where lone Echo gives the half

To some wight, amazed to hear
Jesting, deep in forest drear.

On the fairest time in June
You may go with light of moon
Or the seven stars to light you,
Or the polar ray to right you.
But you never may behold
Little John, or Robin bold
Never one, of all the clan,
Thrumming on an empty can

. . . .

Gone, the merry morris din;
Gone, the song of Gamelyn;
Gone, the tough-belted outlaw
Idling in the "grene shawe"

(15–36)

The language itself is seductively concrete: there is no "mid-forest laugh," no one "thrumming on an empty can," no "song of Gamelyn," and, with Keats's energetic realization seeming to cancel the negative, no "tough-belted outlaw."

Tempted as he is toward resuscitation of the dead outlaw past, Keats elaborates his glimpse of "down-trodden" time. Speculating that Robin and Marian might be brought back to life, he sees them not as enticing partners in sensuous subjectivity, as Reynolds did, but as figures of historical and political meaning:

And if Robin should be cast
Sudden from his turfed grave
And if Marian should have
Once again her forest days
She would weep and he would craze
He would swear, for all his oaks,
Fallen beneath the dockyard strokes,
Have rotted on the briny seas.
She would weep that her wild bees
Sang not to her—strange that honey
Can't be got without hard money.

(47–57)

John Barnard has drawn attention to the fact that Keats's poem is "less sentimental and more political" than Reynolds's were,[19] and the point is briskly exemplified. If, says Keats, they were to return, Robin to rise from "his turfed grave" (39) and Marian to revive "her forest days" (41), both materially realized images, they would have a political significance, a critique to make of the impact of modern power: imperial naval policy has denuded the forests for ships, while profiteering on rents, notorious in the period, has led to tenants' being forced to pay for things naturally growing on their holdings.

As Reynolds is the first to see a delightful intimacy between reader and forest dweller, Keats is the first to see these figures as a means of criticizing the inorganic, alienated character of modern society. Both positions will be powerful elements of the nineteenth-century—and the modern—understanding of the meaning of Robin Hood. And though they have since been expanded at great length and sometimes with great impact, they have rarely been as sharply and pithily expressed as on that wintry day in postwar, strife-torn, romanticizing England.

Keats, after his initial negation, accepted Reynolds's proposal to resurrect the outlaws but used that rebirth more sharply than his correspondent. Yet Keats the politician was never long-winded: the poem ends with his position moving closer to Reynolds and agreeing to share, in Robin's honor, the "silver can Of Rhenish" wine:

> Honour to bold Robin Hood,
> Sleeping in the underwood!
> Honour to Maid Marian,
> And to all the Sherwood-clan!
> Though their days have hurried by
> Let us two a burden try.
>
> (57–62)

In effect contradicting his opening, Keats agrees to celebrate—but at a greater distance than the intimacy Reynolds created, and with more linguistic precision: they will sing a burden, an outdated chorus.

Not so for Reynolds: he waxed stronger from this master class by distance-learning and produced a third sonnet, which Barnard understandably judges to be "the best":[20]

Robin the outlaw! Is there not a mass
Of freedom in the name? It tells the story
Of clenched oaks, with branches bow'd and hoary
Leaning in aged beauty o'er the grass:—
Of dazed smile on cheek of border lass,
List'ning 'gainst some old gate at his strange glory;—
And of the dappled stag, struck down and gory,
Lying with nostril wide in green morass.
It tells a tale of forest days—of times
That would have been most precious unto thee,—
Days of undying pastoral liberty!
Sweeter than music of old abbey chimes,—
Sweet as the virtue of Shakespearean rhymes,—
Days shadowy with the magic greenwood tree!

(134–35)

From the start Reynolds accepts Keats's idea about the political value of the hero, but he understands "freedom" as the freedom to visualize and to personalize rather than to offer political critique. The image of "clenched oaks with branches bow'd and hoary" gives the affective physical context, and the "dazed smile on cheek of border lass" sexualizes the relationship with the scene as, in its gruesome way, does the scene of "the dappled stag, struck down and gory": sadomasochism, both human and animal in focus, is a significant element in the romantic rapport that many nineteenth-century writers have with the Robin Hood tradition.

Reynolds seems to realize he has drifted away from political implications into heart-pumping excitement, so he returns to his own distinctly reduced sense of "a mass of freedom" related to, in series, "pastoral liberty" (not political), the national poet Shakespeare (who eschewed Robin Hood), and the sweet music of old abbeys (ignoring the fact that they contained Robin's enemies, those vicious old abbots and monks). These features merely activate cultural values in Reynolds's emotional national mainstreaming of the outlaw tradition. He ends this poem in a self-revealing way, with a line that realizes much of the nineteenth-century Robin Hoodery:

Days shadowy with the magic greenwood tree.

For the early ballads, the greenwood stood for fertility, a food-raising, animal-fattening summer. In gentrification, the greenwood became a pleasure-dome for aristocratic sport; now it is a domain of the imagination for urban fantasizers of worlds elsewhere.

Together Keats and Reynolds put into play crucial features: the beauty and the escapist value of the forest, the fascination and the enigmatic value of history—either as possible critique of the present or as another form of escape and self-authorization. Also of great importance in the nineteenth century, they created a strong flavor of sensual, masculine-focused feeling, which can be political but can also slide into a relished violence that the forest settings make possible. Another innovation of major importance is that without treating Robin as in any way gentrified—no earl, no property, no restoration by the king—Reynolds and Keats took from gentrification the crucial feature of Marian: even the social outlaw Robin, as Keats implicitly understands him, has a partner. This Robin Hood, in history, in touch with politics, realized as a person, sensualized, heterosexual but also homosocial, is a far more modern figure than the contradictory rebellious noble of Ritson's introduction.

The four poems were soon published: Keats's in 1820 in *Lamia, Isabella, The Eve of St. Agnes, and Other Poems* and Reynolds's as early as February 21, 1818, in *The Yellow Dwarf,* the widely read intellectual magazine run by John Hunt, brother of Leigh Hunt. The poems remained quite familiar throughout the century, those by Reynolds as well as those by the better-known Keats; they show dramatically how new ideas about poetry, its topics, and its readers' construction of identity could have innovative impact on the now quite ancient tradition of Robin Hood.

Leigh Hunt, himself a committed radical who had served two years in jail for deriding the Prince of Wales, was apparently inspired by the poems and by his reading in the tradition. Early in 1820 he published four "Ballads of Robin Hood" in his own magazine, *The Indicator.* When they were anthologized in his *Stories in Verse* in 1855, the subtitle *For Children* was added, but this does not appear in the original, and indeed does not seem very suitable to these sometimes politically sharp poems. The subtitle probably relates to the increasing direction of Robin Hood material toward young readers from the mid-century on.

Though the headnote Hunt wrote for the 1855 collection says the ballads are based on Robin's being "of gentle blood," it also calls this a "popular assumption"; the stories themselves re-create the garland tone of boyish social justice.[21] In the first ballad, "Robin Hood a Child," the friars steal his uncle's estate. In the second, "Robin Hood's Flight," the young Robin shoots a deer for a starving peasant and then kills the abbot and two foresters; the ballad has a cheerful tone and a harsh content, a mix characteristic of Leigh Hunt's volatile writing. The short third ballad seems to reflect on Hunt's own life as a radical. The ballad tells no story but merely describes "Robin the Outlaw" as remaining true to his original intention—like Hunt, it is implied:

> . . . we can say, *I* never will,
> False world, be false for thee
>
> (148)

For Hunt, as for Keats, Robin Hood is a totem of value by which the modern world can be tested. The last of the four ballads, "How Robin and His Outlaws Lived in the Woods," describes greenwood activities: being merry, practicing forest martial arts, feasting—the "forest community" image of the early ballads. But unlike them, and characteristic of the nineteenth century, these ballads include women as well:

> A pleasant sight, especially
> If Margery was there,
> Or little Cis, or laughing Bess,
> That tired out six pair.
>
> (149)

The heterosexual dance in the forest is a new feature, quite different from the all-male society of the previous texts, and Hunt recognizes the incompatibility of domesticity and the outlaw life:

> Only they say the men were given
> Too often to take wives,
> And then, twixt forest and a shop,
> Lead strange half-honest lives.
>
> (150)

The inherent improbability of combining masculine forest out-lawry with heterosexual society will haunt the nineteenth-century nov-elists, as Robin and Marian are a settled pair, but also he is a homoso-cial outlaw. By not countenancing heterosexuality, the early ballads had no problem; by making the pair temporary visitors to the forest, the gentrified texts avoided it. Now that Robin is both an active outlaw and a partnered man, the heart of the myth experiences a strain that will not be resolved until the story redefines itself as a love-conflict triangle. The triangle, already developed in the ballad operas, is a feature in which conflict over Marian becomes a main concern of the story.

Hunt ends his last ballad by reviving the idea of outlaw financial redistribution: Robin's joy would be "special"

> To light upon a good fat friar
> And carve him of his purse
>
> (150)

And this sadomasochistic (if also cartoon-like) element is developed:

> A monk to him was a toad in the hole,
> And a priest was a pig in grain,
> But a bishop was a baron of beef
> To cut and come again.
>
> (151)

The final tone is a little more thoughtful; in returning coin to the peas-ants, Robin sees it as their natural productivity restored after alienation:

> Says Robin to the poor who came
> To ask him for relief
> You do but get your goods again
> That were altered by the thief.
>
> (151)

These three Young Romantics, Keats, Reynolds, and Hunt, con-tributed much to the figure of Robin Hood. They stress his youth and charm, his natural connections, and his festal spirit. They imply or outline bold activities as well as innate—rather than in-born—nobility. They also touch on sexuality, with women resident in the forest, and they introduce a taste for violence, themes that will flour-ish as novelists take up the tradition. They also, in differing degrees but with consistent focus, make Robin a distinctly radical figure, connected with contemporary forces of reform.

Much of this pattern will be supported by another writer of 1818–19, the massively influential figure of Sir Walter Scott. Though he had gained high standing as a poet of romantic narratives like *Marmion* and *The Lady of the Lake* and may well have read the Reynolds poems, in 1819 he was still anonymous as the very successful author of the "Waverley" novels. His major impact on the Robin Hood tradition was to relocate Robin Hood within a historical and particularly a national frame of reference characteristic of the historical novel, though he also gave Robin the context of natural values that Keats and Reynolds had established. He was a literary and historical scholar of considerable standing, with an impressive knowledge of earlier material, both elevated and popular. He had met Ritson on several occasions and although their politics were worlds apart, they respected each other's work. Scott certainly knew the Robin Hood materials, and not only from Ritson's collection; he had already shown, in Douglas's archery success in *The Lady of the Lake* (see p. 99), the ability to adapt Robin Hood themes for other purposes. When he decided, mostly for financial reasons, to transfer his medieval fictions to an English scene in *Ivanhoe*, he had just finished *Rob Roy*, a Scottish outlaw story that in its opening pages makes it clear that the English outlaw is a shadowy presence. Even *The Heart of Midlothian* (1818) includes some Robin Hood traces.[22]

In *Ivanhoe*, dated in 1820 though it appeared in December 1819, the Robin Hood tradition has not simply provided a character, the powerful, even awe-inspiring Locksley; it also seems to have offered the basic plot. A noble and fairly young man is stripped of his title and lands by oppressive rulers in the time of Prince John. The hero is driven into the forests, finds friends, defends his own rights and a more general sense of social value, and is finally restored by the returning King Richard. Few would have had difficulty in putting the name Robin Hood to that hero. But to Scott, the distressed aristocrat is Ivanhoe; the whole novel is, in a real sense, a displaced Robin Hood story, much like *As You Like It*. It even begins in Barnsdale, but the figures are Saxon serfs, not Robin and his men. One of Scott's reasons for that displacement may well be that, knowing of the carnival-turned-riot in Edinburgh in 1561 and having had the radical Robin Hood thrust at him by Ritson's edition, he felt the figure was unacceptable for someone of his own innate conservatism. The threatening power of Locksley is always evident in the novel, and this may well be Scott realizing his own inherent fears of such a potent commoner. But there might also be less political reasons: he was too good a linguist (unlike most later authors and film directors) to offer Robin, or Robert, as the major name of a hero who, in this new departure in English historical fiction, had to be unimpeachably Saxon; only late in the text does Locksley reveal his better-known identity. Ivanhoe's name itself was originally more emotively Saxon: Scott planned to call him Harold, to remember Hastings, but decided that Byron's "Childe Harold" had preempted the name, so called him Ivanhoe after an Anglo-Saxon village name.[23] This was first and last a story based on theories of nationality and value or—more simply and more revealingly—race. All the other features of the text follow the crucial division between Norman and Saxon.

So a major new feature emerges in Robin's mythic biography: he is quintessentially, racially, English, and proves this by his hostility to the Norman French. The idea stems from the "Norman Yoke" theory of history, popular from the seventeenth century onward,[24] arguing that a relatively free, prosperous Anglo-Saxon peasantry was cowed into impoverished serfdom by the military triumph of the Normans in 1066. The idea was a weapon for eighteenth-century radicals such as Tom Paine, who influenced indirectly the French revolution and directly the American War of Independence: he linked Normans to lords and dismissed both. Scott shows that the idea can be reversed: what is wrong with the lords in Ivanhoe's England is that they are Normans, not that they are lords—there are admirable Saxon lords, including Ivanhoe. Scott's elegant reversing of the radical "Norman Yoke" theory is just like the way in which setting Robin Hood back into the 1190s made his antiroyalist resistance become acceptable: both maneuvers justify the hero's oppositionist actions and make outlaw strength a platform for renewed tenure of lordship.

In terms of historical fact, the 1190s date invalidated the Norman-Saxon idea: no Saxon lords remained in the 1190s, and though the languages were still separated on a basis of power—French potent,

English largely servile—people did not associate their racial identity with their social condition. Scott, like so many in the period of nationalism, was prepared to brush aside his own historical knowledge to focus his whole text on race—including Jewishness as a secondary theme to the Norman-Saxon encounter in the story of Isaac and Rebecca. Much has flowed from this in the later outlaw tradition: few later versions of the Robin Hood myth have not in some way mirrored Scott's insistence that race is central to the outlaw story.

It is both ironic and predictive of future politics that in *Ivanhoe* the insertion of race into the tradition both restrains Robin's role and makes him more violent. He is known as Locksley—a name from a place, like Ivanhoe—and he is illiterate, a motif that later writers did not pursue but which Scott, a writer and lawyer, used to exclude him from the possibility of real power. He is also not a major character in the plot: Locksley in fact appears in only four main scenes. But his power seems enhanced by that restriction, like the impact of a fine supporting performance in film; Ivanhoe himself is a notoriously dead part for an actor. The jacket illustration for the 1985 Penguin Classics edition has nothing to do with the eponymous hero: it is the expansive Maclise painting of Robin feasting the king—the climax not of the novel's plot but of its secondary use of the outlaw material.

Yet Scott's impact on the tradition is more than a new racializing of the story. He is also a great novelist, and the sense of a human presence that emerges in Reynolds' sonnets is powerfully realized in *Ivanhoe*. The outlaw first appears as

> a stout well-set yeoman, arrayed in Lincoln green, having twelve arrows stuck in his belt, with a baldric and a badge of silver, and a bow of six feet length in his hand. (80)

He is unnamed, but no one could doubt who this is: the depiction combines the condensed menace of the fifteenth-century bandit with the robust iconicity of the woodcuts in the broadside ballads (see figures 2 and 3). Scott leaves the character there, and then brings him steadily but intermittently in from the margin. This vigorous figure accepts the prince's archery challenge and famously wins, but in a new way: when Robin Hood splits the arrow, Scott deploys a fantasy projection of the medieval concepts of "splitting the wand" or "split-

ting the peg"—that is, hitting the wooden objects that held the target. Scott had already used this idea with Douglas in the archery tournament in *The Lady of the Lake*, but here, very influentially, attaches
the idea to Robin Hood.[25] Hubert, Locksley's opponent, has just
landed an arrow in the center of the target:

> "Thou canst not mend that shot, Locksley," said the Prince,
> with an insulting smile.
> "I will notch his shaft for him however," replied Locksley.
> And letting fly his arrow with a little more caution than
> before, it lighted right upon that of his competitor, which it
> split to shivers. (152)

This has become the archetypal Robin Hood moment. Being totally improbable, it is a superhero's achievement, ripe for use in films,
television, and comics. But the feat is also rich with new meaning in
Scott's time: it is racist—Hubert had a grandfather at Hastings, so
this is a Saxon revenge for Harold, who by tradition died from a Norman arrow. But the contest is also a masculine encounter: the deliberate aggression of "I will notch his shaft for him" is rich with the in-
termale hostility that was recognized but contained in the many
"Robin meets his match" ballads. Robin's triumph is evidently a phallic one—not unlike Arthur's drawing the sword from the stone—and
this is underlined in the sequence that follows, as even Prince John
"in admiration of Locksley's skill, lost for an instant his dislike to his
person" (153). The comment emphasizes Locksley's body: throughout
the novel Scott creates images of both class and race with physical and
sensual intensity, but far more so with Locksley than with Ivanhoe
himself.

The outlaw has two more major appearances that both realize his
power and restrain his impact in a tension that gives the character considerable force and fascination. The Black Knight (an alias and idea
borrowed from Malory's Lancelot in the Tristram story) leads the
Saxon assault on Torquilstone, where, with some of the Gothic sadomasochism beloved of the period, we have a besieged youthful beauty
and a raped and maddened older woman, as well as Norman nobles
who can take the blame. But the success of the siege depends heavily
on Locksley's leadership of the archers to cover the Black Knight's

assault in chapter 29, and then in chapter 31 he drives in the assault on the weak spot when he alone sees the signal from inside the castle. Throughout this he is called, by author and Black Knight alike, no more than "stout yeoman," and there remains about him a cloud of mystery that he himself has expressed to Gurth and Wamba: "who or what I am is little to the present purpose" (206). But after the battle, as the outlaws withdraw into the forest again, Scott himself seems finally drawn into the outlaw tradition that he has so far used only at a distance. The epigraph to chapter 32 claims to be from an "Old Play" but is, as A. N. Wilson's note indicates, "usually attributed to Scott himself" (576). It expresses clearly his anxiety about outlawry:

> Even the wild outlaw, in his forest-walk
> Keeps yet some touch of civil discipline;
> For not since Adam wore his verdant apron
> Hath man with man in social union dwelt,
> But laws were made to draw that union closer.
>
> (347)

Yet the following sequence indicates that Locksley is not so much in union with the rest of society as a self-standing unit separate from it. Just half a mile from the destroyed Norman castle of Torquilstone, "Locksley assumed his seat—a throne of turf erected under the twisted branches of the huge oak" (348). Then, addressing both Cedric, the leading Saxon noble, and the Black Knight (whom we all, from our knowledge of the Robin Hood tradition, recognize as the king):

> "Pardon my freedom, noble sirs," he said, "but in these glades I am monarch: they are my kingdom; and these my wild subjects would reck but little of my power, were I, within my own dominions, to yield place to mortal man." (348)

In this utopia, the Saxon serf Gurth is freed, the Saxon lady Rowena comes to offer thanks and unlimited food and drink, firm justice is dispensed to Norman prisoners, and Locksley divides the spoils "with the most laudable impartiality" among his men, so that, as in the *Gest*, the Black Knight is impressed by "the justice and judgement of their leader" (356).

As if his forest authority is exercising control over the story—it surely did over Scott's imagination at this point—the scene continues in Robin Hood mode. There is feasting and a game of buffets from the *Gest*, and two yeomen bring in as prisoner the prior of Jorvaulx "before the sylvan throne of our outlaw chief" (361). In addition there is much celebration of a figure who is to remain throughout most of the modern versions, the jovial friar, eating, drinking, making jokes, and, fully carnivalizing on behalf of the outlaws the learning and dignity of the church.

Moving quickly now, in chapter 40 Scott makes the king announce himself to the outlaws and pardon them; in return, Locksley gives his name as "Robin Hood of Sherwood Forest." The king replies, appropriately enough, "King of outlaws, and Prince of good fellows!" (464–65). The plot has indeed shown Robin to be a fellow—that is, an equal—of the king, because of his military skills and determined character. Later the king calls him "brother sovereign" (471), and it finally seems as if Scott cannot restrain his sense of sympathy for—even identity with—this straightforward, honest, potent character. Like one of the plain-speaking truth tellers of Scott's other novels, Robin in chapter 41 has to put the king straight and stop him from carousing too much. Finally, in a remarkable moment that shows Scott's sense of the dangerous attractiveness of the outlaw figure, the author breaks contact and sends the outlaw back to the world where he found him:

> As for the rest of Robin Hood's career, as well as the tale of his treacherous death, they are to be found in those black-letter garlands, once sold at the low and easy rate of one halfpenny:
> Now cheaply purchased at their weight in gold. (475)

Scott suggests that his real business with Robin Hood was a matter of cross-class literary borrowing. He meant Robin to be simply an illiterate, tough, Saxon non-commissioned officer. There is no Little John, because that is the role Robin is meant to play for Ivanhoe,[26] but the outlaw hero tends to dominate a scene whoever else appears in it—Prince John, the disguised Richard, or the skillfully manipulative historical novelist.

There can be no doubt that Scott's main thematic impact on the outlaw tradition was to make it a matter of race, Saxon versus Norman. He also gave great weight to the "days of bad Prince John" setting, though that did not become absolutely dominant until the days of film. But Scott was also the first novelist to handle the outlaw theme, and, restrained though his Locksley is, he is still a powerful, potently masculine individual. There is no Marian, and so Scott passes on in vigorous form the homosocial pattern of the early texts in both a sense of cheerful revelry and value for male bonding. That too will last, even when Marian joins Robin in the nineteenth-century forest. As a historical writer and something of an armchair warrior (he planned to raise a regiment against unruly workers and call it the Loyal Foresters),[27] Scott also made Robin a military man; in the decades that followed, some lively pages and many less than enthralling ones were produced in that mode.

But perhaps Scott's most important move was to take Robin Hood out of marginal theater, antiquarian anthologies, fugitive garlands, and the private thoughts of poets, and to insert him into the middle of the dominant and massively developing genre of the period, the novel. Much was to flow from that. The first novel actually entitled *Robin Hood* is an enigma. It was published in Edinburgh, in mid 1819, and it uses the Scott-like device of an introducing character who will pass this story on to the reader. Yet this work can hardly be a response to *Ivanhoe*: Scott did not publish his novel until December 1819, and he had been keen to maintain secrecy while writing it, as there were pirated pastiches of his novels about—hardly surprising, as he would not put his name to them. The 1819 *Robin Hood* may simply have been inspired by *Rob Roy*, with its early discussion of the English outlaw. Even if the author had heard that Scott was working on Robin Hood, it is quite different from *Ivanhoe* and should be thought of as yet another product of the Robin Hood golden age in 1818–19. The 1819 *Robin Hood* develops the implications of the Keats-Reynolds romanticization of the hero in the direction of the dominant Romantic prose form, the Gothic novel. Some later novelists will to some degree follow the same path, though drawing their major influence from Thomas Love Peacock.

The 1819 *Robin Hood* begins in fine Gothic mode with a heroine trapped unwillingly in a nunnery; she has the finely romantic name of Ruthinglenne as well. She encounters the outlaws in broad, if not broadside, ballad form—Allan a Dale and Little John turn up at the nunnery disguised as a blind minstrel and his mother. But though Robin is described in the lengthy "Introductory Chapter" as a "free-booter,"[28] there is little actual plundering: Robin comes to dislike being known as a robber ("This name was become hateful to his thoughts," 2:103–4). Most of the fairly intricate action involves the noble family of Pevys Castle, where Will Scarlet is located; he is Robin's enemy and, as it turns out, illegitimate cousin, who has frustrated Robin's "just expectations" to the estate (2:180). The Sheriff of Nottingham is Sir Walter de Clare, father of Claribel, to whom Robin is briefly affianced before finally claiming his true love, Ruthinglenne, "the Mysterious Nun," Claribel's long-lost twin sister.

If the center of the story is the transmutation of the "displaced earl" story into a fairly overheated inheritance drama, there is also a lively element of the Gothic. The story opens in familiar sensational style:

> The night was dark and stormy: the bleak winds of autumn blew the shrivelled leaves from the withering branches of the trees: the countenance of nature was forlorn; and the flitting owl, which screamed dismally in the wood, as it winged its course through the area in search of prey, appeared the only animated being which had not sought shelter from the blast. (1:81–82)

Ruthinglenne is of course also out in the weather; she is the usual sensitive, pale, needing-to-be-looked-after, but also in the end rich and well-connected, heroine. Robin is, unlike in Scott but as normal in the nineteenth century, rather dashing:

> His dress was green, like that of his companions; but it was enriched by a purple scarf thrown across his shoulders, and by a knot of plume in a similar colour which waved in his cap. (1:131)

Less predictably, Robin is a harper and, bizarrely, he has never shot an arrow before but turns out to be very good at it immediately (2:36). Some details indicate that the author refers to other texts: for example, a sequence in which Robin and John are lost in the forest and then meet the captain of the outlaws reads rather like *Gamelyn*, which could have been known through Ritson's notes. In addition, there is mention of the Bishop of Hereford (2:182); the ballad about him was also available in Ritson. Robin plays a harp to "the Merry Men of Sherwood" while they spend "an idle hour with the shepherdesses who tended their flocks on the borders of the Forest" (2:41), an apparent reference to Jonson's *The Sad Shepherd,* also in Ritson's discussion of the sources of the tradition.

Though this is in many ways a hybrid text, with pastoral and Gothic joining the outlaw story, and is not likely to have had much influence, it nevertheless already represents a number of themes that will recur in mainstream outlaw novels. These include the presence of a substantial number of women in and around the forest, including outlaws' wives; the use of much natural setting to manipulate emotion; the familiarity with the modes and meanings of the Gothic; and the obsession with family lineage and various inheritances, including Robin's. His enemies here and in many texts to follow are corrupt aristocrats, not the overeager sheriffs or yeoman enemies of the early ballads, and even the Catholic clergy are less venomous than in the Reformation. In this respect the Robin Hood novels are in line with much nineteenth-century fiction, so often a weapon of the emergent bourgeoisie against the aristocracy they aspired to supplant.

Curious and relatively trivial as it is in terms of the tradition, the 1819 *Robin Hood* introduces into the novel the kind of sensibility that Reynolds and Keats showed in their poetry of the previous year, with the interest in and empathy with individual character that is central to the novel. There is so much use of gothic devices and so little of the sexist or violent elements of the later Robin Hood novels that it seems quite possible that the author was a woman. Though it probably had little direct influence on the tradition, *Robin Hood* of 1819 is strongly indicative of how the outlaw was changing. It is the first of the novels and plays that shape the dominant Robin Hood of the nineteenth century, a gentleman who is in touch with the vitality of nature; he is not very active as a robber, has a lady, and has youthful charm and patriotic energy. Whether actually noble or not, he seems best described as Robin Hood Esquire, a title that indicates the respectable leader of a characteristic English family in this dynamic century, which was as rich and innovative in Robin Hood activity as in so many other spheres.

Lord of the Forest

Robin Hood's noble birth is one of the secrets revealed in the 1819 novel *Robin Hood,* and that social status differentiates the knightly freebooter of the semi-gothic story from the other Romantic re-creators of the hero so far discussed. They neither used Ritson's biographic formulation nor were in any substantial narrative way influenced by the ballads he had gathered and were newly available in the small one-volume reprint edition of 1820—itself probably a response to *Ivanhoe.* But in 1818 one author was at work on a full and ultimately very influential piece of Robin Hood fiction that did accept the challenge offered by Ritson to combine an earl's status with a bandit's adventures. He used yet another genre: after the historical novel by Scott and the anonymous semi-gothic novel, Robin Hood now appeared in the form of the novella. At this time and in Thomas Love Peacock's hands, this implied not only a short novel, but also one that, like the early work of Maria Edgeworth, was heavily influenced by French eighteenth-century *contes morales* rather than by the sprawling English novels of that period. Peacock's interest here, as in his other short works, was to be witty and satiric, and as in *The Misfortunes of Elphin* he used a story from the past as the structure on which to base his elegant and often poetic wit.

Peacock was a whimsical, learned, and liberal man, and by 1818 he had already published *Melincourt, Headlong Hall,* and *Nightmare Abbey*, well-received ironic novellas, when he began working on *Maid Marian*. He stopped writing it to concentrate on starting a bureaucratic career with the East India Company, an imperial trading business, and when the book was published in 1822 he added a note to insist that all but the last three chapters were completed early, presumably to indicate that he was not inspired by *Ivanhoe*. He may have overestimated his early achievement; in fact, the last seven chapters seem to be a unit, and tend to use ballad material as their fairly unaltered source, compared with what has gone before. But in any case there are few signs of Scott's influence.[29] From the start *Maid Marian* is a gentrified text with Munday, presumably via Ritson, as the obvious point of reference. Robin is an earl, and the first scene is his wedding with Matilda Fitzwater; this is disrupted by his enemies, however, and he goes into exile, soon to be joined by Marian and soon after that by her father.

The text is markedly theatrical, not only in the amount of speech that is deployed (as in all of Peacock's novellas) but also in the first emphatic use of a motif that had already developed in the ballad operas: a love-conflict triangle between Robin, Marian, and the chief villain. This extends the threat Prince John provided in Munday and is a pattern much repeated since. Here Sir Ralph de Montfaucon is at first just the king's agent to arrest Robin, who is in trouble for breach of forest laws and for debts to an abbot. But as soon as Sir Ralph sees Marian, he becomes the moustache-twirling, heroine-desiring villain beloved of Victorian melodrama, though even he is not truly bad: he takes on Robin's arrest as part of his understandable careerism, and the text makes it clear that no red-blooded gentleman could resist Marian.

Coming from Munday and the gentrified tradition, she is here given the title "maid" for the first time. Frances Brooke's light opera *Marian* of 1788[30] is really a pastoral with Marian's lover Robin the Boatman being too far from any version of the outlaw for credible recognition. But to be the heroine and in the title does not give Peacock's Marian any real dominance; he was also one of the Young Romantics, and their sensual personalization and male viewpoint is clear. In the first scene she hardly speaks, is called "Sweet Marian" by the earl, and receives a kiss on her lips.[31] She first has a main part to play at the opening of chapter 4, where an extended version of Reynolds's male gaze creates her as a most desirable object:

> Matilda, not dreaming of visitors, tripped into the apartment in a dress of forest green, with a small quiver by her side and a bow and arrow in her hand. Her hair, black and glossy as the raven's wing, curled like wandering clusters of dark ripe grapes under the edge of a round bonnet, and a plume of black feathers fell back negligently above it. . . . Her black eyes sparkled like sunbeams on a river: a clear, liquid radiance, the reflection of ethereal fire,—tempered, not subdued in the medium of its living and gentle mirror. Her lips were half opened to speak as she entered the apartment. (26)

The Diana-like opening motif of quiver and bow is transmuted into sensuously natural images—grapes, feathers, and sunbeams. Though she has some elements of "ethereal fire," they are "tempered" and made "gentle," and, as in so much writing of the century, through to Hardy's Tess, the erotic focus on the woman's lips is insistently masculine.

If Marian is in this way controlled by the narrative, she is not by her father: he is one of a series of irritable but ineffectual fathers that fill the Robin Hood novels as they do the work of women writers from Jane Austen to George Eliot, and a mother remains equally absent. The feature that most nearly justifies giving Marian the title is that Robin himself is surprisingly inactive, especially in the first half of the book. In the later sequences, when Peacock was hurrying to finish for publication, the story moves on through ballad stories and Robin is a good deal more engaged.

Peacock always has an intellectual and ironic element, and here his purpose is to use the medieval legend to criticize contemporary conservatives who sought to justify in past glories their refusal to permit the reform that Peacock steadily supported. He creates a poet laureate called "Harpiton," a none-too-subtle dig at Robert Southey, the contemporary laureate who had become an archconservative.[32] In a long and stagy speech by Brother Michael Peacock reuses, as did Scott, Ritson's potent rhetorical question about the relative rights of Richard I and Robin Hood. But Peacock develops it into a critique of contemporary tax evasion and resistance to social reform, asserting that "William the Conqueror and Robin Hood differ indeed, in this that William took from the poor and gave to the rich, and Robin takes from the rich and gives to the poor: and therein is Robin illegitimate: though in all else he is true prince"(82). As Butler explains, "legitimacy" was the totemic term derived by Burke from the past,[33] and was a catchword of contemporary politics, ripe for Peacock's burlesquing. This kind of argument is recurrent through the novella, and Brother Michael is its usual mouthpiece. There are two friars—a fat, comic, drinking and eating one and another, Michael, who is as good with a staff or sword as with his tongue. Representing the writer in the text (like Skelton in Munday), Michael is Marian's special protector and the prime means of turning this fairly affectionate realization of a medieval myth into a piece of contemporary political banter.

Peacock's medieval renovating outlasted his politics. A skilled plotter, he activates the middle of the novella by neatly condensing the opening events of "Robin Hood's Birth, Breeding, Valour and Marriage" with a chance meeting between Sir Ralph de Montfaucon and Marian. Sir Ralph pursues the outlaws, and besieges Arlingford, Marian's father's castle, in a sequence that looks, from its place in the plot more than its actual detail, like a reworking of Scott's siege of Torquilstone, even though Peacock claimed to have written this before he read Scott. His stitching together of ballads and their action toward the end of the story is elegantly done: later writers would learn a lot about shaping a Robin Hood saga from this version. But they would also see fully formed versions of Young Romantic Robin Hood motifs. Peacock sums up forest life:

> So Robin and Marian dwelt and reigned in the forest, ranging the glades and the greenwoods from the matins of the lark to the vespers of the nightingale, and administering natural justice accordingly to Robin's ideas of rectifying the inequalities of human condition: raising genial dews from the bags of the rich and idle, and returning them in fertilising showers on the poor and industrious: an operation which more enlightened statesmen have happily reversed, to the unspeakable benefit of the community at large. (126)

Here natural beauty merges through metaphor into forms of "natural justice," and a final gibe at the present ranges the author alongside the values of the outlaw. Peacock's position is parallel to that of Keats and Hunt; though his characteristic playfulness may blunt his irony a little, he does offer the greenwood as a source for true values and genuine law, a motif that will become permanent in the tradition.

He also provides an element of plotting that nineteenth-century novelists will often employ. In order to "find refuge" (91) Marian's father withdraws to the Gamwell family home in Barnsdale; this use of a second forest site as a place to locate characters who are not needed or of much interest, particularly women, will prove handy later, especially when the outlaw plots become overcomplicated in long novels. A more important plot element is that hero and heroine remain at the end in the forest: when Richard returns, Robin is restored, as in Munday, but by now neither the novel nor they have any interest in the aristocratic life as such. Peacock quickly takes us on to the reign of bad King John, when they are again exiled and end their days in "their greenwood sovereignty" (14) which, whether they die or not, is the usual conclusion of the novels. Robin and Marian essentially present greenwood virtues. Brother Michael sums them up as early as the end of chapter 2: "They are twin plants of the forest, and are identified with its growth" (20).

That statement is followed by a song about "the slender beech and the sapling oak," and there are many fine lyrics through the text. Readers tend to regard the songs as optional extras, but they were a prime cause of the great influence Peacock held in the nineteenth century. In the same year as it was published, a musical version of *Maid Marian* was performed on the London stage, arranged by the prolific producer J. R. Planché, with music by George Bishop. It was a long-standing favorite: George Saintsbury, writing in 1895, spoke from personal experience that the musical was "extraordinarily popular" and that as a result the novella was read by many who knew nothing else by the author.[34]

Peacock set up for the outlaw hero his new positioning, as a vigorous patriotic English heterosexual, in touch with natural law and noble in both birth and values. Peacock brought wit and light-handed politics to the outlaw tradition, but that element was not widely copied. Crucially for the tradition he combined the status of the noble earl with the dynamic actions of the social bandit: Ritson's stimulus was transmitted through Peacock's imaginative skill.

But Ritson's stimulus had not only been narrative: he had also presented the fullest, though not the first, of the "real" Robin Hoods, those figures whose biography is taken to be more important than their mythic meaning. The late medieval chroniclers had assumed that history and story were the same thing and that fables about a person were part of his public persona. The gentrified writers, on the other hand, had focused their biographicism on tangible remains such as manuscripts, graves, and epitaphs. Ritson, however, had generated a Robin Hood suitable for the new age of biography. Scott, while attracted to a personality for the hero, still wanted to restrain him in a number of ways, especially in terms of social status and narrative presence. And Peacock was the first to develop the Robin Hood historical novel, with speech, character, and motivation—the full Romantic individualist treatment for the outlaw hero, capable of being perceived as a real historical identity.

The Robin Hood who emerged from this crucial period had changed enormously, as is epitomized in two title pages. The 1820 reprint of Ritson's anthology has an illustration on the title page showing Robin fighting a sturdy, broad-shouldered fellow with a quarterstaff. The artwork is a recut version of Berwick's illustration for the "Robin meets his match" duel in "Robin Hood and the Tanner," and it implies a straightforward fighting hero (figure 10). But for the title page of the 1823 reprint a completely different image of Robin is imagined, one closer to Reynolds than Keats, Peacock, or Hunt: the outlaw sits and dreams, and a stag escapes (figure 11). Romantic Robin has been created, a hero who is now decisively national, natural, and masculine. This powerful version of the hero is still with us.

A Novel Outlaw

Peacock's hero is not merely an entry in a biographic dictionary: for Peacock, as for Keats, the hero's historicism has political meaning as a comment on how conflicts of the past cast light on tensions of the present. Two French writers found this an intriguing approach and followed Ritson in their elaboration of Robin Hood, gentleman but also nationalist reformer, who was an admired model. Their main source was a translation of Peacock's *Maid Marian*, as postwar France struggled to reestablish traditional social order without losing some of the gains of the revolutionary period. In 1825 Auguste Thierry included a lengthy discussion on the outlaw in his history of the Norman conquest of England, and in 1832 Edmond Barry, apparently of Scots origin, focused a thesis on the outlaw.[35] The writers who followed Peacock and Scott would almost all see the biographic historicity of Robin Hood as having political meaning of some sort.

Pierce Egan the Younger was a major force in the development of Robin Hood fiction. His father was well known for sporting and adventurous novels, and the son also mined a popular vein. After success

ROBIN HOOD:

A

COLLECTION

OF ALL THE ANCIENT

POEMS, SONGS, AND BALLADS,

NOW EXTANT,

RELATIVE TO THAT CELEBRATED

English Outlaw:

TO WHICH ARE PREFIXED

HISTORICAL ANECDOTES OF HIS LIFE.

LONDON:

PRINTED FOR LONGMAN, HURST, REES, ORME, AND
BROWN, PATERNOSTER-ROW; AND T. BOYS,
LUDGATE-HILL.

1820.

FIG. 10. Robust Robin: title page illustration of the 1820 reprint of Joseph Ritson's collection of ballads

ROBIN HOOD:

A

COLLECTION

Of all the Ancient

POEMS, SONGS, AND BALLADS,

NOW EXTANT,

RELATIVE TO THAT CELEBRATED

English Outlaw:

To which are prefixed

HISTORICAL ANECDOTES OF HIS LIFE.

LONDON:

PRINTED FOR C. STOCKING, 3, PATERNOSTER-ROW,
By J. and C. Adlard, Bartholomew-close.

1823.

FIG. II. Romantic Robin: title page illustration of the 1823 reprint of Joseph Ritson's collection of ballads

with the historical and not unpolitical *Wat Tyler*, about the so-called Peasants' Revolt of 1381, he produced in 1840 the detailed, sprawling *Robin Hood and Little John, or The Merry Men of Sherwood Forest.*[36] Nearly half a million words long, this is three-volume length but its format is popular, appearing in one closely printed volume, with many typographical errors and engagingly naive illustrations, some by Egan himself. Where Peacock wrote a brief, witty, sometimes lyrical novella for a discerning audience, Egan produced a massive, wordy, often clumsily written saga for a mass public. The mythic hero is squarely in the modern publishing marketplace, and his life is extremely popular in tone. Robin's father was "a soldier of good family" who turns out to be the Earl of Huntingdon (following the spelling of the place, not Munday's character), while his mother's family "valued themselves upon their pure descent from a Saxon monarch" (5). He has youthful attractiveness that verges on the erotic:

> He was slightly but well-formed; his limbs, though slender, had that easy set—that freedom of action which, in youth, indicates coming strength; his chest was open, even to an unusual breadth—his uprightness of bearing giving it an expanse in appearance which it, perhaps, did not really possess; his head and face were round, and well set upon his shoulders; his eyes were a deep hazel, large, full and bright to a degree (9)

And he is found deep in the forest by a great oak:

> Here was the monarch of the woods, with its principal gnarled branches twisted into straggling but admired disorder; there the tall beech, with its thin elegant boughs; the graceful acacia, the stately elm, the dark pines, the larch and the gentle willow with its drooping stress of pale green leaves, like unto the aerial draping of a fairy; the earth was carpeted with a turf, whose tint and smoothness made it difficult to believe that it was grass and not velvet the feet were pressing; there was profusion of flowers here, there, and everywhere (42)

These trees could not grow in the same place; Egan's purpose is a romantic, even mythic, forest effect, not dendrological accuracy.

Robin lives in this rural utopia with Gilbert Head, also known as Hood; this name is also found in the 1819 novel *Robin Hood,* and both presumably derive from Ritson, who reports its presence in *Looke About You*. But before long we discover that Gilbert is only a foster father and that the child Robin was the real inheritor of the Earl of Huntingdon. If inheritance drama is a familiar mode in the popular novel, another is sensuous, even titillating, excitement. Herbert Clare (also a surname in the 1819 novel), warder of Nottingham Castle, has a pretty daughter Maude, who comes to the forest and will eventually be the wife of Will Scarlet, but throughout the opening development Robin is repeatedly kissing her lips, which are like "rare, tempting fruit" (143). Marian herself has "pulpy lips" that promise good kissing (19) and Robin is already heart-struck by her, but through Maude he seems to demonstrate both virility and a curious relationship with Will, who also kisses Maude a lot. This erotic rivalry between two handsome men, with several intimate combats and encounters in which the woman is as much a mediator of desire as its object, is a regular feature of the Robin Hood story from Egan on. It started, in a mild form, in Peacock, and it invites exploration into Robin Hood's ambiguity of gender. This ambiguity appears to fit very well with Eve Kosofsky Sedgwick's argument for the widespread development of erotic homosocial relationships in fiction around the turn of the eighteenth and nineteenth centuries.[37] The illustration of Robin and his rival, both separated and linked by the phallic sword, is a classic instance of Sedgwick's thesis (figure 12).

Apart from these variously romantic realizations of Robin, there is frantic activity: a fight at Gilbert's cottage, much as in Peacock; enemies coming and going through the forest; many burials at the forest oak; and escapes and alarms inside Nottingham Castle. The melodramatic novel, like the Hollywood film, does much more with the castle than the forest-focused ballads ever did, though even Errol Flynn never tangled with a villain as extreme as Egan's Caspar Steinkopft.

Marian rarely appears, but after six years she and Robin exchange vows, eventually marry and—the Victorian domestic idyll has its own force—have a child, as do the other couples in this curiously bourgeois forest. But the outlaw hero's story does not permit a sentimental family: the child dies, and Marian spends much time with Robin's great-uncle Gamwell at a place called Barnsdale Hall, in the spare forest, that parking lot for unwanted characters, which

FIG. 12. Robin and rival, by Pierce Egan the Younger from *Robin Hood and Little John*, 1840

has under the pressures of Victorian respectability become a gentleman's estate.

Most of the second half of the book involves Robin and the other outlaws in versions of the ballad adventures made more militaristic; at one point twelve Saxons kill a hundred Normans in a brutal and much-relished set-piece battle. Then King Richard returns and pardons Robin, but there is not much to pardon him for: Robin, it transpires, has actually preserved the king's deer, not poached them, and why he was outlawed in the first place is never clear. Like the Robin Hood of Reynolds, Keats, and Scott—and implicitly Peacock—he somehow belongs in the forest. Toward the end, the outlaws, now a part of the royal armies, are attacked in the forest and Marian is shot and killed by accident, not unlike the good-natured barmaid in a cowboy film. Savage vengeance is taken, and only three of one hundred Normans survive. The novel has a striking undercurrent of such sadomasochism, including some cruel treatment of animals, reminiscent of Reynolds's dying stag—examples of what A. N. Wilson, in his edition of *Ivanhoe,* calls "the often violent medieval fantasies of middle-class nineteenth-century England."[38] Finally Robin is betrayed by the prioress, a dangerous sexualized woman who loves Guy of Gisborne's brother. Robin dies and is buried at the forest tree; the novel ends with Keats's lines about "Honor to Bold Robin Hood" (with "honor" spelled the American way).

Dynamic and slipshod at the same time, touching most points in the Victorian moral and sensual reflexive system, Egan's *Robin Hood* is a major disseminating force of the reconstructed outlaw; it was often reprinted and is the vulgate form of the tradition in its new period. Here Peacock's elegant new structure is sprawlingly re-created; his few moments of sexism are lavished over many pages; his elegant wit becomes blunt moralization and masculine self-admiration. The occasional silliness of Egan (such as a villain in search of Marian's body called Sir Tristram Uggeleretsch) and the clumsiness of both his style and his drawings tend to domesticate the outlaw myth. Egan seems to be a massive version of the many printed garlands and chapbooks that were still appearing with clumsy block prints and bizarre adventures: in one recurring chapbook story Robin dresses up as a young woman and persuades a wealthy young man to take him off into the forest for sexual purposes—then robs him. Egan's novel is in touch not only with the new ideas of gentrification and Saxon-Norman conflict but also with the sweltering currents of popular culture at their most muddled, elaborate, and psychically potent. A direct result of his success was the production in 1849 of a partner volume, *Maid Marian, The Forest Queen.*[39] The author was Joachim

H. Stocqueler, a jobbing writer of prose and drama with a lively imagination and wide experience. He had worked for twenty years in
India, produced some military narratives, and went on to a new life
in America, not the English death recorded by the *Dictionary of
National Biography*.[40] More fluent than Egan but handicapped by the
fact that he could not, in a companion volume, duplicate the mainstream material already used, Stocqueler just made things up.

This novel opens with Marian alone in the forest. Peacock's lush
reification of the female is more fully developed; she is armed but still
elegant:

> Although the green tunic, the russet boot and the close fitting
> hose—the broad felt hat, and the black hackle plucked from
> an eagle's wing—the bugle, the staff and the *couteau de chasse*,
> or hunting knife, would have denoted a man, and he a lawless
> forest ranger; the face, the delicate limbs, the rich ringlets
> which covered the hand on which the small head reclined, left
> no doubt that the recumbent form was that of one of the op-
> posite sex. (2)

She is seen as "queen of the wood" over "the merry thieves" (Keats's
phrase reappears) because Robin, whose "maiden bride" she is (3), has
gone away on crusade, having lost his social position for some unclear
reason (but apparently involving debts). A villain-rich plot develops:
Prince John, disguised first as a pilgrim then as "Edric the Saxon," is
prowling the forest, looking for women. His favorite, apart from
Marian, is Edith, daughter of Hugo Malair. The name Hugo is borrowed from Scott; Malair is a characteristic Stocqueler joke. Edith
probably comes from Thomas Miller's *Royston Gower* (1838), where a
chronologically displaced Edith Swan-Neck (in history the lover of
King Harold) is at risk in the forest. Stocqueler stirs up this piquant
stew: John presses Edith for sexual favors and she weakens—the writing is quite highly charged with eroticism—but eventually, after having his way with her, the prince throws her out of the castle window
to death in the moat. Marian is also captured, having been, with more
erotic and sadistic effect, gored by a boar in the forest.

Several military and bloodthirsty chapters—seeming almost like a
lull after the hectic forest action—detail Robin's role in the taking of

Acre, and he returns with an Arab couple, father and daughter. Much Orientalism follows, with a dancing girl and mysterious male threats, followed by an encounter with a local witch (Minnie Eftskin, no doubt of theatrical origin) whom Marian visits for a love potion as her returned beloved is so distant to her. Stocqueler does not develop the "false Marian" possibilities, perhaps because his text lacks the kind of reticent masculine neurosis that empowers such a formation. Rather, he sweeps on with a lively mix of sensational events and characters, including a rich Jew and his daughter out of *Ivanhoe*. But instead of reverting, as Peacock and Egan did, to ballads for the second half, Stocqueler invents a new distressed gentleman, Wilfrid (not, however, surnamed Ivanhoe), with his own beloved, whose hair is done by Maid Marian—something of a comedown for the erstwhile heroine. After much engagement with this new, space-filling pack of gentry and their problems, we eventually have Richard's return and the reinstatement of Robert Fitz Ooth (from Ritson) as Earl of Huntingdon. Stocqueler does not reenact the ending of the story but merely gives a quasi-scholarly account, drawn entirely from Ritson, of Robin's death and Marian's sad aftermath—as in Munday, her hounding by John and her death at Dunmow. Stocqueler finds his way out of the story in the literary mode that led him into it as a sequel. But along the way he has demonstrated how ripe the outlaw myth was to illustrate the many ideologies dear to the heart, at least of the Victorian male.

Not all the treatments in the nineteenth century were so melodramatic or even erotic as those by Egan and Stocqueler. A literature for children was evolving in the late eighteenth century, and some of the nineteenth-century Robin Hood chapbooks, with large print and small format, may have been directed toward children. In fact, the outlaw story itself may have been an initiating element in the growth of children's literature, as Bennet A. Brockman has argued.[41] An early version of the possibility of the outlaw story at this level is by "Stephen Percy"—that is, John Cundall—in *Robin Hood and His Merry Foresters,* which appeared, like Egan's novel, in 1840. The Cundall story seems clearly directed to younger readers through the simplicity of style and the naive woodland morality. A fuller move in the same direction was by George Emmett: his *Robin Hood and the Outlaws of Sherwood Forest* appeared in 1869 in fifty-two weekly parts in the

"Young Englishman's Edition"; it also appeared in one-volume form by binding together the parts.[42] The writer (whose name did not appear on this first edition) claimed to have done "immense research . . . among the ancient manuscripts and pamphlets" (2), but Ritson and G. P. R. James (see pp. 143–44) seem to be the sources of the stories. Robin Hood is "a bold yeoman who has erroneously been termed a robber" but he hates "with a thorough Saxon hate, the Norman oppression of the English nation" (2). Youthfulness is endemic: the ballads themselves, Emmett argues, had "a love of all that is manly and brave, and a contempt for all that is cowardly and mean; thus they appealed to the hearts of the freeborn, manly youth of England" (2). In this spirit he commends his work "not to the critic, but to the youthful lovers of manly worth and gallant deeds" (2).

The material that seeks this lucrative youth market in this spirit of moralized jingoism combines old ballad stories, such as the archery competition, with a "gentle blue-eyed" Marian (3). The language is creakily archaic—"A murrain on ye, ye knaves" is a typical remark (5)—and most of the Victorian features of Robin Hood Esquire are mentioned along the way—the beauty of the forest; the healthy sports; the military basis of the hundred-strong band; rescuing maidens from rape, peasants from eviction; and, that touch of legitimated violence again, whipping an exploitative landlord with a "stout deer-hide thong" (12).

Adventures multiply and the characters grow more exotic: Robin is advised of the sheriff's misdeeds by a Wood Demon, straight out of pantomime, and later in the forest meets first the Duchess of Lancaster and then, drifting in from *Ivanhoe*, though possibly suggested by Stocqueler, Isaac and Rebecca. In fits and starts the story finds its way to the hero's betrayal and death at Kirklees, but the account is never more than an opportunistic and erratic engagement with the tradition: the author seems to be making up each episode at the last minute, and some of the illustrations have strayed in from other texts. Middle-class in its earnest sense of respectability and definitely popular in its sentimental and excitable features, the collection was successful; it was even reprinted, under a different title and with different illustrations, in 1885.[43]

Emmett had many successors with popular and youth-oriented

outlaw sagas, such as the Rev. Edward Gilliat with *In Lincoln Green: A Merrie Tale of Robin Hood* (1897) and Joyce R. Muddock (a man) with *Maid Marian and Robin Hood: A Romance of Old Sherwood Forest* (1892), but there was better-focused, better-finished, and far more influential work than Emmett's at the youth end of the outlaw market. The classic Robin Hood children's book was the work of Howard Pyle, a young American book illustrator who wrote his own text to go with a set of handsome full-page illustrations in the tradition of William Morris. Combining strength of line and decorative detail with a lively sense of the youthful vigor of the hero (figure 13), these fit well with the garland-like title, *The Merry Adventures of Robin Hood*. A substantial, large-page production, Pyle's saga took the story of Robin from his encounter with the hostile foresters outside Nottingham through many separate but sequential adventures on to the traditional death by "the treachery of his cousin, the Prioress of the Nunnery of Kirklees."[44] Pyle was not influenced by Scott, Peacock, or any of the literary re-creation of the nineteenth century but clearly found his source among the prose garlands and chapbooks, that domain to which Scott returned Locksley, and which had at the popular level maintained their presence throughout the century.

Pyle's tone is both quasi-medieval and fanciful. His preface invites his readers and viewers to "give yourself up even for a few short moments to mirth and joyousness in the land of Fancy." He offers "innocent laughter" and the chance to see "good, sober folks of real history so frisk and caper in gay colors and motley." And he modestly, but truthfully, says that this imaginative delight is simply "bound by nothing but a few odd strands of certain old ballads (snipped and clipped and tied together again in a score of knots)" (vii).

There are villains in "greedy priests, the vengeful sheriff and his agents" (27), and the whole moves to a somber close with Robin's death, but it gives final credit to the hero who "showed mercy for the erring and pity for the weak through all the time of his living" (296). In his lively illustrations and his naively vivid prose Pyle renews both the trickster-like spirit and the ethical simplicity that the outlaw hero had shown from the beginning, however much his biography and myth had been sidetracked in the service of other interests. The explosion of Robin Hood stories for children in the following fifty years

FIG. 13. Howard Pyle's jolly Robin, from *The Merry Adventures of Robin Hood*, 1883

and the transition of the myth into film, comics, and television owe a good deal to Pyle's masterly reestablishment of the antique bases of the hero's appeal in a charmingly simplistic medieval context. Stripped of any politics beyond a general feel-good morality and homosocial, occasionally brutal, fun,[45] this was a Robin that teachers, parents, and filmmakers could transmit without hesitation.

Pyle brought the simplest, and strongest, of Robins back into the publishing mainstream, and a similar impact was achieved by the successful and highly influential musical *Robin Hood* with libretto by Harry Bache Smith and a fine score by Reginald de Koven that opened in America in 1890. It was a great success there, and did well in London, where it was renamed *Maid Marian*—presumably because there were so many English stage versions called *Robin Hood* (though there was also Planché's very well-known *Maid Marian*).

Claiming to be founded on "A Mery Jest of Little John"—presumably the *Gest*[46]—the Smith–de Koven *Robin Hood* tells how Robin tries to win back his title as Earl of Huntington, which the Sheriff of Nottingham has been holding while Robin has been a minor. The sheriff is trying to give the estates and title to "a young country lout known as Guy of Gisborne" (1890, iv), and Robin joins the outlaws led by John Little. Marian, a royal ward, will also join the band, dressed as a boy, for love of Robin: she has been promised by the departing King Richard to the Earl of Huntington. The action starts with an archery contest that Robin wins on the day he comes of age, but his lands are seized and he takes to the forest. As in Egan, he flirts with Alan a Dale's girlfriend, here named Annabel. Then the sheriff and Guy come to the forest, looking for Robin, disguised as tinkers—this is theater, not political realism. They get drunk and are involved in comic adventures: Dame Durden, an innkeeper and mother of Annabel, claims the sheriff as her husband because he is disguised in her husband's suit. Among these and other comic confusions, the plot reemerges: Robin is arrested and Guy is to marry Marian, but Friar Tuck and the outlaws effect a rescue. Suddenly the king returns, pardons the outlaws, and restores Robin to his lands.

This pattern has become very familiar because it underlies so many of the major Robin Hood films of the twentieth century, though they tend to use exciting action rather than the comic business of the stage. Nor do they use the music of the original that was much admired at the time. Robin's solo "Oh! Promise Me," with words by Clement Scott, is the lead song, which entered the popular imagination with its hymn-like romanticism:

> Hearing love's message, while the organ rolls
> Is mighty music to our very souls
> No love less perfect than a life with thee
> Oh! promise me; Oh! promise me.

> (1890, 35)

The musical tradition was to disappear, though in the mid 1930s MGM planned to film this version with Jeanette MacDonald and Nelson Eddy; the major impact of the musical, which made de Koven's name and fortune, was to pass on its story pattern.[47] It offered an authoritative model of Robin as a distressed lord to be reinstated finally by the king and as part of a love triangle with the villain and a vulnerable partner, Marian. That conservative, masculine, and sentimental structure was to dominate much of the popular Robin Hood material that was to follow.

Those features were already present in a major but often unnoticed Robin Hood text written by Alfred, Lord Tennyson, poet laureate and moralizing phrase-coiner to the Anglophone public. His Robin Hood play *The Foresters* has been substantially overlooked, notably by Tennysonians, but it has a good deal of interest and influence. Tennyson wrote the play, a quasi-Shakespearean mixture of verse and prose, for Henry Irving, with Ellen Terry in mind as Marian, but he declined it in 1881, probably because it lacked enough action for his bravura acting style. It came into its own, however, in a production obviously stimulated by the Smith-de Koven success: the flamboyant producer Augustin Daly mounted a splendid production with music by Sir Arthur Sullivan, which played with great success across the United States from 1892.[48]

Robin's status is clear from the start: Sir Richard Lea, from the *Gest* but now father of Marian, says: "There never was an Earl so true a friend of the people as Lord Robin of Huntington."[49] He is youthful: the first big scene is his thirtieth birthday, and his love for Marian is pure; hearing that Prince John has designs on her he says:

The high Heaven guard thee from his wantonness,
Who art the fairest flower of maidenhood
That ever blossom'd on this English isle.

(753)

They are betrothed but will not marry until King Richard returns; yet Robin's own Saxon Englishness is in no doubt: Marian
likens him to both Harold and Hereward. This is a familiar and now
standard Robin, combining Munday's social status, Peacock's youthful energy, and Scott's racialization with Tennyson's own sense of
moral weight. As is usual in gentrification, there is outlawry, but
through no real fault in Robin. A message arrives announcing his dis-
grace, and he merely admits unwise generosity:

I have shelter'd some that broke the forest laws.
This is irregular and the work of John.

(756)

Tennyson at once adds, as might be expected, the nature motif in full
force as Robin hears of the outlaws he plans to join:

They hold by Richard—the wild wood! to cast
All threadbare household habits, mix with all
The lusty life of wood and underwood
Hawk, buzzard, jay, the mavis and the merle,
The tawny squirrel vaulting thro' the boughs,
The deer, the high back'd polecat, the wild boar,
The burrowing badger—by St Nicholas
I have a sudden passion for the wild wood—
We shall be free as air in the wild wood

(756)

Patriotism appears, as the foresters sing, without much subtlety:

There is no land like England
Where'er the light of day be;
There are no hearts like English hearts
Such hearts of oak they be.[50]

(757)

There is a neat contrast with Keats's skepticism about the value of
cutting oaks down for ships; here the nautical reference in "hearts of

oak" and the suggestion that England is wherever the sun shines ties Robin Hood's generous nobility to the English imperial mission. Robin himself sees things more subtly when he celebrates his new life, in which he is

> . . . all the better
> For this free forest-life, for while I sat
> Among my thralls in my baronial hall
> The groining hid the heavens; but since I breathed
> A houseless head beneath the sun and stars,
> The soul of the woods hath stricken thro' my blood
> The love of freedom, the desire of God,
> The hope of larger life hereafter, more
> Tenfold than under roof.
>
> (757)

The speech powerfully enfolds the force of nature into the mainstream value of Victorian life, and clearly suggests the liberating power of the greenwood against the constraints of civilization; the word "groining" has splendidly negative-sounding groaning connotations. What Reynolds called, following Keats, "a mass of freedom" is given an almost ritualized celebration—not as a mass of people, but as a natural religious service. The nineteenth-century coupling of Robin, and indeed Marian, with the force of nature—so powerful an image then and still—is brought to a new poetic height.

Not much of the rest of the play operates so well. After some tiresome wooing between Little John and Marian's maid Kate, and a less than enthralling action sequence derived through Peacock from the lively ballad "Robin Hood and the Bishop," Marian escapes to the forest, disguised as her brother. She has no fight with Robin (as distinct from "Robin Hood and Maid Marian"), but in an uninspired exchange she and Robin pledge chaste love. The most startling moment is when Scarlet rushes in and thinks she is a witch, a brief recurrence of the motif that expresses deep-laid male anxiety about the strong woman.

Some quasi-Shakespearean fairy business and some ponderous social moralism—false beggars are robbed, honest tradesmen spared—occur, in none of which there is any sense of the roguish, tricksterish Robin Hood. Finally King Richard returns and sorts out matters, including the problems of Marian's father, the knight of the *Gest*. Now Robin will return to court, as the displaced earl should. Yet this is not where the nineteenth-century audience, inherently an-tiaristocratic, likes to think of Robin Hood, and the play ends by em-phasizing the natural thrust of the hero's meaning—the only element that seems to have fired Tennyson's imagination throughout this un-dramatic play. First Robin says that the forest will remain, when they are gone, both from it and life:

> . . . farewell
> Old friends, old patriarch oaks. A thousand winters
> Will strip you bare as death, a thousand summers
> Robe you life-green again. *You* seem, as it were,
> Immortal, and we mortal. How few Junes
> Will heat our pulses quicker! How few frosts
> Will chill the hearts that beat for Robin Hood.
>
> (782)

In this male world even the oaks are patriarchs, but it is to Mar-ian that Tennyson gives the last, and finest, word; while Robin laments mortality in the face of the cycles of nature, she reminds him, and the audience, of the undying honor that Keats celebrated in the outlaw's name:

> And yet I think these oaks at dawn and even
> Or in the balmy breathings of the night
> Will whisper evermore of Robin Hood.
>
> (782)

And she makes some claim for political value in their activities:

> We leave but happy memories to the forest.
> We dealt in the wild justice of the woods.
> All those poor serfs whom we have served will bless us,
> All those pale mouths which we have fed will praise us,
> All widows we have holpen pray for us.
>
> (782)

Out of this somewhat Darwinian naturalizing of the fame of the out-laws she, like Robin before, sees a mystic continuity:

Your names will cling like ivy to the wood,
And here perhaps a hundred years away
Some hunter in day-dreams or half asleep
Will hear our arrows whizzing overhead,
And catch the winding of a phantom horn.

(782)

As an epitome of the Victorian gentrified Robin Hood and the furthest development of romantic naturalism, this final image of the greenwood value of the Robin Hood tradition survived the dullness of much of Tennyson's *The Foresters*, and it pointed the way for a number of so-called Georgian poets of the early twentieth century. Drinkwater, Newbolt, Noyes, and Squire all wrote about Robin Hood in terms of natural values with various added attributes, such as poetry and patriotism.[51] But whereas Tennyson saw a combination of forest mysticism and Christian spirituality, accessible to those who escape the "groining" of modern society, Alfred Noyes spoke for the last gasp of nineteenth-century Romantic Robin Hood poetry when he saw the outlaw as an exciting but regrettably distant figure in his famous anthology piece "Sherwood":

Merry, merry England is waking as of old
With eyes of blither hazel and hair of brighter gold.[52]

And Noyes glances toward the ballad action in militarized form as:

. . . the boughs begin to crash
The ferns begin to flutter and the flowers begin to fly
And through the crimson dawning the robber band goes by

But where both Reynolds and Keats, not to mention all the other nineteenth-century writers, were happy to admire, re-create, and honor the value they both found and inserted in the outlaw story, Noyes, writing in the twentieth century, can feel only loss. At the end of his poem, what Tennyson's Marian thought was a continuing reminder of social reform and spiritual value is for Noyes only regret for what is lost, an echo, a memory of Robin's bugle:

Calling, as he used to call, faint and far away
In Sherwood, in Sherwood, about the break of day.

From Ritson and the Young Romantics to the Georgians, there is a "long nineteenth century" of a revised Robin Hood. He stands for Englishness, now firmly, racially, even imperially conceived. In this tradition he also stands for youth, vigor, good breeding, manners, and energies. He acknowledges the value of women as a source of pleasure and sometimes partnership, though he is hardly involved in the complexities of sexual and familial life and has strong homosocial, even perhaps homosexual, values. He is firmly associated with the natural world; for the Victorians, one of the virtues of the medieval nature of the story is that it is inherently hostile to towns. The hero often has a military side and may well facilitate sadomasochistic and erotic features. As a gentleman he is kind to the poor but remains distant from any real political conflict. In short, Robin Hood has been re-created as Robin Hood Esquire, a nineteenth-century gentleman, for good or ill, for all that the role might mean.

Outside the Mainstream

The nineteenth-century Robin Hood Esquire was powerful, and still is. But Robin Hood Esquire was not the only version of the outlaw to appear in the nineteenth century, as the varied energy of the tradition combined with the renovated mainstream figure.

Influential though Ritson and Peacock were, Sir Walter Scott was also a force in the land, and largely through his impact—though partly also for political reasons—the figure of the social bandit, the tough yeoman Robin Hood, did not disappear, especially among those with reformist sympathies. Thomas Miller was an all-purpose writer, later to help G. W. M. Reynolds with churning out his *Mysteries of London*, and in 1838 he produced a long and slow-moving historical novel, *Royston Gower*.[53] Miller was trained as a basket weaver and like many craftsmen of the period had radical sympathies, which his writing reflects. While he accepts fully Scott's Saxon-Norman division, he makes his titular hero a tough old soldier and Robin Hood a hard-handed friend of the oppressed. The Normans are vile and come to variously nasty ends, though there is little of the enticing violence of the gentrified novels. Anti-Norman and antiaristocratic politics are basic: Robin marries a Saxon girl, Elfrida, known (with a nature-myth suggestion about the etymology of Marian) as May-rain. Robin and Elfrida have sturdy sons, and in later years Robin is said to have "performed many a bold deed, and feathered many a shaft at the hearts of the invader, let loose over England by King John" (3:250).

Robin Hood plays a similarly restricted but potent role in a better-known novel, G. P. R. James's *Forest Days* (1843).[54] The title phrase is from Keats's poem, though Reynolds also used it in his third sonnet. James's wide reading included an essay in the *London and Westminster Quarterly* in 1840 signed with the initials "G. F."[55] While this was ostensibly a review of Egan's novel, its main thrust was to argue that the dating of Robin Hood in the 1190s was wrong, and that Walter Bower's location of the outlaw in the mid thirteenth century was correct. By linking Robin with Simon de Montfort's resistance to Henry III, "G. F." connected the outlaw's value of natural justice with the development of parliamentary democracy; it was widely believed, by liberals at least, that de Montfort's "Provisions of Oxford" in 1258 were effectively the beginning of the English parliamentary system. This new turn in politicizing the history of a notionally real Robin Hood was very attractive to liberals as a validating myth, and this is the story James chose to tell.

As in *Royston Gower* (and *Ivanhoe*), Robin Hood is absent from the title and much of the action; occasionally he appears as a warlord, with 140 armed men under his command in Sherwood and Barnsdale. He is employed to hold together the archers on one wing of de Montfort's army at Evesham, an incident obviously borrowed from Scott's bold yeoman at Torquilstone, though his full name, Robert of the Lees by Ely, involves both the *Gest* and Munday. He in general reacts to the various members of the aristocratic Ashby family (who, oddly, include an heir to the earldom with a Saxon name, Alured); their mutual hostilities are the central business of the plot. This Robin, like Scott's, has no closely observed personality or personal life and is not connected with a woman; though a sexualized and fallible female, who becomes the villain's mistress, is from Robin's area he shows only a calm pity for her. None of the other regular outlaws appear; the main supporting character is a long-armed dwarf named Tangel who seems to owe more to Victor Hugo's hunchback of Notre Dame than to any earlier English story.

But though he is more an instrument for nobles to use than a noble himself, James's Robin, like Scott's Locksley, does have the capacity to disturb. In a striking final scene, more sharply focused and memorable than many of James's rather pasteboard efforts, King Henry finally decides to forgive the vile Sir Richard de Ashby for all his treachery, and indeed murder, because he is noble and might reform. But at that moment:

> a loud, clear, powerful voice, which was heard echoing over the whole field, exclaimed in the English tongue, "This for the heart of the murderous traitor, Richard de Ashby!—whom kings spare, commons send to judgment!" (3:303)

Ashby dies by an arrow marked with the name Robin Hood: enacting summary justice is hardly revolutionary, but the scene conveys a clear sense of rectifying aristocratic weakness, as when in *Ivanhoe* Robin, the image of a practical, even bourgeois, man of business, stops the king from reveling too much. G. P. R. James's story may mostly involve aristocrats, but it has an underlying democratic irritation with them that is in keeping with what his source, "G. F.," saw as de Montfort's espousing of "the political aspirations of the burgers" (433).

The same position was taken by J. M. Gutch. In 1847 he produced a new collection of Robin Hood poems, which were reprinted and widely read throughout the rest of the century. As an anthology it is notable in part for bringing "Robin Hood and the Monk" into wide availability; the manuscript had been one of the few works not known to Ritson.[56] But the anthology also added a series of apocryphal texts, such as the made-up "Birth of Robin Hood," which worked the hero's name into a well-known ballad ("Willie and Earl Richard's Daughter")[57] to make him respectable and romantic from birth, and less interesting texts, such as "Robin Hood and the Peddlers." The latter appears to be one of John Payne Collier's forgeries, though it was printed by Child, who expressed more distaste for the plot (Robin is made to vomit after a fight) than doubt of its validity.[58]

Useful as it was as a transmitter of texts, Gutch's edition was most striking for its first volume, containing full accounts of scholarly positions on the outlaw's identity and meaning. Gutch gave a full résumé of Ritson's introduction, an account of Thierry's support for the gentrified thesis, the texts of both the "Sloane Life of Robin Hood" of about 1600, and the recent essay by "G. F." Gutch added his own comments and made no secret of his disagreement with Ritson, especially his wish to "controvert the noble lineage which Mr Ritson . . . has ascribed to him."[59] Like Robert Evans in the 1810 edition of *Old Ballads*, Gutch was bothered by Ritson's "sneers" at Christianity (1:xxvi), and, like Percy, resisted the gentrified Robin Hood as the original basically because the yeoman material predated the gentrified texts.

Gutch's own position was a generalized liberalism, feeling that Robin, the yeoman turned outlaw, "was led into such a course of life by a noble struggle for liberty and independence" (1:iii). But Gutch's main interest was that of an archiving scholar gathering, somewhat indiscriminately, whatever he could about the hero and passing it on. However, his very full knowledge of the tradition, including its doubtful margins, does not seem to have shaken his faith in a real Robin Hood from whom these stories started. He may correct Ritson and reprint "G. F." without real comment, but he does not doubt that there was a person behind the whole story. This is a new form of historicism, that confident Victorian belief in real archival history and in real human decision making behind all the deeds and words that can be assembled.

The process of personalization moved a step further in five years, when the doyen of Victorian archivists, Joseph Hunter, published his still startling account of his researches into Robin Hood. An archivist from what was briefly called "Hallamshire"—now South Yorkshire—Hunter worked for thirty years in the newly established Public Record Office and among many other activities turned his skills and patience to the Robin Hood question.

In the *Gest* King Edward comes to Nottingham and the forest and meets Robin Hood, who goes back to court with him but then leaves: amazingly, Hunter discovered that in 1324 King Edward II was in the Midlands and the North and among his household was a "valet de chambre" called Robyn Hode, who left the king's service "because he could no longer work."[60] Of course, as those who have sought an even earlier real Robin have said (see pp. 193–95), there is no sign that this character was an outlaw, and Robert or Robin Hood was not a very unusual name. But the finding was the sort that gave empiricist historicism some credibility. Hunter shows no interest in the poetry itself; for many in his age it seemed more interesting to find facts about individuals. In the excitement of the scholarly quest, there is a myth of its own, a myth that tangible, material knowledge about real people is all we need to know and to believe in this modern world. Hunter is the Enlightenment utilitarian of the Robin Hood tradition, and he has had many followers among historians.

But if there was a myth of materialism to be located in the hero's biography, there was also a myth of myth, which would deny the existence of any real Robin Hood or the usefulness of even thinking about one, and that argument was also realized richly in this dynamic period. Gutch was too early for Hunter's work, but he had read and, in his scholarly way, included in full the first clear argument for the mythic status of Robin Hood, Thomas Wright's essay "On the Popular Cycle of the Robin Hood Ballads."[61] Gutch would no doubt have agreed with his comment that Ritson's *Life* "is the barren production of a poor mind" (2:201). Wright also dismissed Barry and Thierry, the French followers of Ritson and Peacock who saw Robin Hood as a gentrified liberal reformer, in part because they were inconsistent with the early texts but also because he saw the essence of Robin Hood elsewhere. Wright placed great stress on place-names and local heroic and magical associations. He did not know much about the play-games but would have deployed these as well as the May games in his account of "the legends of the peasantry" (2:208) in support of his conclusion that we can "place Robin Hood with tolerable certainty among the personages and the early mythology of the Teutonic peoples" (2:208).

The argument depends on probabilities: Robin is associated with spring and nature, and there are parallel Germanic mythic figures with vaguely similar names such as Hudekin and even its German equivalent, Witikind (2:207). At one stage Wright does allow for a possible real Robin Hood, but sees the developed figure as fully mythic; he could be "the representative of some northern chieftain whose actions had gained a place among the national myths, and who had become an object of popular superstition" (2:204). The newly biographized hero has vanished into myth, a view that would have other adherents in the twentieth century and that would resonate through some of the fiction and films about the outlaw hero. This is not really a matter of right and wrong, or Wright and Hunter, but more a sign of the variable ways in which the values embedded in the character—especially now that they stressed both nature and a personalized hero—could be taken from different viewpoints to suggest contradictory values.

But there were even more Robin Hoods than the liberal earl and the threatening yeoman, the identified real man and the misty mythical force. There was also a theatrical Robin Hood: in 1795 O'Keeffe added the outlaw to the newly popular harlequinade (see pp. 92–93), and more theatrical surprises were in store for the hero. One was at the hands of the egregious sometime novelist Joachim Stocqueler and his collaborators, C. W. Brooks and C. L. Kearney. His autobiography (a curious document, published in India and withdrawn from publication probably because it was rude about a Viceroy) tells that in 1826 he had seen in Paris an opera called *Robin des Bois*, the French for Robin Hood.[62] It was in fact Weber's *Der Freischütz*. Although it is set in a forest and there is much hunting, it is with guns, not bows and arrows, and the story has nothing to do with Robin Hood; still, it was published in 1800 in French as *Robin des Bois*. This indicates the wide spread of the outlaw story, probably in theatrical form, even before Scott and Peacock. Though he presumably remembered the opera, Stocqueler was not heavily influenced by it. *Robin Hood and Richard Coeur de Lion,* which he cowrote in 1846,[63] is a witty, slapdash entertainment in which the wicked sheriff is building horrible brick houses in Sherwood; Robin, backed by the Algerian Abd El Kadir, the "Old Man of the Mountains," various nymphs, and a quarrelsome King Richard, manages to frustrate this modern urban crime in a conclusion drawn from *Macbeth* when the forces of good, equipped with boughs like Robin's troupe in the old play-games, defeat the villains. Full of amusing verbal wit (much better than the usual crass punning), the pantomime gives the theatrical Robin an energy and verve not seen since the late medieval plays—but with a difference: Robin is played by the manager's wife, no doubt an imposing figure in well-filled tights. Principal Boys, women in tights playing the male lead, in pantomime are still with us, but more surprising is to find that in 1846 Little John, Scarlet, three forest figures called Nuthook, Scut, and Kestrel, as well as Richard's minstrel Blondel, were all played by women. At one point Stocqueler, who obviously could not resist any sort of joke, has Robin helping Little John off the stage in tears.

Gender complexity—and mockery of noble outlaws—is rich in these pantomimes and musical plays: in F. R. Goodyer's Nottingham-based "Fairy Extravaganza" of 1868, *Once Upon a Time or A Midsummer Night's Dream in Merrie Sherwood*, Robin and Alan a Dale are played by women, and Widow Hardcash is a male pantomime Dame. The core outlaws remain male, but both Oberon and Titania are played by female dancers.[64] This was not always the case: the 1860 *Robin Hood* with book by John Oxenford and music by "Professor" G. A. MacFarren casts according to gender, with the only women being Marian and her maid, Alice; perhaps the fact that both actresses were French added enough spice for the audience's pleasure. In the 1851 Manchester pantomime *Robin Hood* Maid Marian is played by a male, presumably a boy soprano, while only Alan a Dale and the fairies are female (a lot of French names appear among them too).[65]

Just as the very early Robin Hood was involved in transgressive play-games, the theatrical Robin Hood and his friends took many bizarre shapes, from Stocqueler's tearful transvestites to Tennyson's somber liberal political couple. As a spirit of fun and wonder, a sort of forest Harlequin, this Robin was in touch with at least some of the playful and energetic elements of the tradition, that could in other areas be historical, ideological, even spiritual. But there were wider possibilities: the American interest in the tradition was striking. Early in the nineteenth century Washington Irving let his Geoffrey Crayon find in the outlaw a figure who could stand for values and actions appropriate to the new American nation.[66] Writing in 1862, not long before his death, though the essay was not published until 1880, Henry Thoreau found in the idea of greenwood a parallel to his own sense of the need for natural values.[67] In 1876 Mark Twain made Tom Sawyer a reader and imitator of the outlaws.[68] Australian outlaw ballads of the nineteenth century referred to Robin Hood and the Irish Brennan of the Moor as famous predecessors to native heroes such as Bold Jack Donohoe and above all the home-grown, and home-executed, Ned Kelly. For Dumas, writing his two Robin Hood pot-boilers in 1872 and 1873,[69] the hero's name did not need translating to

Robin des Bois, but he represented an élan and sense of freedom highly inspiring in those dark post-Prussian war days.

Wide and curious as the Robin Hood phenomenon and its varieties of biography and myth were in the nineteenth century, a consistent sense of the normative mainstream figure remained. With its unproblematic celebration of the heroic individual and his dependent lady, this middle-of-the-road Robin Hood did well in America in 1890 and was very influential. It probably prompted Daly to mount the Tennyson-Sullivan *The Foresters* in 1892, and its simple plotting and potent appeal seem to have stimulated several early films.

Robin Hood came out of the nineteenth century in multiple form, highly popular, strong in his masculine, even masculinist, mythic biography involving domestication of a genteel sort and an exciting life *au naturel*, equipped with a range of up-to-date sentiments and combining, through developments in both the novel and the theater, a sense of deep-laid value with a vividly surviving sense of fun. The outlaw myth was ready for the twentieth century and, above all, a natural for film.

 C H A P T E R I V

Robin Hood of Hollywood

The Outlaw on Screen

A Visual Image

By the end of the nineteenth century Robin Hood, now at least five hundred years old, had taken many identities relating to the periods, contexts, and genres in which he had appeared. But whether he was bold yeoman, rueful lord, or rural gentleman, he had not so far been the focus of a major work of art. Each version of the outlaw hero had received at least one solid, lucid, and surviving representation, but there was no masterpiece to enshrine and to transmit the meaning of the hero, no Robin Hood equivalent of Malory's *Le Morte D'Arthur* or Tennyson's *The Idylls of the King*. Though that reduced cultural profile might suit the idea of an outlaw, eluding the fixity of great literature as much as the constraints of a sheriff and his jail, it also helped to make the tradition all the more flexible and mobile. Because something as ironic and insubstantial as Peacock's *Maid Marian* was for nineteenth-century writers the most authoritative source available, they felt all the more free to let their imaginations roam. So they re-created the outlaw in terms of contemporary activities and liberties, from imperial military adventures to the inter-male delights of rural, and sometimes cruel, sport.

That fruitful flexibility and the related low profile of the Robin Hood texts changed in the twentieth century, as one medium became dominant and provided several technically powerful and highly popular re-creations of Robin Hood's story. Each of these tended to dominate the following versions and to pressure them into being either pale copies or deliberate, and sometimes forced, rejections of the dominant contemporary image of the hero.

The newly potent medium, was, of course, film, and then its junior relative, television. In these, a new and authoritative image of the hero was created, drawing on the earlier versions but clearly different in a number of ways. Less aggressive than the social bandit, more active than the displaced lord, more leaderly than the rural esquire, Robin Hood of Hollywood strides, smiles, leaps on and off his horse, brandishes his bow, speaks with large gestures and noble sentiments, and always, unlike both the social bandit and the distressed gentleman, dominates the scene entirely. Addressing his men from on high, swinging through the air to menace the Normans, taunting his enemies from a battlement, standing with arrow ominously poised, he is a theatrical figure, but one that the magic of cinema can make, in one swift cut, both potent at a distance and intimately exciting in close-up.

Robin Hood of Hollywood is an action hero. What in the novels was a matter of lengthy explanations of sieges and battles—scenes that only a skillful novelist like Scott could realize with real excitement—is in film a matter of images of speed and thrill. What in the plays is a slow-moving exchange of feeling, which can work well if the writing is poetical enough—as Munday's is occasionally and as Tennyson's is very rarely—in film is a tender two-shot, with symbolic foliage, emotive music, and appropriately low lighting. Film can combine the two aspects of Robin, not only an active man, a fighter, a leader of men but also gentle and understanding in personal relations with the poor, with his male friends, with Marian. Film, curiously, both elaborates and fulfills the implications of the very early ballads, which also operate by cut, montage, change of focus, by suggestive dialogue rather than novel-like elaboration. It is no accident that the best comparison with the *Gest* is with the major films of the twentieth century, nor that a remarkable resemblance exists between the early and broadside ballads and the pacing and impact of a television series: each takes little time to experience, each deals with a few interlocking scenes, and each focuses on one aspect of the hero's identity and his relation with a few other characters.

Modern film and ancient ballad are both performance genres, devoted to telling a story to a substantial and wide-ranging audience. They do not expect the close attention of the novel-reader or the playgoer; they need to seize and to keep attention to transmit meaning through rapid movement and broad strokes, both by the hero and the artist. But what in ballad would have been added by voice, gestures, and probably by additional music from the performer, in film is created by various techniques—color, camera work, design, music, and the engaging presence of the actors.

The Robin of the twentieth century was re-created in film, and though Britain made a significant contribution, the outlaw focus moved from Sherwood to Hollywood. At the same time, Robin's name changed, subtly but decisively. While British people still call him Robin Hood, two words with equal stress, to North Americans he is Robinhood, with a firm stress on the first syllable: the metrics of the new name are the same as those of Hollywood itself.

More dramatic and memorable changes than that have come upon the hero in film. His body is now a central feature. Whereas the tights were originally deployed so that nineteenth-century actresses playing Robin could show their legs, the male body became the focus of display in the early films. In the 1922 film Douglas Fairbanks represents Robin Hood at first as a heavily armed, fully dressed nobleman. But after he returns from crusade and is outlawed, his body is liberated from the stiff concealments of robes and armor, and he wears an acrobat's revealing costume to match his darting leaps, slides, and triumphant salutes. With Fairbanks the protruding chest is as important as the legs and arms, but with Errol Flynn in *The Adventures of Robin Hood* (1938) repeated emphasis is on powerful thighs, whether gripping his horse, poised suggestively close to Marian, or placed in direct, and sexually challenging, opposition to Prince John. Cinema and television have always selected men with figures and features that are romantically exciting; as well as Fairbanks and Flynn, John Derek, who starred in the fairly unexciting *Rogues of Sherwood Forest* of 1950, and Patrick Bergin, of the 1991 *Robin Hood*, both have classic matinee-idol looks, while Michael Praed, who stirred many a heart with the 1984 television *Robin of Sherwood*, offers the most dramatic profile of all.

While the body of the sexualized Robin speaks directly to the audience, the plot of the films usually celebrates the gendered triangle story, both heterosexual and homosocial, which had developed in the nineteenth century and was passed on from the theatrical tradition. As Kevin Harty indicates,[1] at least three of the seven pre-1914 Robin Hood films had this story in some form. The 1912 *Robin Hood* made by Eclair has a Smith–de Koven based story about Guy of Gisborne's determination to marry Marian, which leads to his capturing Robin; getting tied to a tree is the interestingly phallic mode of capture (as well as a cowboy motif), and that is how Guy himself ends up. The 1913 *Robin Hood* by American Standard has a triangle based on Will Scarlet and Christabel, daughter of the sheriff; her name seems to descend from Egan. The British and Colonial Films *Robin Hood Outlawed* of 1912 has Robin rescue Marian "from an evil knight," as Harty's synopsis puts it (455). In the Fairbanks film the rival is Guy, played as a silent villain with black-rimmed eyes, lurching from violent threat to craven defeat. Though this film gives no suggestion that Guy and Robin have a close relationship mediated by Marian, the 1938 film depicts Sir Guy as an attractive alternative hero. As Sir Guy, Basil Rathbone is a villain with an admirable military stance, especially compared with the cowardly sheriff. Guy finally fights Robin Hood as an equal in a classic sword fight, which even involves near-embracing between the two well-matched males; the scene illustrates the feeling "between men" that Eve Kosofsky Sedgwick has outlined (see p. 128). The triangle's secondary, male-bonding, force—or perhaps in this and some other cases its primary force—recurs vividly in the television series *Robin of Sherwood*, in which both the sheriff and Guy of Gisborne are depicted as inherently gay. Both have a pronounced interest in the conspicuously handsome Robin; only the sheriff's lumpish and clearly undersexed brother, the abbot, has any interest in Marian, and that is merely for her money.

But a love triangle that includes male-male bonding is not the only emotional structure that is developed. Robin is also involved in a symbolic dysfunctional family, and "outlaw" can be read as if it means alienated child. None of the details surviving about the pre-1914 films seem to bear on this aspect of the story, but the 1922 film clearly constructs Robin at the start as a kind of son for King Richard. Wallace Beery, who usually played heavies and presumably was cast not to outshine Fairbanks physically, presents the king as a jovial if insensitive supporter of the boyish hero. After Robin defeats Guy in the opening tournament, the king insists that he obtain his prize from Marian, Queen of Beauty. Robin demurs; the caption reads, "Exempt me sire, I am afeard of women." The remark has provided the title for a discussion of gender anxiety based on male homosociality in the tradition.[2] But Richard insists on "normal" gender behavior, like any father urging sexual maturity on the unwilling son, and in a bizarre sequence Robin nervously moves his head about until Marian finally manages to surround it with a crown. If this did not itself suggest unwanted entrapment, implicitly sexual, by women, he is then the center of a mob of young beauties who want him to wear their favors in battle. Escaping from this flapper riot, he dives into a river, only to surface facing a washerwoman; he thinks, "Another woman!"

The young Robin's passage into heterosexual identity is pursued in the scene before the crusaders depart: all the other men seem to be in dark corners, making energetic farewells to their beloveds, while Robin is alone. But then he rescues Marian from Prince John's unwanted overtures and sees her as something different: "I never realized a woman could be like you." She is indeed different from the others, as she resists Prince John, calls Robin back from crusade to help save the people of England, even fakes her death to protect herself, showing a proto-feminist strength in Marian that has not been matched until very recently. This may be a testimony to Fairbanks' sense of partnership with Mary Pickford (though she did not play the part), but may also generally indicate the new awareness of the role women could play when men were away at war.

This film brings a full-blown family drama, focused on Robin's sexuality, into the tradition, and this recurs in different forms in the more serious versions. In the 1938 *The Adventures of Robin Hood* King

Richard treats Robin and Marian like children, and though his return brings sanction to their wish for marriage, in the final scene they escape from him. In a surely conscious replay of the early sequence in which Robin escapes from the hall full of Prince John's soldiers, he and Marian elude the congratulating king and his men and like newly sexualized children, scamper out together, presumably to bed.

A different kind of family drama occurs in the 1991 film starring Kevin Costner. Here the sheriff rival is made ridiculous through Alan Rickman's overacting, and he himself kills Guy of Gisborne. So although the sheriff goes through the Marian-stealing ritual, there is little actual tension and no contradictory rapport with Robin. A new Hollywood-style homosocial development emerges, however, in Will Scarlet's strained relationship with the hero. The idea of an outlaw who is unwilling to accept Robin's leadership goes right back to Little John in "Robin Hood and the Monk," though the recalcitrant follower is also a standard feature of male action films, especially westerns and war stories. Here he is Will; tension exists because he and Robin are half brothers but Robin's father abandoned their mother. Sibling rivalry simmers, sustained by Christian Slater's skill with teenage sulking (his presence as a handsome deutero-Robin and youth idol played a major part in the film's success), and is not resolved until the end, where Robin can embrace Will and say, "I have a brother." The family melodrama is resolved in masculine rapport, without even needing Marian in between. Again a paternal role is played by the king, but the producers kept secret in the titles the identity of the actor who played the king: it was the vigorously authoritative Sean Connery. Perhaps his name was suppressed to retain Costner as the unrivaled star, but part of Connery's impact was that he was the actual father of someone who had recently played Robin Hood: Jason Connery took over the role from Michael Praed in the television series *Robin of Sherwood.*

These instances show how film has added a new element to Robin Hood's identity: a set of personal and familial tensions that belong inherently to the film genre. The tensions have the effect of adding sensitivity—with partner, parent, and other men—to the hero and making his final triumph a personal success as well as a social one. Robin the twentieth-century individual, finding identity through relationships as well as achievements—the archetypal Hollywood man—is realized in those structures.

But the twentieth-century filmic Robin has an identity wider than his attractive body and his sociosexual interactions; as in earlier versions his inherent resistance to some form of authority always gives his role a kind of political meaning. This varies considerably but in general charts an expanding role for the hero, so that twentieth-century Robin Hood of Hollywood becomes a political figure with concerns much broader than the local and regional significance of the late medieval figure; indeed, his impact transcends the English national significance that he developed in the nineteenth century.

A striking symbol of the 1922 film is realized in the historically conscious title sequence. We see at first lines from Charles Kingsley:

So fleet the works of men
Back to their earth again;
Ancient and holy things
Fade like a dream.[3]

The initial meaning is a medieval-modern contrast: this fiction will reactivate the fleeting medieval world, and there is nothing inherently different from Scott's work in that. But as the film begins and continues, a quite different, America-focused form of renovation seems to be under way. First we see a ruined medieval castle, in England, on a hilltop. Then in a montage suddenly the castle appears as new. We are not just admiring the ruins of the past; we are seeing them rebuilt in America. This is more than a metaphor. The first set seems massive, and it was indeed, not just a small gatehouse and a matte, like the castle on a hill we see several times. Fairbanks's production team, including his engineer brother, built a ninety-foot-high castle entrance on Santa Monica Boulevard.[4] It long stood there, providing massive proof of the way in which America can, with both financial and technological power, create anew the grandeur of the past.

The same sense of splendor dominates the opening sequence, in which—unlike in almost all other Robin Hood films—we do not start in the forest. In fact, the film is nearly half over before Robin becomes an outlaw. The massive crowd scenes and the march of the men to a tournament and off on crusade are all part of the grandiose style of early cinema that was very much connected with, and creative of, the myth of Hollywood. From D. W. Griffith to C. B. de Mille, and with Fairbanks's *Robin Hood* marking an important stage along the way, film realized the new American sense of power and splendor: the castle had been renewed only because it had (like many real castles) crossed the Atlantic.

But this splendor was not simple, either in its nature or its direction. As the crusaders marched off to war overseas, film watchers in 1922 must have been reminded of the American departure to fight in Europe only five years before. But the outcome in film is different. As the strongly gentrified Earl of Huntingdon, Robin is proclaimed Richard's second in command on crusade, but he returns home soon at Marian's request. He is branded a coward because of it; his royal father figure is much saddened by the apparent fault. Robin's decision to return must have contemporary political meaning: by 1922 the principle of American isolationism was well established, and the story tells us that, whatever the immediate opprobrium, it is right to sort things out at home, not engage in costly adventures overseas. This Robin is not only a Hollywood appropriation of masculine and aristocratic grandeur; he is also a true modern American. The film showed how new Robin could be, but it also indicated that Robin Hood pictures could make real money.[5] For that reason alone it was a crucial step in the re-formation of the outlaw as a twentieth-century and international hero, one to be widely imitated in film.

A political meaning for the outlaw myth is also to be found in the 1938 film starring Errol Flynn. Abandoning the idea of starting with a tournament (though as Behlmer shows, some at Warner Brothers thought an audience would expect it),[6] this plunges Robin from the start into resistance. The film opens with a peasant killing a deer, the Normans descending on him, and Robin resisting them and setting him free. The peasant-poacher motif is found in Henry Gilbert's 1912 retelling of the stories (see pp. 175–76), and this has become the standard opening in visual form; it is no doubt a major reason why many people now think the forest laws are a central part of the myth. Robin's resistance is clearly on behalf of such little people: the men who pass messages to meet Robin at the Gallows Oak are old, bowed down, marked by suffering. Some commentators have felt that this is more than general good deeds. Ina Hark has argued that as Robin shows the increasingly sympathetic Marian around his base, and especially as a group of poor all praise and bless him, just away from the main feast, we are looking at a medieval version of a New Deal camp, those Roosevelt-inspired systems of public support for the unemployed in the mid 1930s.[7] Hark argues that this would not be contrary to the attitudes and even interests of the Warners themselves at this time, who were sympathetic to Roosevelt's program.

That interpretation provides a credible local meaning for Robin's resistance to oppression, but several commentators go further, suggesting that the Normans are represented in many ways like the storm troopers who were causing so much legalized disruption in Germany at the time. The fact that Warner Brothers's own agent in Berlin had been beaten to death in 1935 for being Jewish makes this a credible argument, and events in Europe were certainly influential in many ways: Wolfgang Korngold's decision to stay in Hollywood and write the score was itself conditioned by Hitler's move against Austria.[8] The association with the brownshirts is easy to make when watching the film, and an antifascist Robin is an appealing idea; yet some of the scenes most suggestive of Nazism, such as the scene in which Norman soldiers smash up shops, are also found in the 1922 film. The antifascist interpretation may have more to do with the political context then and now than with any conscious plan on the part of the filmmakers.

Errol Flynn's fine rhetoric as a Saxon resister has a widely applicable democratic meaning, as in his statement to Prince John "We Saxons just aren't going to put up with these oppressions any longer" and in the oath he administers to the outlaw band:

> You the freemen of this forest swear to despoil the rich only to give to the poor, to shelter the old and the helpless, to protect all women rich or poor, Norman or Saxon, and swear to fight for a free England, to protect her loyally until the return of our king and sovereign Richard the Lionheart, and swear to fight to the death against all oppression.

Such a vaguely right-thinking politics may be all that most people take away from the film; in many ways its greatest strength is as a

FIG. 14. Robin and Sir Guy of Gisborne, from *The Adventures of Robin Hood*, 1938

memorable re-creation of the Robin Hood of the modern period, firmly national, strongly natural, and more masculine even than usual, with Flynn's insouciant charm, powerful thighs, and masterful style with the beautiful if immobile Olivia de Havilland. But in terms of gender, the film also provides the strongest "between men" pattern of all, with Basil Rathbone, who often was the active heroic lead in films, playing Sir Guy of Gisborne with great power: the final sword fight vividly re-creates the special tension between the two men in a highly intimate encounter (figure 14).

Whatever the politics of the 1938 Robin—and at this distance they seem gendered rather than sociopolitical—the film has been long-lasting and deeply influential: more than sixty years later it still shows on prime-time television, and a remastered print was successfully released in cinemas in 1998. Flynn's Robin dominated the field for some time; in fact two later productions (in 1946 and 1950, starring Cornel Wilde and John Derek) presented their heroes as being his son. And in what might seem a third case, *Son of Robin Hood* (1958), the son was actually a daughter. The John Derek film of 1950, *Rogues of Sherwood Forest,* avoided using the name Robin Hood in its title, but as if to clarify dependency it cast as Little John Alan Hale, who had already played the part in the Flynn and the Fairbanks films.

The dominance by the Flynn film was evident in the lackluster quality of a number of nevertheless fairly successful Robin Hood films of the 1950s and later. The first was Disney's *The Story of Robin Hood and His Merrie Men* (1952), which starred Richard Todd, better known then and since for playing modern military men. This film was made in Britain, as were others: inexpensive films with less than authoritative Robins were made by Hammer Studios, notorious for cheap but intense horror films. In these Robin Hood films the hero was an amiable, democratic, and rather unheroic figure, played by fairly obscure actors such as Don Taylor in *Men of Sherwood Forest* (1957) and Barrie Ingham in *A Challenge for Robin Hood* (1962). These films and actors were overshadowed not only by the Flynn vehicle but also by the version that most people remember from the 1950s—in the bulky shape of Richard Greene from the Associated Television series that began in 1955.

The Adventures of Robin Hood has always been felt to be a very English affair. Greene was a well-spoken, pleasant-looking officer type; he had in fact worked in Hollywood, as in the 1939 *The Hound of the Baskervilles,* but was best known for various forms of stiff-upper-lip British derring-do. Quaint as the series looks in black and white, with small sets, fixed cameras, and actors doubling up as in a repertory company, it was well written and well acted.

The sociopolitical meaning of the series derives from its period. Robin returns home from crusade and finds that his house has been taken and the country is in very poor shape under the greedy Normans. A relationship with the postwar British decision to dispense with Churchill and the Tory government seems close. The thrust of the series is to reject oppression against the ordinary people of England; corrupt tax collectors and legal officials misuse their authority, and Normans in general are represented as an oppressive class rather than a race. The ideology of postwar Britain seeking social reconstruction and personal liberty is strong, and Robin comes across like one of the many ex-officers who won parliamentary seats for Labour in the 1945 election.

This might well seem a reclaiming of the English outlaw from the internationalism of the American films, but the actual situation is more complex. ATV had decided on Robin Hood as the topic of one of a set of drama serials they planned to produce, and they had access to some writers who were happy to work even for low British salaries; the writers had been blacklisted as a result of the collaboration between American studio owners, including Warner Brothers, and the House Un-American Activities Committee under the inspiration of Senator Joseph McCarthy.

The story of these events is still not fully told, but Ring Lardner Jr. is on the record as having written, with Ian McClellan Hunter, about twenty of the first year's scripts, using a number of pseudonyms.[9] Many of the first episodes were by an otherwise unknown "Eric Heath," and so the series appears to have been established by writers whose understanding of sheriff-like oppression was a good deal sharper than even the most liberty-loving English of the period. The situation of these writers has been imaginatively realized by Michael Eaton in his script for the semi-Robin Hood film *Fellow Traveller* (1991), and there is some irony in the fact that the return to England of a Robin Hood with a genuinely radical feel—albeit with the social position of gentleman—is due in large part to the internationalization of the story. The series was released in the United States at the same time as in Britain and was well received: the audience in the two countries was reported as thirty million people for each episode in the early part of the series, which included 143 separate stories.[10]

Most of the twentieth-century Robin Hoods of television and film are in some way a gentleman. The twentieth century may have been the century of the common man, but there is rarely anything lower-class about the hero. American versions might make him seem less lofty; Errol Flynn is named "Sir Robin of Locksley," which has a friendly, youthful (if inaccurate) ring to it, and Kevin Costner has a strongly democratic air to his character. But the implied consensus is that it is perfectly appropriate to have a man of noble birth leading a popular movement—and of course the leaders of the Democrats in America and the Labour Party in Britain would not contradict that view.

Varying the Pattern

But if that was until the early sixties the mainstream pattern, it was soon to be questioned, and indeed much of the Robin Hood film-making in the later half of the twentieth century can be seen as resisting in some way an archetypal "Hollywoodized" Robin, that hero who is noble, handsome, gentlemanly, rashly brave, violent in the service of good, blandly representative of national and even international liberalism, devoted in a slightly distant way to his lady, leader of a loyal band of ready and lower-class fighters who are often comic and even a little oafish. Most of the films from the 1960s and later overtly or implicitly criticize at least some of those positions—in part just for filmic innovation, but also to express a range of ideas about other identities and values Robin Hood might have and other politics he might represent.

Some of these variations are simply carnival-like, such as cartoon representations, including Warner Brothers's own *Rabbit Hood* of 1949 and *Robin Hood Daffy* of 1959. In the Disney version of 1973 Robin becomes a dashing fox with a suave English voice; in the 1981 Muppet version he is represented as "a bold and chivalrous frog," equipped with his own Lincoln green skin. In both cases the filmmakers are essentially playing with and so effectively promulgating the archetypal Robin Hood of Hollywood, though neither film is without some sense of ideological value. Disney combines a sense of vigor, even vitality, in the Anglo-American voices that play the most robust parts and traces of racism and sexism in portraying the villainous figures as ugly and usually African animals, wearing frilly costumes. The Muppets movie is less politically dubious, locating in Miss Piggy what seems the first trace of feminism in the tradition: she rescues a less than bold Robin-Kermit by leading an army of gallant chickens against Sheriff Gonzo. Kermit's embarrassed refusal to give her even one "kissy" in return, while usual in Muppet-dom, is at least an exposure of the woman-avoiding masculinism embedded in so many of the texts.

Warner Brothers's *Robin and the Seven Hoods* from 1964 is in one sense a tribute to the outlaw tradition, but the title implies that the tradition could be updated to an American present, symbolized by a different meaning of the word "hood." Two following visual versions suggest more strongly that it is time for a break with the romantic heroics of the Hollywood outlaw. One is little known and hard to trace: released to cinema in 1973 as *Wolfshead*, it was made by Hammer Studios for London Weekend Television in 1969 as a pilot for a series presenting Robin as a yeoman who is involved in realistic and bloody rebellion against the Norman lords. Using the cinema vérité style of the day, with dark, rainy settings, realistic costuming and context, and offering a left-wing political agenda, this is a new reading of the hero, very clear in the darkly handsome but definitely rough and ready figure of David Warbeck.

Despite being little known, *Wolfshead* both marked a new phase of British Robin Hood realism and can be seen as a direct stimulus to a much better-known film, *Robin and Marian* (1976). This was directed by Richard Lester, with a script by James Goldman; Dudley Jones credits the latter with the unusual features of the film.[11] As Kevin Harty remarks, this is a "marked departure from other Robin Hood screen efforts" (437). Robin is very different in appearance, demeanor, and meaning from the Fairbanks-Flynn-Greene archetype. First, he is older: he has been on crusade for some twenty years and has returned tired and slow-moving. He is also no gentleman, a man of the people on a par with the equally big, tough, and battered Little John. Sean Connery and Nicol Williamson play the roles with robust relish, far from the smooth sophistication they so often had to don for the stage or screen.

But if the film celebrates a renewed resistance by senior citizens as Robin unwillingly responds to Norman oppression (personified by an equally soldierly and weary Robert Shaw as the sheriff), a bigger surprise is in store for the well-trained filmgoer. Robin does not survive: here is no happy ending with marriage and celebration, stoups of wine and merriness. The film follows the pattern of the *Gest* as Robin dies at the hands of the prioress—but there is a grand twist. The prioress, elegantly and touchingly played by Audrey Hepburn, is Marian herself, who has taken to a busy life as a nun and healer after Robin left her for crusading. With some initial reluctance, she rejoins the man who deserted her for war, but when, in a final combat with the sheriff, Robin is badly wounded, she decides that they should die together, and pours out a poisonous potion. The love-death from

Tristan and Isolde is grafted onto the outlaw myth in a powerful ending, well handled by Connery as a gruff, sergeant-like Robin Hood who realizes this is the best way to end, at his moment of triumph: "I'd never have another day like this, would I?" he acknowledges, after sharing the fatal cup with her.

Time, class, divided loyalties, and deep passion are for the first time woven convincingly into the Robin Hood story, along with the solid realism that *Wolfshead* brought forward: Sherwood Forest can be cold, Robin's band includes weak men and cowards, and battle is a slow, awkward, agonizing affair. But such a challenging Robin—a direct opposite to the Hollywood hero—was a risk, and this is the Robin Hood film that lost money, especially in America. Star casting, fine techniques, and strongly original scripting cannot make up for the fact that Robin Hood grows old and dies; the outlaw hero across time is essentially a figure of youthfulness and summer, not vulnerable to age, wounds, or, usually, women. The film's acceptance of all these negative forces was one step too far for the Robin Hood faithful, and this version of the myth was outside the biography that most people acknowledge for the forest hero.

But the impact of realism was not forgotten, merely diluted. *Robin of Sherwood*, the successful and influential television series made for Harlech Television, also dissented from the Hollywood myth but had enough of its own romanticism to be an acceptable new biography of the hero. Here Robin is a peasant boy whose innate resistance to the Normans who killed his father and burned his village is activated when Much kills a deer. Richard Carpenter, an experienced writer of action television series, including series for children, combines the innovatory force of *Wolfshead* and *Robin and Marian* with the shape and feeling of the Hollywood pattern. Instead of being distinctly mature, Robin is definitively young, and Michael Praed plays him like a student radical with swinging dark hair and casual clothes, always eager, adventurous, idealistically insistent.

The series offered other innovations. It reflected contemporary interest in the supernatural, with Robin magically confirmed as "The Hooded Man" by Herne, a horned nature god from the mists of Anglo-Saxon myth (and as Cernunnos, the Horned One, from Celtic myth before that). The sound track by Clannad, an electronic folk-rock group, emphasized this element, and the action was fast; some of the first filming with handheld cameras followed the outlaws running through beautiful local settings. Young, roguishly handsome, committed to resisting the Normans, Robin himself was a figure of nature. In one scene, as the outlaws gloomily sit, after a setback in which two have been killed, the ever-aggressive Will Scarlet (played powerfully by the young Ray Winstone) asks why they are undertaking this seemingly futile resistance. Robin stands, spreads his arms to the green forest below them, and says, magnificently, if enigmatically, "For this."

If a vague ecological libertarianism is part of *Robin of Sherwood*'s politics, another element, with equally unclear focus, touches on contemporary concerns. Relations with the Arab world had become an emerging theme, through the Arab-Israeli wars, the oil crises, and, most visibly, the influx of Arab buyers into Western property markets. In the feature-length pilot for the series *The Sorcerer* the worst villain is not the rather ineffectual, scheming sheriff or the bungling upper-class lout Guy of Gisborne but Simon de Bellême, returned from crusade with many bad habits, like a rogue officer back from Victorian India. His magic has enslaved a giant servant, whom Robin liberates as Little John, and the villain is, naturally, going to put the titian-haired youthful beauty Marian to all sorts of nameless indignities. Robin defeats him in his vile foreign lair—and then, at the end of the long pilot, as the outlaws, including Marian, shoot fire arrows to remember their dead colleagues, they are joined by Nazir, Bellême's Arab servant, who becomes a loyal member of the Sherwood band. Robin, like so many in the period, is both hostile and friendly to the Arab world.

Carpenter's scripts involved Robin in the traditional robberies and rescues, but also brought in medieval magical realism (Marian saves the outlaws from the "Witch of Eldon" by courage and supernatural assistance). In addition, the hero's power traced back to ancient Blakean myth and the sword of Albion. Most critics feel the series fell away after Praed left and Herne, with some convenience, crowned a new Robin in the Earl of Huntingdon, played by Jason Connery. As a whole, however, the series retains considerable impact. Still alive—in fact, very popular—on websites, *Robin of Sherwood* brought back youth and idealism to twentieth-century Robin, as well as a new manifestation of the technical brilliance that helped empower the 1922 and 1938 versions. In terms of the tradition, the importance of the program may have been to show that the classical Hollywood image could be updated without dismaying the dreams of the audience. The potent mix of realism and romance in *Robin of Sherwood* seems to have influenced following versions, just as the success of the British show in the United States in the mid 1980s apparently persuaded several studios that real money could be made through investing in yet another major outlaw epic.

In the late 1980s the media forests were humming with rumors about Robin Hood projects; at least three had been mooted, and several major actors were connected with the role, including Alec Baldwin, Tom Cruise, and Mel Gibson. Eventually two films were made, *Robin Hood: Prince of Thieves* by Morgan Creek in collaboration with Warner Brothers, starring Kevin Costner, and *Robin Hood* by Twentieth Century Fox, with Patrick Bergin in the lead. The Costner film, much more expensive at $60 million and stronger in publicity, became one of the top-selling films of the 1990s; the Bergin film was only released to television in the United States. Commentators often have denigrated the Costner film, attributing its success to the star's personal following and even to the international success of the theme song, "Everything I Do, I Do It for You";[12] at the same time commentators often argue that the Bergin picture was more lively, more vigorous, and in some way more authentic.

In fact, though *Robin Hood: Prince of Thieves* does lack the lucid, well-paced drama of the 1938 film—director Kevin Reynolds mixes overly elaborate set pieces with languid human-scale scenes—the film is still a dramatic and often gripping version of the events covered in the Flynn film, with some interesting variations. As Robin, Costner does not seek the dashing trickster-like image of Fairbanks and Flynn; he is more serious, seemingly a little older, and he dresses in a credibly bulky and dull-colored costume rather than the stagy, body-revealing traditional outfit. Nevertheless, Costner is not unmasculine, and we, like Marian, are able to admire his naked form—or that of his body double—as he is bathing. In the same multiple way he cuts a more thoughtful figure than his predecessors; the earnest involvement of Costner's successful role in *Dancing with Wolves* is in part being reprised, and yet, as in the climactic scene in which he is catapulted into the enemy castle, the hero retains an element of swash-buckling adolescence.

While in some ways the image of Costner's Robin is restrained, the film also offers a new level of intensity that sometimes borders on melodrama. The forest scenes are more detailed—Robin trains his men in a distinctly military way—but they are also broader. The battle with the Celts, for example, blends the cowboy tradition with some *Star Wars* touches. Character is also more boldly drawn than before: Tuck is a larger-than-life buffoon and Little John a less than sharp-witted English provincial; the previous major films gave Robin a group of supporters who were less able and exciting than he was, but still capable and sensible in their activities. Marian, though, is a stronger figure than even Enid Bennett played in 1922, and far more so than the only intermittently active Olivia de Havilland in 1938. In *Robin Hood: Prince of Thieves* Marian's first appearance is to fight Robin in armor, and to make a good job of it; the ballad "Robin Hood and Maid Marian" may well have been in the mind of the scriptwriter, Pen Densham. But in spite of early spirited moments, she becomes a prisoner in the villain's tower in a final scene very similar to that in the 1922 film, requiring a through-the-window rescue equally rich in daring and improbability. Her oppressor is the sheriff, but his attempt to marry Marian at the end stems from his lust for the crown (she is the king's cousin), not from any triangular sexual excitement, which would itself be excluded by his grotesque overacting. But this lack of homosocial excitement is compensated for by the strongly emotive fraternality of Robin and Will Scarlet.

Intense male melodrama is also found in the forest fight, where the outlaws' treetop fortress is burned and acrobatic heroics ensue, and in the final rescue of the outlaws about to be hanged. Both are typical Hollywood big-stage scenes, bringing to the long tradition of Robin Hood combats the remarkable skills of modern technicians, elaborating the outlaw myth as once did the waterworks, fireworks, animal displays, and scenery transformations of the Victorian theater. But the film also has a thoughtful side, a distinct position in terms of contemporary politics. The by now traditional quest for Saxon freedom is pursued in the spirit of international democracy—which does not extend to the Celts, who are crudely stereotyped as bestial enemies. By this time, however, Arabs are seen in a light less simplistic than in traditional Orientalism, and from the start Robin is given a new partner, the wise, skilled Moor Azeem, with whom he escapes from a Saracen jail in the opening scenes and who stays with him throughout the film. The figure was perhaps suggested by Nazir from *Robin of Sherwood,* the Arab who leaves his evil master to support Robin. This new Little John represents a range of Eastern wisdom—science in his telescope and explosives, medicine in his skill with childbirth, as well as warrior skills and general wise advice. The Arab element of Azeem also has contemporary meaning: links with the Gulf War and Orientalism have been outlined by Kathleen Biddick:

> Military images of the Gulf War invaded the film. . . . The missile-nose view of targets that became familiar to a television audience watching the trajectories of scud missiles translated into the film's signature special effect—arrow-nose views of "medieval" archery. . . . The presence of Azeem in the film can be read in a number of ways. He is the "good" ally like Syria or Kuwait and represents the "best" of Orientalism. . . . Others would read Azeem as a sign of the new Orientalism, governed by a new imperialism that pits progressive Arabs against Islamic fundamentalists.[13]

Azeem's internationalism has a domestic meaning as well, because the part is played in gravely distinguished mode by the African American actor Morgan Freeman; this black Muslim takes a role like Kicking Bird, the Sioux wise man in *Dances with Wolves.* The figure's meaning in terms of American race relations is emphasized by the sheriff's seizure of Robin's father at night, in a scene that includes torches and Ku Klux Klan robes, though the deer-killing peasant motif is also present, as usual, to initiate Robin's outlawry.

The other film of 1991 was less elaborate in production values and less wide-ranging in reference. It was simply called *Robin Hood,* though the film indicates that the hero's real name is Robert Hode and that he makes the mild change of name when driven to the forest by a breach with his friend the sheriff over—of course—a peasant killing a deer. Many viewers found Bergin more lively than Costner, with his bright, ironic eyes and his cheeky, almost self-bristling, moustache. The film has a strong Marian in the already impressive person of Uma Thurman: the director permits her to ogle Robin coolly from galleries and windows. Her possession of the sexualized gaze transmutes into her own plan to impersonate a boy to join the band and to escape her unwanted suitor, Sir Myles de Falconet, played in highly inappropriate Prussian style by Jürgen Prochnow. Intriguingly—and alarmingly—this strong Marian seems to dredge up from the scriptwriter's unconscious the motif of female sorcery as Marian is impersonated to trap Robin.

This false Marian is played by the sheriff's mistress, as if her sexual nature itself makes her untrustworthy, and she calls to Robin in enticingly witch-like tones. The real Marian, as a boy, breaks the spell; this leads to an exciting chase when he/she and Robin escape. That might sound as if the unsexualized woman saves the hero from the dangers of sexualized femininity, but there is a twist: in triumph at their escape the "boy" kisses Robin—to his instant pleasure and nearly instant dismay. The scene at once supports and sophisticates the sexism that underlies the "false Marian" sequence: the dangerous kiss offers both homoerotic feeling and heterosexual release, just as in the traditional "between men" triangle.

This is as intricate as the film gets, moving toward contemporary notions of complex sexuality via the forceful heroine. It also includes apparent references to the politics of 1980s Britain, no doubt inserted by John McGrath, the radical Scottish playwright who reworked the American script, as well as a strong realism of setting and a concentrated vigor between Robin and Marian. But the film loses pace after the "false Marian" episode, and the conclusion, in which the outlaws seize the castle by impersonating carnival revelers, confirms the sense that the most significant thing about Robin is the twinkle in his eye and his boyish charm. In Flynn and the more mature Costner, by contrast, those qualities are used to combine credibly international liberalism with excitingly perilous fighting.

Not only the power of a star and massive funding made *Robin Hood: Prince of Thieves* the more successful and influential of the 1991 films. Though the Bergin film has, especially in its leading actors, the potential to renew the vigor of the myth, that possibility is never adequately developed. Liberal abroad and at home, maturely engaging and managerially skilled, Costner's Robin Hood resonates with the

1980s sense of frustration at the impact of right-wing governments in the West and established another major piece of filmmaking in the grand Hollywood tradition, both politically contemporary in significant ways and basically faithful to the persona and deeds of the hero's traditional biography.

Alternative Screen Robins

While Hollywood was updating the hero in serious fashion, other visual versions were less respectful to the tradition—and in several ways responded with ironic directness to those new canonical forms. Whereas the 1960s mood had been for added realism, later dissent took ironic forms. *The Zany Adventures of Robin Hood* of 1984 was made by the people who had parodic success with vampires in *Love at First Bite*. George Segal plays an indecisive Robin with baggy tights, Morgan Fairchild gives an inspired reading of a Marian not at all happy to be a maid, and Janet Suzman plays Eleanor of Aquitaine, mother to Kings Richard and John, with controlled ironic comedy. Essentially the film mocks the pomposity of major versions, with moments combining farce with postmodern transgression, as when Robin rescues Marian from a castle with the welcome and efficient help of Israeli commandos.

Farce can have a slightly sharper critical edge and an even less imposing Robin, as in *Maid Marian and Her Merrie Men*, a short series made for BBC television in 1988. The series in part parodied the romantic masculinism of *Robin of Sherwood*, and in part was simply British pantomime. Shown at children's viewing time, this cartoonlike feminist reversal of the traditional pattern was written by Tony Robinson, of *Blackadder* fame, who also chose what has become the plum part of the sheriff, and may have influenced Rickman toward burlesque villainy. Marian, a sensible, sleeves-rolled-up, provincial English lass, confronts the demented sheriff and to protect herself takes hostage the tailor who is designing Prince John's new (very large) underpants; any risk to these is unthinkable and she escapes to the forest. The tailor is one Robin of Kensington, a cowardly enthusiast for royalty and the enterprise economy; he is played by Wayne Morris, an actor whose

FIG. 15. Marian's merry band, from "Robert the Incredible Chicken" in the BBC series comic book *Maid Marian and Her Merry Men*, 1988, *by Tony Robinson. By permission of Tony Robinson and Paul Cemmick.*

long dark hair, deep dark eyes, and exaggerated profile were a deliberately chosen hyperbole of Michael Praed's good looks. So the band is established, and expands comically, to include an aggressive dwarf called Little Ron and Barrington, a marijuana-drenched London Rastafarian; it is conceivable that this wry city black might have influenced the concept and casting of Freeman in the Costner film.

Naively comic in the English "carry on" tradition, with a pair of London louts as Norman soldiers, this series both carnivalizes the contemporary claims of *Robin of Sherwood* and made a feminist statement that was essentially muffled by the farcical nature of the show; it went readily into cartoon form, rich in complication but well short of any complexity (figure 15). Yet the series and its structure did show that as soon as feminism had a voice in the tradition, the role of Robin was radically changed: this first cowardly Robin Hood falls into a stream through fear of the ferocious bridge defender (Little Ron), not through his manly sporting spirit. And when this motley band of outlaws goes to the archery contest, Robin is disguised not as a bold tinker, like Flynn, or a stalwart peasant, like Costner, but as a large chicken—and it is Marian who wins the contest. While some might find this degrading to the timeless hero, these are the first signs of a major change of position in the whole myth, and the beginning of a decidedly new stage in Robin's mythic biography. This stage will be developed more strongly as writers of feminist fiction consider what they might contribute to the outlaw tradition.

Gender is also the starting point of dissent for *Robin Hood: Men in Tights*, directed by Mel Brooks and released in 1993. Responding directly and often in detail to *Robin Hood: Prince of Thieves*, this is in the Brooks tradition of mocking an identifiable genre—as in his groundbreaking *Blazing Saddles*—and develops an idea that the young Brooks had written for Sid Caesar's parodic series *When Things Were Rotten* on 1970s television. It is a complete story: Robin rescues Marian from the sheriff of Rottingham (Roger Rees valiantly trying to parody Rickman's self-parody), is rescued himself from the gallows by the arrival of King Richard (Patrick Stewart as a cut-price Sean Connery), and finally marries Marian by the doubtful authority of Rabbi Tuckman (Mel Brooks playing himself). Throughout, Robin has the support of his outlaws, but this is of limited use as they are primarily a male chorus dressed for the centerpiece song and dance, "We're Men, Men in Tights." This foregrounds the homosocial, even homosexual, elements that have long lurked in the tradition, but the film is more cautious than its title might suggest. None of the outlaws is permitted to be actually gay; even Little John, though thoroughly cowed by Maid Marian's huge Germanic servant, accepts a hetero-sexual, if subservient, role with her.

This is not the only ultimately traditional feature of the film. Although it is full of parody and nonsense—Cary Elwes says, "I am the only Robin Hood who can speak with an English accent," and a tiresome running gag involves the blind outlaw Blinkin—it makes repeated reference to other Robin Hood films.[14] In a roundabout and ironized way, the film subscribes to the hero's standing, including his masculinity: only he will unlock Marian's chastity belt, with however much difficulty. Within the farcical structure of this film the core image remains of the dashingly masculine, improbably theatrical hero who has intrigued audiences for six centuries; though small and often baffled, Cary Elwes is a perfectly formed Robin Hood who never quite loses his dignity.

This is not so clearly the case in *The New Adventures of Robin*

Hood, a television series made by a Franco-American consortium in Lithuania and released by Warner Brothers, "who," says Jeffrey Richards, "should really have known better."[15] Shown around the world in 1997–99, and drawing on the success of the television series *Xena: Warrior Princess* in combining antique fantasy with kung-fu style action, this promoted to hero standing in its first season Matthew Porretta, the actor who had played Will Scarlet O'Hara in *Robin Hood: Men in Tights.* His version of Robin is closer to soft-porn film than to outdoor adventure, with luxuriant mustache and tight clothing, and he has a leather-bikini-clad, stockily handsome Marian to reflect inactively the impact of Xena in living rooms around the world. The second season had a more mainstream Robin in John Bradley, whom Richards describes as "a muscle-bound WASP hunk."[16] Magic transformations and highly improbable fights with melodramatic villains made this an exotic mix combining the tones of modern fantasy fiction and nineteenth-century pantomime, even though it was filmed in Lithuania, presumably for financial reasons. But the personalized politics of Western modernity also appeared: in one second-season episode the outlaws are caught in a castle of their own fears, and only with Robin's stalwart aid against the oppression of negative thoughts (the internalized sheriffs of modern psycho-babble) do they learn to believe in themselves enough to triumph over their own anxieties. The series pushed the hero close to bathos, and if his authority survived at all it may have had more to do with the long tradition of the outlaw myth than with the nature of this cheaply and often clumsily made series. And yet here too the hero's authority was remade, if in a banal way.

Even here and even in Brooks's hands, the myth survives. What-ever happens to Robin Hood in film, whether he is an acrobat, a slightly overweight officer type, a fox, a frog, a stylish coward, even the leader of a Californian burlesque troupe, Robin Hood still retains a certain heroic standing. Just as Robin Hood has given vigor to the cinema, so cinema has given him a face, a physique, action, drama, and extended politics both domestic and international. Essentially, Hollywood and its relatives in the visual fiction business have made Robin Hood a figure of international standing, yet his many changes and developments, even his vicissitudes at the hands of some filmmakers, have not radically changed the shape of the original hero. He remains noble but welcoming to all comers, physically powerful but never oppressive, serious but always to some degree smiling, sexually attractive but never fully or finally partnered with either gender, and, most important, in all but one case still alive.

Robin Hood in Fiction

A Schoolchild's Hero

Nineteenth-century fiction, whether adult or juvenile, developed and amplified a fairly consistent figure of Robin Hood—active, gentlemanly, English and rural, settled deep in the forest among his male friends, only remotely connected with the politics of his time. In the twentieth century wider variations molded the hero's career in fiction, shaping him first as a fatherly figure for children, then as a more historical hero involved in more or less credible political and military maneuvers, and most recently as a figure seen from the double viewpoint of female authors and of a substantially strengthened Marian.

To study the range of Robin Hood's identity in the early part of the twentieth century is to be immediately struck by the extraordinary amount published for children in the first three decades. To some extent this is because the market for all children's literature expanded massively during this period as children's literacy and education became major social concerns. Stories about a boyish and English Robin Hood were felt to be appropriate reading for the young; the healthy activities of Robin and his friends, politically neutered as he largely was by his gentrification, were a model for young English boys and also, no doubt, girls. And if the coded phallic symbolism and the overt homosociality of the stories entertained the young readers in darker directions, that was hardly something that teachers were likely to be conscious of or blamed for in those days before depth readings of texts.

The Robin Hood materials had another appeal, descending persuasively from Scott's potent concept of Robin Hood as English; the world the stories enshrined was that of an ideal England, unmodernized, nonurban, naively charming, ethically simple, free of the entanglements of modern civilization and contemporary moral complexity. It is hardly surprising that this pastoral Robin was popular in England, where antique forests and villages could still be visited, and where the booming motor and petroleum industries gave strong support to internal tourism (Shell led the way with its maps and handbooks). But the emergence of the same phenomenon in America, or at least the Eastern states, was less predictable. The English material was rapidly republished in America, and a good deal of local work was produced as well. Pyle's *Merry Adventures* became a significant forerunner to the patriotic pastoral Robin, and the great libraries of the United States are filled with plays, stories, and poetry anthologies of the same kind. The young Stephen Vincent Benét ventured a classically Georgian poem on the hero with the refrain:

> There's many a forest in the world,
>   In many lands leaves fall;
> But Sherwood, merry Sherwood,
>   Is the fairest wood of all.[17]

The widest influence derived from the frequent reprinting of story collections, updatings of Pyle. Henry Gilbert's *Robin Hood and His Merry Men* of 1912 was an early and widely read version. It suggests liberal politics: the preface starts by saying, "Once upon a time the great mass of English people were unfree."[18] Gilbert's retelling combines a fairy-tale simplicity with an insistent sense of need for reform politics, and his hero has some of the strength of Hardy's Gabriel Oak added to Georgian pastoral:

> His head of dark brown curls was covered by a velvet cap, at the side of which was stuck a short feather, pulled from the wing of a plover. His face, bronzed to a ruddy tan by wind and weather, was open and frank, his eye shone like a wild bird's, and was as fearless and noble. Great of limb was he, and seemingly of a strength beyond his age, which was about twenty five years. In one hand he carried a long-bow, while the other rested on the smooth bole of the beech before him. (12)

This young-old Robin is a yeoman with his own sizable farm, but he loves beyond his class: Marian is an earl's daughter. Robin becomes an outlaw not through naive action as usual but through a series of acts of resistance to the Normans, who oppress the local people and try to abduct Marian. In somewhat Georgian mode, Robin gets support in the forest not only from serfs opposed to the Norman lords but also from "little people" whom he has helped, led by Hob o' the Hill and Ket the Trow—though they are more like Celtic survivors than the fairies from Noyes's play *Sherwood* (1911).

Gilbert develops the book by substantially expanding the action of the major ballads, with several lengthy episodes from the *Gest*, but the detail and the recurrent sense of politics make this more like a historical novel than a children's text. Its climax is a Scott-like siege of Evil Hold, the fortress of the wicked Isenbart de Belame; he has murdered Marian, who, as in the Victorian tradition, has become Robin's wife. After Marian's death, Robin maintains his representation of the poor and oppressed:

> Never was there a cruel deed done by some lord on his vassal but Robin exacted some recompense from the haughty knight; and when a poor man's land was invaded by a stronger, it was Robin's hidden archers who made the place too hot for any but the rightful owner to dwell upon it. (359)

This somewhat military and political Robin does eventually die at the hands of the wicked prioress, but he leaves a legacy of resisting oppression, rather than a legacy of playful trickery or gentlemanly pursuits more common in the nineteenth century. Distinctly liberal, and representing Robin as the leader of an anti-feudal police force, Gilbert keeps alive some aspects of the social bandit, crossed with a distinctly modern sense of social justice.

Most of the anthology-style retellings were, though, more conservative in message and stuck more closely to the ballads themselves. Particularly popular, distinctly bland, and still widely available in secondhand bookshops, is one by J. Walker McSpadden and Charles Wilson. Their 1921 *Robin Hood and His Merry Outlaws* resembles Pyle in scope but lacks his bold artwork, his exciting rhetoric, and his underlying sense that the medieval world has much value to contrast with the bleak present. The introduction notes that the original stories are now hard to read but were also "more or less disconnected and obscure to our modern thinking,"[19] so the authors planned a lucid collection about a hero who "was not simply a robber and brawler" (11) but was "a Saxon who stood out for the rights of the people," who was "fair in war, a protector of women and children . . . courteous, moreover to noble and peasant alike," with some Georgian manly magic: "a man of frank, open countenance, singing among the lights and shadows of the good greenwood, and jesting in the face of death itself" (11–12).

McSpadden and Wilson present the ballads in a logical order, starting with a euphemized account of Robin becoming an outlaw by arguing with the foresters (he kills one of them) and including the encounter with the king in Sherwood. A wedding with Maid Marian is slipped in here, in accordance with nineteenth-century tradition, but because "this is a true account" (283) the happy ending is succeeded by the death ballad. Simply told, brightly illustrated, and many times reprinted, McSpadden and Wilson's version offers a Robin Hood full of a natural manliness that is neither "disconnected or obscure"—and so is comfortingly unlike the experience of 1921 itself. The slightly stilted dialogue and the sketchy historicizing of the stories make more acceptable the naive representation of the hero.

A later anthology of more recent and widespread influence is *The Adventures of Robin Hood* by Roger Lancelyn Green (1956). The educational link is evident: he dedicates the book to a woman who was his schoolteacher—"In memory of Robin Hood and many other end-of-term plays"[20]—and he has constructed a scholarly compilation starting with his own "The Birth of Robin Fitzooth." The latter draws on the improbable Ritson-disseminated genealogy and on the spurious ballad "The Birth of Robin Hood," which Green probably found in Arthur Quiller-Couch's *Oxford Book of Ballads* of 1910.[21] Peacock's influence is evident early on as Robin's marriage to Marian is disrupted by a rival, here Sir Guy of Gisborne, and Robin fights his way out into outlawry and the forest. In a scene strongly reminiscent of the 1938 film but also referring to the *Gest,* Robin makes his men swear a remarkably long oath to resist bad Prince John, rob the rich to feed the poor, and protect women in the name of Mary (45–46).

A well-rationalized sequence of ballad adventures follows: Green locates the atypical "Robin Hood's Fishing" very late, arguing that Robin wandered to Scarborough on his way north after a last escape from King John. Most of the major ballad stories are covered, and Green pays occasional attention to a significant role for Marian. She enters the Pinder of Wakefield story from the play, not the ballad, and not only fights Sir Guy (again drawing on Peacock but renaming the villain) but actually defeats him. In the context of Marian's success with a sword, it is perhaps less than surprising that the false-Marian theme emerges immediately: the next chapter tells the story of Maudlin, the witch of Papplewick, from Jonson's *The Sad Shepherd*.

In spite of this seemingly automatic moment of witch-based sexism, Robin and Marian are married, and she is present when he dies. Green finally frames his simple account with a Georgian moment, by briefly telling a story: Henry III, out hunting in Sherwood, met two old hermits, and realized they were Little John and Friar Tuck. Green imputes immortality to them as much as to the myth he has been reworking. The story of Robin the noble (in both status and ethics) conveys the vigorous spirit of English freedom and masculinity—a model for the young English person to honor and, depending on gender, either to imitate in manly mode or to admire and to support in what little role is offered to a woman.

But some of the collections were less general in their impact. In his long career as a children's writer, Geoffrey Trease wrote a first novel that was especially political. *Bows against the Barons* (1934) in title and story is rich with the leftist enthusiasm of the mid 1930s. With vigorously populist chapter titles such as "Comrades of the Forest," "The People Speak," and "When Sherwood Rose," Trease uses a young boy called Dickon as focus. He is caught killing a deer—the device surfaces again—and runs to the forest, where he sees Robin, who has "keen blue eyes like steel," a "foxy-gold beard," hands that are "friendly but strong" and who "laughed musically, deep in his chest."[22] This Robin's paternalism runs to left-wing politics; he addresses his men as "comrades," sends Dickon with a message to a revolutionary meeting in a Nottingham cellar, and then leads the people to assault Nottingham jail in a scene more reminiscent of the workers' rising in *Battleship Potemkin* than the siege in *Ivanhoe*. Robin sums up by saying, "It was hammers and sickles did it, today, not the bows and bills of Sherwood" (61), and the illustration in the first edition shows an insurgent crowd, with, in the foreground, both a hammer and a sickle (figure 16).

FIG. 16. Radical Robin, from Geoffrey Trease's *Bows against the Barons*, 1934. *By permission of the British Library.*

The evil baron is Sir Rolf D'Eyncourt (Trease probably knew this was a Tennyson family surname), whose actions are negatively described in a chapter entitled "Mailed Fist"; the peasants organize guerrilla war against him with the cry "Sherwood Rise, for the day is here" (125). Despite his enthusiasm for a Marxist reconstruction of the peasants' cause, Trease does not completely ignore history: the peasants are defeated by a combination of the army of the Duke of Wessex and treachery among the Nottingham populace. Some are hanged, and others escape to the North; at the end Robin is killed at Kirklees by a prioress hoping for a reward from the duke. Little John recognizes the political problems: "I reckon things will come about slower than we thought" (152). Dickon, the youthful focus to the end, commits himself to a long struggle: "We'll go on working to make Robin's dream come true" (152). Neither time nor politics have been kind to Trease's Robin as a peasant Lenin, and Trease himself mollified his text somewhat in the 1948 second edition,[23] removing the recurrent use of the words "comrade" and "workers" and replacing the propagandist illustrations with the romantic historicism of C. Walter Hodges.

A more conventional historical approach was taken by Carola Oman, the daughter of Charles Oman, professor of history at Oxford, and the wife of Lord Lenanton. Though she clearly had an establishment position—the biographical note to *Robin Hood* says she had three dogs named after the Plantagenet kings Edward, Richard, and John[24]—this did not prevent her from transmitting with clarity and good historical context the story of the social bandit found in the ballads. She fits the ballad adventures skillfully into the framework of the *Gest*, with some variations, such as holding back Robin's killing of Guy for his last feat, and inserting a marriage to Marian at the end. Marian is, as the ballad about her relates, a lady, but Robin is not gentrified in this version. Oman ends with the elegant historian's idea of making Wynkyn de Worde and the young Copland discuss the value of printing the ballads, and Copland himself tells the story of Robin's death. Wynkyn thinks it is sad, and so insists on including it only in brief form, so explaining one of the oddities of the *Gest*. Oman's collection, which has often been reprinted, stands as the most successful modernization of the medieval Robin Hood.

A more conservative account comes from Antonia Pakenham, later known as Antonia Fraser, daughter of the liberal Lord Longford, who produced early in her literary career *Robin Hood* (1957). Robin is first heard of in a way accessible to children: "He loved to harry the Norman barons with his pranks," and his first appearance is with a boy:

> "Hooray for Robin Hood!" cried one shrill voice. Robin of Locksley bent down and patted the boy on the cheek.
> "Why do you cheer me, boy?" he asked gently.
> "Because you saved our father from the wicked Sheriff and his men," said the boy boldly.[25]

Authoritative but gentle, Robin, like his stories, encourages the young to be bold. With illustrations showing the hero as a combination of handsome and homely and with subtitles every few pages, the novel invites the young to share this comforting world of firmly defended right, swiftly punished villainy, and general delight: ". . . life in Sherwood was gay and carefree, with much merry-making and feasting to while away the time when the men were not out trapping or shooting food" (33).

Combining manly rectitude and licensed violence, with a villain named Oswald Mountdragon (a curiously Saxon first name for a Norman), Pakenham offers a fluttery Maid Marian who faints when ambushed: "Robin chafed her wrists gently and was relieved to see the pink creep back into her white cheeks" (51). But such innocence can be deceptive. This Marian is a false Marian, being on a mission from the wicked Oswald to guide him to the outlaws. However, Robin notices her leaving a trail, and in any case she has a change of heart when she sees "the merry life of the men of Sherwood." She weeps and Robin comforts her—yet again "gently" (53).

Marian is now under the paternal authority of Robin, and so is no longer false, but that does not mean all women can be trusted. Her friend, tellingly known as Black Barbara, desires Robin sexually, it is implied, and launches a set of witch-like plots, including his imprisonment, which are frustrated by Marian's new loyalty and the courage of Robin's friends. For Lady Antonia the malign feminine has endurance; in the final priory death scene, as Robin feels himself growing weaker, out of the wimple stared not the meek features of a holy nun, but the burning eyes, the diabolical features, stamped with hatred and vengeful joy, of Black Barbara herself! (191)

There are many more children's versions, usually linking the ballad stories, often using a youthful perspective—which tends to make Robin rather paternal, for the first time. With the sharp exception of Trease and to some extent Gilbert and Oman, they offer a rather vague mishmash of nature, liberty, and English manliness as the core motifs of this much admired hero. Yet these versions do not entirely conceal the currents of nationalism, homosociality, sexism, and indeed sexuality that lie beneath to intrigue the schoolchild more than parents and teachers might know, or like to know.

The Outlaw in Historical Fiction

Though the children's fictions do set themselves in history, the history tends to be a matter of a king's reign, some generalities about evil lords and forest laws, a few fairly gothic locations, and a more or less fustian style of language. But there is also historical outlaw fiction that attends in some detail to the events and personnel of the past and tries to weave a credible web around a fictional figure in history, as Scott had done. Surprisingly few Robin Hood fictions of this kind exist, however, perhaps because for many publishers the story is inherently a juvenile one, perhaps because to commit oneself as a writer to a fully historical project is to move away from the mythical. In these texts the material of the ballads is largely abandoned for a set of new events tied much more closely to history.

The pattern of innovation and historicity evolving together is visible in Jay Williams's *The Good Yeomen* (1956). Though this certainly might be read by adolescents, it has none of the hallmarks—illustrations, short chapters, youthful focal figures—of the children's fiction, and the first edition is not presented in that context: the back cover reviews and the blurb firmly locate this as a historical novel. Unusually, the focus of the story is Little John—itself a sign of a historicist urge to withdraw from the traditional pattern of the hero myth. John is a bondsman who has killed a beadle, a legal official, and he escapes to the forest. The Robin he meets—on a bridge (Williams does include some ballad events)—at first seems like a Victorian wood demon, dressed all in green with black hair and "a thick, uncombed black beard."[26] But myth is not the mode here: Robin is the son of a land-owning franklin (neither a peasant nor a lord), has been a soldier, and was outlawed for debt. He is called, rather oddly, the "heued" of the outlaw band, the Old English word for head, which Williams suggests was misunderstood as "Hood" (270).[27] Saxon though the title might be, Robin is essentially gentrified: John and Robin are socially distinct rivals for the same girl, Agnes, the daughter of the knight from the *Gest*.

Despite these significant innovations, *The Good Yeomen* is basically a full and faithful reworking of the *Gest*, elaborating the inserted character of Agnes. She has a physical liaison with Little John (another sign this is not juvenile fiction), but then, as he lies wounded, she falls in more substantial love with Robin. The battles and actions of the *Gest* are fully amplified with credible detail, but John remains the focus. He finally refuses to go with the pardoned Robin and the king, because he still distrusts royalty and his mission is to work for a rising that will free all serfs like him. At the end he and Tuck (whom Williams inserts into the action of the *Gest*) agree to go off together to further their political aims in Kent—a forewarning of the Peasants' Revolt, which effectively started there. With a subtle touch, Williams makes John invent the ballad-story of Robin Hood's death, so that he will be remembered as an honorable outlaw, not a man who, as John says judgmentally, "went to live with the king and passed his days in ease as the king's lackey" (284).

Honor to the outlaw but also a sense of his limitations in political history is a recurrent theme in the historical novels, but one that rarely works as faithfully to the ballad materials as in *The Good Yeomen*. The 1983 novel *Locksley*, by "Nicholas Chase," a pseudonym for the brothers Anthony and Christopher Hyde, depicts Robin as a remarkably flexible figure, as he explains on the first page:

> I've been Daniel Delore, owner of a stew of whores; Robin Hood an outlaw; Alwyn White, a sailor. I've been a banker, in company with a Jew; a friend of kings; husband to a queen.

Indeed, I've been so many different men that my true name and
bearing are almost lost—and yet not quite. I can still tell the
world: I am Robert Godfrey Bouvier Atheling, Knight Equerry,
Fourth Earl of Locksley, Verderer of the Royal Forest at Sherwood by Decree.[28]

Not unlike Egan and Stocqueler, Chase fills out the Robin Hood
story with materials not found in the ballads, which are for the most
part ignored. Robin's life and work are manifold, and even his name
is a curious hybrid, his aristocratic French forenames being followed
by "Atheling," the Anglo-Saxon for "prince." This improbable part-
Saxon aristocrat heads off on crusade with King Richard; he then
meets Eleanor of Aquitaine, is present at a major battle, saves King
Richard's fleet by decoding a cipher, and falls in love with Richard's
queen-to-be, Berengaria, who, in the context of Richard's homosexuality, shares Robin's feelings.

He then returns to England loyal to King Richard. In the middle
of the novel, however, a brief version of the traditional materials appears, as Robin's lands are seized, his people distressed, and he sees
Norman savagery. Local battles follow which have some relation to
the tradition and involve his sister Marian—a new idea, which permits his relationship with Berengaria. The rest of the book follows
Robin and their friends across Europe in many contrived adventures.
The book radically reshapes Robin Hood and the other characters
into a roller-coaster historical melodrama, as if the English and early
materials are too dull to explore in any detail.

More faithful to the tradition, but also spinning off into an "I was
there" set of fantasies, is Parke Godwin's pair of novels entitled *Sherwood* (1991) and *Robin and the King* (1993). Godwin takes the
Norman-Saxon story seriously enough to locate it in a credible period: his Robin Hood inhabits the late eleventh century and has a
firmly Saxon name as Edward Aelredson (Robin's father in the 1984
Robin of Sherwood was, perhaps not accidentally, Aelred). Born in
1050, Robin becomes Thane of Denby (a small town in Derbyshire
not far from Nottingham) and becomes firm, indeed homosocial,
friends with Marian's former admirer, a Norman. Just as he, Ralph,
rejects the worst brutalities of William I, Robin resists simplistic and
self-seeking rebellion, using his knowledge of the law to claim his own

rights and to support the legitimate claims of other Saxons. Shadows of the American civil rights movement seem to appear throughout this material. In another scene, Robin refuses to join in a rising against the Normans because he feels it is "a naked bid for personal power rather than restoration of an English crown,"[29] much like those liberal whites, and indeed blacks, who rejected the Black Panthers' violent resistance to racially based authority, and instead deployed legal and politically manipulative skills similar to those of this reformist Robin Hood.

Like Chase, Godwin hardly deals with the traditional story materials, and indeed seems to strain to fill out his second volume, *Robin and the King.* Halfway through he sends Robin into exile overseas and begins a long "I was there" sequence about the wars in Normandy, with the hero serving William Rufus. It is well done, but hardly a link to the myth of the outlaw hero. In general Godwin seems more interested in Norman history and its conflicts as a version of modern tensions than in the outlaw figure and his traditional values. This is characteristic of the historical fictions, which usually employ Robin Hood the outlaw as a focus for the audience's experiencing of exciting events rather than as a representative of particular values.

Marian Takes Over

If the historical novelists tend, through their interest in events and their contexts, to downgrade Robin's traditional mythic career in favor of other activities and characters, another more recent movement in fiction has significantly redefined the role of the hero. As David Lampe comments in the best survey made so far of the feminist material, "The most interesting pattern in contemporary fiction is the handling of Maid Marian."[30] Though some earlier novelists gave Marian a place in the title and some films developed a sense that she might be able to plan, act, and resist effectively, Marian's role remained basically that of a vulnerable ornament likely to be purloined by Robin's enemies and to require rescuing. She was never much more than a trophy for Robin and a medium to link him with other exciting men.

As feminists approached the material, they encountered the challenge of reorganizing gender power seriously in a myth that was so committed to a masculine viewpoint and to masculine motifs such as comradeship and conquest. Feminist farce such as the Muppets film of 1981 and the BBC series of 1988 simply reversed the structures so that a potent woman supported and rescued a feeble man. Amusing and stimulating as it was, the comic tone itself tended to dissipate the force of the myth, and recent feminist revisions have taken a more serious and subtle approach. These works have brought Marian into play as a heroic figure—not one who denigrates the myth but rather, in differing ways and degrees, both supports and gains strength from the male hero.

Traces of a feminist position are evident in Peacock's Marian and even in the ballad "Robin Hood and Maid Marian," and there is a tomboyish force about the Maid Marian found briefly in the forest in T. H. White's *The Sword in the Stone*, the first part of his Arthurian omnibus *The Once and Future King*.[31] But these are little more than gestures. Robin McKinley is the first author to rework the material significantly from an identifiably feminist position. A successful author of fantasy and children's fiction, she reports her long fascination with the outlaw myth in her afterword to *The Outlaws of Sherwood* (1988). She also mentions her sense, through reading J. C. Holt's book, that "the tales of Robin Hood have always reflected what the teller and the audiences needed him to be *at the time of the telling*."[32] In *The Outlaws of Sherwood* Robin is a young Saxon forester and fletcher; his mother is close to him, and he sees a good deal of the half-Norman Marian. As well as being "lithe and slender" (77), Marian is a fine archer and capable of decisive action; she steals back Robin's father's bow from the sheriff's guards. In the usual American way, family dramas emerge. Her father, Sir Richard (from the *Gest*, as in Tennyson), has a difficult and violent son; Robin's mother was courted by the chief forester but scorned him. Robin experiences pressure in both contexts. He kills a forester by accident, takes to the woods, and meets Little John (on the bridge, of course). A few familiar adventures follow, including an archery contest (Marian wins, but is wounded by Guy), but most of the action is invented, focusing on

Cecily, a warrior maid, who joins the band, and on Marian's problems with her proposed marriage to someone named Nigel. Some other names have a ring of fantasy rather than outlaw tradition, such as a horse called Windwing or a favorite Sherwood location named Growling Falls.

Like fantasy fiction itself, the plot tends to ramble, and Marian, for all the text's interest in her, does not act as a central agent for any set of events; she watches, and primarily acts as a messenger between the forest and the outside world. She has real value to the outlaws, however. At one stage Robin says they may be "hiding behind a woman's skirts" (172), and she grows in strength toward the end of the text; in fact, the king wants her to be the new sheriff (294). But she never really dominates: for example, we never follow her gaze examining Robin or find her describing his physique. This is a lively and entertaining novel, but it seems to alter Robin's role very little beyond making him young and sometimes uncertain. The novel does not create enough new action to make Marian a convincingly strong partner for him, and the plot develops interpersonal action in the forest among mostly invented characters rather than recasting the tradition in a bold and redefining way.

That step is clearly taken in Jennifer Roberson's *Lady of the Forest* (1992), a lengthy and well-thought-out book with a cover encomium from Marion Zimmer Bradley, the feminist rewriter of the Arthurian tradition, who calls it "a beautiful synthesis of the Robin Hood legends."[33] Roberson starts boldly, with a scene from late in the action: Marian, imprisoned by the sheriff and visited by him in her cell, is offered a choice between marriage and trial for witchcraft. She refuses him and identifies herself: " 'Robin Hood's whore,' she answered. 'And grateful for it.' " (16). This Marian is sexually desirable and experienced; she can face death bravely, and Roberson develops plot to match that repositioning of the heroine. In her account Robin has, as so often in the historical novels, been on crusade, but here he has not returned to a ruined land; rather, he has come back as a ruin of a person. Marian's eyes are the intelligence of the novel as Robin, at his father's welcoming festivities, never smiles: "The son merely waited in watchful silence as each guest approached. He clasped arms if they insisted, murmured something back, but his mouth never curved. The eyes never lightened" (27). Only to Marian does he respond, gripping her hand with fingers "taut as wire" while "she saw rage blossom in his eyes" (32).

The reason for the rage is that Robin, in Roberson's version, saw Marian's father die. He himself was taken prisoner, and feels that her father died in his own place; he has returned a haunted man. A strong sense of post-Vietnam angst is woven into the novel. Marian turns out to be strong and enduring enough to support Robin back to operational vigor, to fight for the king and for the poor. The ingeniously reworked plot both weakens him and strengthens her, and in the climactic moment of the novel, as the sheriff by luck disarms Robin and is about to cut his throat, Marian attacks with a crutch and breaks the sheriff's sword-wielding arm.

But that feminist plot is not all that Roberson offers. Although the sheriff is sexist enough to accuse Marian of witchcraft (a sign of Roberson's understanding of the traditional masculinist response to a strong Marian), and though he imprisons Marian and eventually pays for it with his life, he is not all evil. One of Robin's many burdens returning from crusade is a message to Marian from her dying father that she should marry the sheriff, because he will protect her and her inheritance. Marian sees glumly that this could very well happen. Part of her spirit of resistance is derived from another woman, the sheriff's daughter, whom Roberson constructs—not in very feminist terms—as a nymphomaniac who insists on satisfying her sexual desires and is widely reviled for her independence. But this highly colored strand in the novel is not needed; Marian herself is able to sense and to express, to Robin, the lack of choice that women have in the face of "a spoiled, powerful man who knows what he wants, and who is convinced *he* is the only one who knows what is best for the woman" (190).

Inherently the novel radically resituates Robin: he is handsome and noble, but also damaged by postwar trauma. Haunted by the Acre massacre (480), he feels that the Saracens effectively castrated him (459), and Marian's own resemblance to her dying father torments his conscience (426). Both Robin and Marian are understood in contemporary terms, and the writing and plotting largely sustain that recasting of the story. While it lacks the depth, range, and much of the powerful spirit of Bradley's *The Mists of Avalon*, Roberson's *Lady of the Forest* is a creditable and basically successful attempt to reshape the Robin Hood tradition in terms of feminism and to reshape Robin as a man with the weaknesses of masculinity and the need for the support of a genuinely good and strong, heroic woman.

Roberson has followed up this novel with *Lady of Sherwood*, which takes the story into the time of King John.[34] Marian is now fiercer than before, saying, "I shall declare war on the Sheriff of Nottingham" (124), and both the sheriff and Guy are more two-dimensional figures, thoroughly deserving to be treated as enemies. Throughout the novel both Robin and Marian are involved in resistant action, though she still manages to avoid too much violence. An element of modern romance remains: Robin and Marian marry, but are often separate, and, in a somewhat underdeveloped strand, she has several miscarriages. The novel contains a good deal of exciting action, but it focuses less on Marian's psychological motivation and on her perceptions of the limits to a woman's action, and in general is a less imaginative and less intelligently updated version of the outlaw story than *Lady of the Forest*.

Other women writers have taken other paths in restructuring the story. Something bolder, more generically familiar, and not entirely unserious is Gayle Feyrer's *The Thief's Mistress* (1996). In appearance a bodice-ripper with a lurid cover and a sexually outspoken approach, the novel has content to match. Unlike Roberson's Marian, whose father saw no reason to teach her how to use a sword,[35] Feyrer's heroine, or hero, learned swordplay from her grandfather, and the novel opens with her dramatic, even sadistic, revenge killing of the man who ordered the rape and murder of her mother.

Later she has other exciting experiences. She meets Sir Guy, whom she finds very attractive, and with him enjoys this genre's usual highly colored sexual encounter. She is ambushed by outlaws and meets Robin, who steals a kiss; then, as the novel says, "a rush of heat swept through her."[36] They part, but before long, unable to resist this sensitive man, Marian ventures into the forest and, having enjoyed more paperback sex, goes on to help him develop his resistance, deciding Guy is too cruel in spite of his appeal. In this story the dynamic is not between the two men in the triangle; rather, the woman selects from the two men. The action through the rest of the novel is fast and furious; Marian fights and kills again and rouses the outlaws to action. The detail is generally historical, but there is also neo-Georgian romantic magic here. Robin "had the look of faerie about him" (177) when they met in the forest, and at the end, in the most whimsical of Marion Zimmer Bradley's voices, "a portal opened between the land of mortals and the ancient land of faerie" (423). Overheated in every sense and at times based on cartoonlike improbabilities—Marian is "hawk fierce, woman tender" (389)—this is in some ways a run-of-the-romance-mill novel. (Lampe ironically draws attention to the author's advertised skill in making chocolate desserts.)[37] Yet the Feyrer novel shows very clearly how far and how quickly the refocusing on Marian has traveled.

Theresa Tomlinson's novel *The Forestwife* (1993) is completely different in rhetoric and narrative, yet it also creates a determined, self-sustaining woman who reduces Robin, in this case by their joint decision, to a producer of occasional pleasure and assistance. This is presented as juvenile fiction, like her other work, but, as *The Times Educational Supplement* said in its review, it is a "vigorous and purposeful story, with intriguing practical details."[38] Tomlinson lives in Yorkshire and sets her story in a somewhat extended Barnsdale, reaching into the Derbyshire Peak District—Little John country. Mary de Holt runs away from home because her father is forcing her to marry an unpleasant older man; it is the Alan a Dale story from the woman's viewpoint (as in Roberson), and she resolves the problem without male help. Her old nurse leaves with her, and they stay with the "forestwife," a wise woman who helps the people of the forest villages with medicine.

Soon she dies, and the nurse takes over her role; she also renames the girl as Marian, "the beautiful Green Lady of the woods" (35). In addition to medical help these brave but ordinary women provide small-scale legal and political help to the neighboring people, assisting the strong wife of the local smith to resist lordly outrages. The story apparently refers to the vigorous activities of miners' wives in the 1984 British coal strike, but not all the action is so practical. In a sequence that is notably melodramatic, even semi-magical, and therefore unusual in this low-key novel, they help a group of nuns to relocate themselves deeper in the forest to escape various forms of male harassment. Along the way Mary sees a man lying in the forest; at first she is struck by his beauty, "her mind drifting into a dream of the Green Lady and her forest lover" (53), but reality breaks in:

> Suddenly he groaned in his sleep and muttered, twitching restlessly. She bent close, wrinkling her nose at the rank smell of sweat and sickness, and saw bruises on his face. His cloak was good homespun, but ragged and torn. How stupid she'd been. This was no fairy lover, and he was ill, not asleep. The skin on his cheeks was white beneath smudged dirt and glistened with moisture. He was real enough for he stank, and was somehow familiar. (53)

She knows Robert from village life in the past, and he and his handful of friends begin to help the women. He and Marian grow close, and live together for a while. But when Marian's nurse dies, she decides that she herself must become the forestwife, and there is no place for a man beside her. Robin consents to this readily enough; effectively he has become a New Man, respecting his partner's professional ambitions, and the short but well-imagined novel ends with his promise to help her: "Fat bishops and rich lords who travel the great roads shall all make a contribution." In return she envisages a continuing relationship between them, in myth if not in person: ". . . though the Forestwife may not be wed, each May Day she shall dance with the Green Man" (166).

Like Roberson, Tomlinson has followed up her success with a sequel, *Child of the May*.[39] This focuses on the daughter of Little John and Emma, called Magdalene, but known as Magda. Her mother has died, and the young woman, large like her father, is involved in outlaw activity against the sheriff. The action of this short novel is closer to the ballads than is *The Forestwife*, and its regendering of the traditional story is more simply active—Magda finally shoots their enemy, Fitz Ranulf. Again as with Roberson, the sequel is lively and an effective statement of how a woman can play a role in history. But the sequel does not match the first novel's imaginative feminist rewriting of the tradition.

From Saxon revolutionary and warlord, through fatherly forester and rustic reformer, to strong woman's plaything and health professional's part-time assistant, Robin has come a long way in the fiction of the twentieth century. The extremes are a good deal greater than those to be found in visual form, as the special audiences of fiction can have sharper interests than the blurred-focus mass audience required for success on screens large and small. The separation is not complete, however: in 2001 elements of feminist fiction found their way onto the television screen in "The Wonderful World of Disney," with the film *The Princess of Thieves.* In the film Gwyn, daughter of Robin and Marian, deploys, as the publicity material informs us, her "dazzling archery skills, quick wit and indomitable passion" to rescue her father and his men from the dungeons of evil Prince John—who is seizing power from Prince Philip, a son of King Richard I unknown to history.

Attractive but a little boyish, played by Keira Knightley looking like a Britney Spears of the medieval forest, Gwyn guides the outlaws to rescue her distinguished-looking but emotionally distant father—a version of the modern American professional—and is finally united with Prince Philip. A substantial dilution of outlaw feminism, with some resemblance to the 1958 *Son of Robin Hood* (including invented quasi-historical characters), *Princess of Thieves* indicates how the modern Marian-focused narrative has moved into the mainstream.

All of the twentieth-century outlaw fiction writers have imported to their view of Robin Hood some valued interest, from Marxism through chauvinism of both kinds to magic, good sex, and various forms of female power. Most of the texts make at least a respectable attempt to historicize the hero with factual material, and all of them have to varying degrees consciously redeveloped the myth and its fictional imaginings. But the period also included other voices. Just as the brutal social bandit and the effete distressed gentleman coexisted in the seventeenth and eighteenth centuries, so in the twentieth century Robin, both cinema star and novelist's hero, stood sensitive cheek by sturdy jowl with a figure weighed down with facts, history, location, and his own elements of wishful thinking and values—the real Robin Hood of historicism.

History and Myth

Outlaw Identifications

Any formal talk, media interview, or even conversation about Robin Hood will generate the inevitable question "Did he really exist?" The question itself deserves interrogation. It is a modern one: Wyntoun and Bower, like other medieval writers, felt that entities existed if they were talked about and believed in, and for them Robin Hood, like King Arthur, Herne the Hunter, the devil, the saints, and even God himself all existed because of their manifold presence in human life and culture. That is not good enough for modern materialist people who seek empirical identity for all things, and so by implication for themselves. Reductive as this approach might seem to literary scholars, and vulnerable to parody as it can be—as in the U.S. *Sun* (see p. xii)—this intoxicatingly "real" Robin Hood remains a potent part of the hero's biography. Highly respectable historians as well as enthusiastic amateurs are enticed into this quest for a satisfying material identity at the core of the otherwise elusive and illusory myth.

Joseph Hunter's method of searching the apparent dross of the archives and finding a fourteenth-century Robin Hood (see p. 145) has been followed by some twentieth-century scholars, not with quite the striking results that he published but with a few specks of possible gold. In 1936 L. D. V. Owen published a report[40] of his discovery in the York assizes record for 1226 of a person called Robert Hood whose goods had been confiscated because he was a fugitive; that is, he had been declared an outlaw for nonappearance at court in answer to a summons in the previous year. The fact that St. Peter's church in York brought the case also seemed to fit with the early ballads. Either more puzzling or more supportive, depending on your point of view, was the fact that in the margin the name "Hobbehod" was written.

Some have thought that this is a variant outlaw name, to be associated with the recurring figure "Hobbe the Robber," mentioned in *Piers Plowman* as well as the contemporary "John Ball Letters" of the 1381 Peasants' Revolt.[41] Owen contends that this figure from 1225–26 is the actual person on whom the tradition became based. Such an argument is based on the location of York and the outlawing of this person—no more. There were in fact other people about with the same name: if historical priority is to be a guide, there might be a case for the Robert Hood who worked for the Abbot of Cirencester and killed a man called Ralph there between 1213 and 1216. Perhaps that is too far west (and in play-game, not ballad territory), and Robin the social bandit certainly did not work for the church—but this candidate is only a little less likely than Owen's man.

Support for Owen's case has come from two sources. David Crook, like Hunter a professional archivist, revealed in 1984 that he had found in the legal archives of Reading (a play-game town) two records on the seizure of property of a fugitive from justice, William, son of Robert Le Fevre (or in English, Bill Smith).[42] In 1261 he was simply mentioned under his own name; but when the justices looked again at the case a year later, his name was given as William Robehod. This change was the work of a clerk, and Crook interprets his action:

> The fact that the fugitive's father was named Robert, or Robin, must have suggested the alteration to him. The version of his name originally written down lacked the element "hood", which was brought in when the name was changed. It is most unlikely that the person who changed it knew anything of the individual concerned and whether "hood" ever formed any part of any form of his name; he must have been drawing on whatever he had heard of Robin Hood. (259–60)

On this basis, Crook argues that the tradition of the hero already existed, and so Hunter's early fourteenth-century man could not have been the real Robin Hood. In further support of that view he cites J. C. Holt's extensive arguments for a thirteenth-century Robin Hood, based in part on the striking discovery of the name Gilbert Robynhood in Sussex in 1296.[43] To use the full name as a surname suggested to Holt that this man was identified with the hero—either for being a bandit or for singing outlaw stories. Neither Crook nor Holt considers the more likely possibility that Gilbert derived his name from playing Robin's part in a local play-game.

But Holt also argues for the thirteenth century as being the appropriate context because of the habits, institutions, and even equipment that are found in the *Gest* and other early ballads. In particular he asserts that the strong hostility to the sheriff, the idea of widespread and oppressive forest law, and the emphasis on archery all belong to the thirteenth rather than the fourteenth century, and he is skeptical about Hunter's identification:

> The one hard fact in it was that the king's journey described in the *Gest* matched Edward's progress of 1323. The rest was a hypothetical reconstruction. And it can be proved wrong. (47)

Holt points out that Hunter's Robin Hood was only a royal servant, not an outlaw, and that there is only supposition in Hunter's linking of this man with the Wakefield Hood family. Basically, Holt is saying that Robert or Robin Hood was not a very rare name, that finding the original outlaw requires evidence of crime, and so Owen's man from 1226 remains "the only possible original of Robin Hood, so far discovered" (54).

Holt naturally welcomed Crook's support for the 1226 York man, stating in a later essay, "The discovery of this evidence by David Crook in 1984 was decisive."[44] The word "decisive" seems a little strong for the elaborate interpretation of one name in one document, and Holt went on to move this alleged fact into the realms of speculation: "This gives some credence to John Major's date. It is further supported by the appearance of Robert Hood, fugitive, who failed to appear before the justices at the York assizes in 1225" (28).

History here has become remarkably stretched. The 1262 "Robehod" reference can indeed, as Crook argues, support the idea that York in 1226 saw a real Robin Hood. But how can a real Robert Hood who becomes an outlaw in 1226 also be the noble robber of Major in the 1190s? He has to be outlawed twice, the second time in advanced years. Holt is casting about for fragments to shore up the thirteenth-century outlaw argument, and as it does so often empiricist history merges into wish-fulfilling myth. Adding a note of sheer improbability, Holt comments that Thomas Gale, Dean of York, "left among his papers a note of an epitaph which recorded that Robin died '24 Kalends December 1247.' " As has been suggested (p. 85), this is a nonsensical Latin date and apparently a joking reference to Christmas Day. Nevertheless, Holt offers 1247 as the death date of this now entirely imaginary Robin, though he does admit that this is "a somewhat tendentious reconstruction, and a shadowy biography" (28). The myth of historicist biography can hardly go further: there is an urgently felt need for a figure, and a gathering of scattered, unrelated details to suggest his existence. It is in fact extremely improbable that if there had been a developed myth of Robin Hood in the thirteenth century there would have been no references to it other than the 1262 one, itself of dubious weight. Historiographically speaking, the "real Robin Hood" historians have made life difficult for themselves by assuming that the outlaw of the ballads must be the original figure. It is far more likely that this social bandit is a special creation of a specific context, the towns of the Midlands and North, and that the play-game figure is the original Robin Hood, real only in the sense that he is the focus of a real myth.

Another experienced historian has challenged Holt's argument about the thirteenth-century context on historical grounds. J. R. Maddicott, in a lengthy essay called "The Birth and Setting of the Ballads of Robin Hood" (1978), starts by noting the late medieval shape of much of the context of the ballad (which Holt concedes early in his essay).[45] Then Maddicott insists that arguments about an underlying thirteenth-century structure are historically wrong: he cites evidence concerning Holt's allegedly thirteenth-century knights, sheriffs, and forests and asserts that they are in fact all represented in fourteenth-century forms. He concludes that "There is, then, nothing in the *Gest* or the other early ballads which would place them at all certainly in the thirteenth century."[46] Maddicott's essay is so far a professional historical discussion, bringing counterevidence to dispute Holt's claim, and it appears to have the better of the debate. But we are only on page four, with eighteen to go. What we discover is that Maddicott's purpose was not to speak about the fourteenth-century political or social meaning of Robin Hood, but to focus in a new way on Holt's own dream of a biography for a real person. In the rest of the long essay Maddicott discusses in close detail people who, he feels, might have become characters in the outlaw tradition. Empiricism runs rampant through contenders for sheriff, abbot, prioress, and a number of real outlaws—but no mention of Robin Hood. Although Maddicott's rebuttal of Holt's thirteenth-century basis would appear to reestablish Hunter's man of the early 1320s, Maddicott shows no interest in that figure. To his own satisfaction he places the birth of the tradition in the 1330s, but, as he finally admits, "the central figure is still missing" (254). He prefers to imagine Robin as being "a blend of fact and fiction" (254), based on one of the several outlaws he has been discussing. It is quite true that Hunter's man gave no sign of criminality, but he did have the right name, he did exist within Maddicott's period, and he did have dealings with King Edward in the right part of the country: a rigorous historicism should surely discuss him. But Maddicott is more independent, more original, more mythic than that. The individual who is in fact constructed in historicist empiricism appears to be not Robin Hood but the wished-for identity of the historian himself.

Yet the tradition of Hunter has not been entirely overlooked or rejected. In 1952 J. W. Walker, a medical man and prolific amateur historian from Wakefield in Yorkshire, published *The True History of Robin Hood;* this has a title much like that of a chapbook, and like many of them is a gathering together of disparate materials. Walker uses real or invented ballad titles for his chapters; thus Hunter's material on Robin as a Contrariant supporting Thomas, Earl of Lancaster, against Edward II is entitled "How and When Robin Became an Outlaw."[47] Other chapters use ballad titles and retell their stories, with ample quotations. The format, titles, and general tone of Walker's booklet neatly indicate how "true history" is part of a mythic structure, a feature that is effectively concealed—or perhaps subtly emphasized—in the cool prose of a Hunter or a Holt, but which is essentially understandable as a quest for human identity that both realizes and ratifies the identity of the writer who traces it.

A less elaborate version of post-Hunter scholarship has been produced by Percy Valentine Harris. His booklets have appeared in many editions, but they all purport to tell *The Truth about Robin Hood*, a truth appealing to Yorkshire, not Nottingham, accepting Hunter's identification of Robin as a Wakefield man. Harris's booklets also go further into empirical identifications, finding Roger of Doncaster who lived near Kirklees and a dubious nun called Alice le Raggede at Kirklees in 1315.[48] Hunter's tradition has been re-enshrined finally in the techniques of modern scholarship by John Bellamy, whose book *Robin Hood: An Historical Inquiry* follows a trajectory very similar to Maddicott's but places Hunter's man at its center. The book is particularly useful for its survey of all the discussions about the "real Robin Hood," but the narrative then vanishes into the heavy undergrowth of archival identifications, with more than a hint of the *Sun*'s fetishization of fact.[49]

But at least Hunter and Bellamy deal in terms of identities with evidence, a myth technically based on empiricism. In *Robin Hood— The Man behind the Myth*[50] Graham Phillips and Martin Keatman start by accepting Hunter's Wakefield connection but lurch off into the Bermuda Triangle style of suppositional argument by linking that Robert Hood with the Knights Templar, largely through the alleged cross on his alleged tomb, supported by his habit of wearing red (for which the evidence is both thin and late). In seeking an alternative real Robin, they are tempted by the Fitz Odo family, who owned the Warwickshire village of Loxley. They then touch another note of popular excitement in suggesting that there was an even earlier Robin Hood, whom they call "The Third Man." Deeply improbable as this argument is, it is less extreme in supposition than Phillips's opinion in *The Search for the Grail* that Robin was identical to Fulk Fitz Warren and that Marian was originally nothing less than the chalice of the Holy Grail in Fulk's possession.[51] At this stage of fantastic elaboration, historicism gazes at its own mythic creation in its own mirror.

Outlaw Politics

There is, however, more to history than historicism. Several historians, more interested in social forces than in identification of a displaced self via archives, have tried to establish what were the original politics of the figure of Robin Hood in the ballads, and what kind of audience would have been centrally interested in him and his resistant values. This approach was rejected by F. J. Child, who insisted that Robin Hood "has no sort of political character,"[52] though a number of writers, from the nineteenth century back to Bower in about 1440, had associated Robin with various public manifestations of resistance. Those writers had done so, however, without calibrating that resistance against any scholarly sense of the actual dates and nature of the ballads' production.

The first person to put politics and the history of the texts together was Rodney Hilton, a distinguished analyst of medieval labor. In his essay "The Origins of Robin Hood," published in 1958 in the British historical journal *Past and Present,* he states that Robin Hood's "historical significance does not depend on whether he was a real person or not" and he reviews and effectively dismisses "the recurring effort to manufacture an authentic, documented individual called Robin Hood."[53] Through the references and events of the early texts Hilton seeks contact with medieval political events. He interprets "yeoman" as a form of servitor, not necessarily a serf, sees the sheriff as an agent of government and the abbot as a representative of landlords, and attributes a thirteenth- or fourteenth-century origin to the ballads. He then relates all of these elements to the "agrarian discontent" that "was endemic through the country" (207). He sees the 1381 Rising as the focal point of this discontent and relates the texts to that movement's forceful spirit of resistance to authority, within respect for the king.

This revolutionary Robin Hood has occasionally been seen in the twentieth century as in Trease's *Bows against the Barons,* Jack Lindsay's unpublished *Robin of England,* performed by Unity Theatre in London in 1946, and Sir Michael Tippett's ballad opera *Robin Hood* of 1933, but Hilton's intervention was a drastic remodeling of the hero among scholars, and it met resistance. Maurice Keen, another left historian, agreed with Hilton in 1961,[54] but in a 1962 essay published in *Past and Present* J. C. Holt disagreed completely.[55] Holt's essay made a number of telling points, many of them through the careful attention to the texts that has always been a feature of Holt's work on the outlaw. He pointed out that agrarian issues in fact play no part in the story of any of the early ballads; there are no laborers among the outlaws, and the only dispute over land is caused by the knight's son killing a man. Holt showed that the early ballads made no reference to robbing the rich to give to the poor, a point missed by many (including E. P. Hobsbawm in his influential book *Bandits*).[56] He also noted that the 1381 Rising was largely confined to the South, while the ballads are set in the North.

Holt also challenged Hilton over the meaning of the word "yeoman": he asserted that it can also refer to the lower levels of the landowning class. Centrally, he argued that the ballads have a higher social level of audience than Hilton identified. Holt saw their themes as expressing the discontent of modest landowners and those who aspired to those levels, all of them identifying in the outlaw story their own sense of a need for resistance to royal law and to clerical oppression.

The strength of Holt's argument is that it deals with the texts and understands that an audience's interests in a text may depend on a crucial difference between audience and text. However, this view takes no account of the role of town and forest in the texts and does not explain why the ballads remained so popular with urban audiences through the seventeenth century. It therefore seems unnecessary for Maurice Keen to have recanted his pro-Hilton position in order to espouse Holt's views.[57]

A more nuanced response to both the limits of Hilton's account and to Holt's range of arguments was offered in 1985 by Peter Coss, a sociocultural historian. Coss has a strong sense of the multifarious nature of texts in the period, both their availability at many levels and the variety of responses to them. He feels "The *Gest of Robyn Hood* carries within it the social crisis of late fourteenth-century England though not perhaps in quite the way Hilton once envisaged."[58] He sees the *Gest* as responding to a world of social dissolution and opportunistic oppression, as envisaging in the forest a better world:

> a secular commonwealth of the free bereft of (corrupt) administrators and of the religious, where there is free access to the beasts of the forest and the "foules of the ryvere", where status distinctions are considerably reduced and where the king is dutifully and courteously acknowledged as lord—but not to the extent of compromising one's freedom. (340)

It is a view derived from the issues and symbols of the text, and one that seems valid for a good deal of the Robin Hood narratives, including the films of the twentieth century.

Coss's general reading of the symbolism of Robin is parallel to a more specific but also basically "Utopian" reading of the texts, "The 'Mistery' of Robin Hood: A New Social Context for the Texts" by Richard Tardif (1983). Tardif sees the forest not as a distant romantic escape but as a nearby and available place of freedom, real and imagined. Through tracing contemporary movements in England and France, he argues that urban journeymen, skilled tradesmen who had no means to set up a business but had to hire themselves out as workers, were the prime audience of the texts; his title links the mastery of a trade to the puzzle of Robin Hood's political-historical meaning and context, and he sums up:

> It seems that there were two somewhat contradictory images of collective action available to the class of urban-serving-men seeking wealth and power—that of the fringe-dwelling gang, and that of the suppressed journeyman. . . . A gap has opened up between their actual lives and the dominant ideological forms in their society, which no longer accounted adequately for those lives. The array of associations that arise from the Robin Hood band and are constituted in the Robin Hood ballads form a network of paths traced across this gap.[59]

Like Hilton's connection with 1381, Tardif's localization of the point of origin of the ballads may be too precise to account for all the developing features and all the popularity of the ballads; Henry VIII was imitating Robin within a few decades (see p. 46). But Tardif is the only commentator who has understood how literary genres develop—in a gap of collective self-consciousness that must be both ideologically and generically filled. He also is the only commentator who has given any account of the role that towns might have played specifically in the development of the ballad outlaw Robin Hood as different from the benign local hero of the play-games. Whereas some historians have produced some of the most limited and intellectually self-centered of the accounts of the hero's biography, others have generated searching accounts of just what Robin Hood might have stood for as the stories were created, and what he might still in various ways represent today.

A Forest Spirit

The historians always thought there was either a real person or real politics at the foundation of the myth. But for many writers and commentators, Robin Hood was in no way so concrete an identity. The mythic Robin Hood—that is, a figure whose myth is actually mythic, not nationalist, or masculine, or historical, or political—has been a recurring and potent figure, especially in the twentieth century. In a true outlaw moment (see p. xiii), Sir Sidney Lee described him in the individualistic fortress of the *Dictionary of National Biography* as "a mythical forest elf."[60] Lee's view was repeated at some length in the very influential eleventh edition of *Encyclopedia Britannica* in 1910,[61] was central to the fairy context of several of the Georgians, notably Noyes and Drinkwater, and was buttressed by the assertions of folklorists such as Robert Graves ("the founder of the Robin Hood religion")[62] and Margaret Murray ("the god of the Old Religion").[63]

A less excitable mythic reading was given by Lord Raglan in his well-known book *The Hero*, which treats Robin as a version of "the Traditional hero." Raglan identifies him as "Robin of the Wood," a fertility figure, and feels that his stories, like those beneath some Celtic narratives, "are suggestive of an ancient system by which the king reigned from one May-day till the next, when he had to fight for his title, if not for his life, and in which the queen became the wife of the successful combatant."[64] The reference to May Day is a weak point, however, and unless the appearance of Marian in a few of the play-games, as at Kingston in 1509, is a trace of a queen-marriage motif, it is noticeable that the restoration of the king (not of Robin) and the hero's marriage tend to appear only in twentieth-century materials—not that such a leap across time would deter a determined mythicist.

From being a figure promulgated in canonical reference books early in the twentieth century, the elf Robin seems to have largely disappeared for half a century in the face of the human patriotic hero of the films and fiction—though there are still playful, semi-magical elements to his tricks, disappearances and sudden amazing feats. But he resurfaces in *Robin of Sherwood*, via the mystical magic of the Herne sequences, and is firmly realized in John Matthews's book *Robin Hood: Green Lord of the Wildwood* (1993) which confidently asserts:

> Robin Hood and his followers are not only the bearers of a single part of the greenwood tradition—they are not the entirety of that tradition. Yet in their diversity and vitality they kept the belief in the Green Man and the Green Lady alive in the land. In the end May indeed triumphed . . . preserving sufficient of the old ways to keep them alive into the present time.[65]

In his final chapter, "In the Heart of the Forest," indicating with an epigraph from Noyes's verse-play "Robin Hood" his contact with the Georgian mythicists, Matthews sums up:

> Robin is really a Springtime aspect of the Green Man—he who holds the land in thrall, breaks free of his more ancient, darker aspect, adopting the light guise of Green Jack. His marriage to Marian, Queen of the May, is a whole-hearted celebration of life and creation, of burgeoning sexuality, and of the creative urgency of nature itself. (164)

In these terms, only the gentrified narratives, which include the wedding of Robin and Marian, really fit the mythic interpretation, and they are not medieval, where Matthews locates the origin of this green outlaw. Few filmgoers or novel readers, let alone those who just understand a headline about Robin Hood or immediately identify the iconic bow and green hat, would take such a firmly mythic view of the hero's identity. His general meaning, worldwide as well as domestic, has much more to do with resisting the sheriff. And yet it is not easy to see why a limited English tradition, located in particular places and a restricted set of activities, would have become first national and then worldwide in its appeal without deeper forces that can operate in terms of pure myth as well as politics. Lorraine Stock has recently summarized the material available and argued for a "Green

Man" element in the hero;[66] the topic deserves more attention and more systematic analysis than it has received.

A good start in this direction is a little-noticed essay by the folklorist Joseph Nagy, a reading of the figure in structural anthropological terms as "not so much a figure who exists outside society as one who exists *between* culture and nature, and several other opposed pairs of categories as well."[67] Finding liminality in pairs such as town-forest, human-divine, man-woman, human-animal, stealer-giver, ruler-anarchist, and classed-cross class, Nagy concludes that:

> The Robin Hood narrative tradition originated in medieval English society, but the values which these narratives communicated were relevant in the post-medieval world as well, and the liminal context in which they were expressed continued to exert fascination. (425)

Reading myth in Levi-Straussian terms as a set of ways in which people interpret their world, and so can cope with it, Nagy's account of the mystic tone of Robin Hood is both less exotic and less improbable than that of the hard-core Green Man theorists, and is also a good deal more flexible. In the absence of any purposive or fully developed Freudian, Marxist, or gender-based interpretations (all of which might be possible, but have so far made only fragmentary appearances),[68] only Nagy—and the other mythicists, if they can be believed—have offered the kind of deep explanation of the power of the tradition that might explain at least some of the appeal of the forest hero in so many contexts and cultures.

How Many Robin Hoods?

Killer and gentleman, myth and everyday hero, village symbol and international liberal, joker and rebel, nature lover and fierce hunter, boyish charmer and father figure to children, man among men and helper to strong women—Robin Hood's identity seems to undergo endless variations in verbal and visual texts. And yet there are other Robin Hoods, figures stranger and yet more intimate than those which are, so far, recorded.

Danny Spooner, an English folksinger living in Australia, liked to preface his performance of "The Death of Robin Hood" with a story, told in sad, serious tones.

> Robin Hood was dying, in Kirklees Abbey. The Prioress it was, his own cousin, who had betrayed him. Little John held him in his arms.
> "John," Robin whispered, "John, bring me my bow, and wherever the arrow lands, bury me there."
> John brought the bow and Robin, growing weak now, drew back the string as far as he could, pale fingers holding the arrow. He glanced in pain at John.
> "Where the arrow lands . . . bury me."
> So they buried him on top of the wardrobe.

The irreverence somehow added to, rather than ruined, the plangent sadness of the ensuing song.

Another piece of Robin Hood apocrypha is a "Test Your Character" story that was going around offices worldwide in the 1980s, before e-mail and the Internet existed. In photocopied form it has surfaced in several places. First you read a story:

> Robin was captured by the Sheriff, who decided to hang him in the morning. Marian went to the Sheriff and begged for Robin's life. The Sheriff said he would free Robin if she would sleep with him.
> She agreed, and did so, and the Sheriff freed Robin. Next morning, as they were riding away from the castle Robin asked Marian how she saved his life, and she told him. He was appalled and abandoned her in disgust. Little John rode up beside Marian; he said he had always loved her and asked if she would be willing to become his partner.
> She agreed, and they rode off together.

After reading the story, your task is to list the four characters in the order in which you value their behavior, best first. You then can turn to the responses that identify your character. Discussing the matter is liable to cause chaos at dinner parties, especially between couples.

That puzzle shows clear signs of feminist relativism, but male chauvinism still exists in the myth. Though Robin Hood never came to Wales (the national bandit is the sixteenth-century anti-Tudor trickster Twm Sion Cati of Tregaron—Tom Jones, son of Katie), Welsh culture includes something that sounds much like play-game activity. In Barry, a moderately tough South Wales port, an annual carnival takes place in early summer. Robin Hood and his men appear, like Morris Dancers. They caper through the streets, and occasionally their leader blows a horn. When this occurs, the men all gather around an attractive woman, shouting and jumping. Then the horn is blown again, and the men dance away; the leader brandishes a set of lacy lingerie.

Heroism burlesqued, gender-prejudice explored, gang-rape celebrated as carnival—Robin Hood in the modern popular mouth is hardly a mild flavor. If a modern F. J. Child were to ransack the English-speaking countries—and very likely others as well—an encyclopedia of Robin Hood apocrypha would no doubt testify both to the extraordinary richness of the popular imagination and to the deep-laid perseverance of Robin Hood as a channel for many varied forces. These forces range from the beauty of nature to the violence of oppression and in the myth combine with many varied reflections on gender, race, politics, time, and even the supernatural.

Robin Hood's biography is mythic in that the multiform figure does not have physical identity—and it seems highly improbable, or at least unprovable, that a Mr. R. Hood ever existed. But his biography is also mythic in that it has the scope, variety, and dynamic continuity of a myth. Yet a study of the elements of the myth indicates that this is not itself natural; there is no cosmic law that there must be a Robin Hood. What has happened is that elements of the myth have interested creative minds in different periods in different ways, and each has driven the myth in a new direction—essentially, driven it onward, given it new vigor.

When somebody—associated with guilds, perhaps—turned the antiauthority pranks of the festive village fertility figure into the basis for a town-forest myth against oppression, and the Robin Hood ballads were born, a major step was taken: the outlaw moved from fugitive organic experience into recoverable culture. Without those narratives that can live on paper and in the mouth, away from the performance of the village green, the myth would have died with other communal medieval practices. And when Renaissance writers, from John Major on, gentrified that tradition, they gave it a new social level and glamour, which has made it more acceptable, from the stage to star-loving Hollywood. Finding backing for a Sir Robin film has been easier than obtaining funding for, say, one about Tom Paine. And again, if the Romantic writers had not meshed, through the medium of Ritson's crucial edition, the biography of a lord with the excitement of a bandit's deeds, the myth would never have extended to the present in so strong a form.

In the twentieth and twenty-first centuries, there can be little doubt that the international power of the outlaw myth is based not on the intriguing novels, comics, and school-play readers, but on the striking suitability of the Robin Hood story for the screen. And the more technically subtle the visuals become, the more potent the myth becomes. At the same time, however, the magic fighting of *The New Adventures of Robin Hood* may take the technical possibilities one step too far into burlesque, and the moral weight of the hero has generated sardonic responses in *Time Bandits* and *Shrek*.

Like all myths, that of Robin Hood survives both across time and through time; it is constantly remade and varied in ways that authors, directors, actors, and even readers and audiences feel—rather than think—is appropriate to their own contexts. The intensity of this attachment appears to vary over time, however. It is noticeable that there have been several periods of high activity in the Robin Hood tradition. The 1980s, the years between the two World Wars, and the 1820s—as well as perhaps the 1840s—were all periods of high Robin Hood activity. Drawing similar conclusions about earlier eras is more difficult, but evidence suggests another period of busy production in the 1660s and 1670s, as well as perhaps the 1590s, the early 1500s, and even, conceivably, the late fourteenth century.

What is notable about these periods of increased Robin Hood activity is that they are all times when government has been overtly and consciously repressive. It is easy to see how the Robin Hood stories of the 1980s, including the films of 1991, are aware of the political character of the Reagan-Thatcher years and respond to it with vigor. The Robin Hood myth has operated in times of political stress as a means of expression for people conscious of kinds of oppression, including the postwar conservatism of the 1820s, the witch-hunting Restoration of 1660, even against the increasing paranoia of the late Elizabethan period and the growing repressive bureaucracy of the world of Henry VII. Thus, the "rhymes of Robin Hood" that Langland spoke of may be ultimately, if indirectly, related to the disturbances of the sociopolitically very troubled late fourteenth century. Hilton's speculation about Robin Hood and 1381 was too specific and too unliterary to receive full assent. But to read the tradition over time makes it seem likely that Hilton, most of the literary commentators from Child to Ohlgren and among the historians Maddicott, Bellamy, and, essentially, Dobson and Taylor, are right to think that this symbol of resistance to oppression originated in a century both terrible and magnificent—when in social, economic and literary terms England and its culture began to separate from the legacy, and the shackles, of antiquity.

To study Robin Hood is to study over five hundred years of the development of modern concepts of heroism, art, politics, and the self. It is an exciting and enthralling domain of study, that can in itself become a guide to the changing patterns and dynamics of society and culture over that enormous period. Robin Hood is always there, lurking at the edge of court culture, slipping through the forests of Romanticism, jumping over the wall of bourgeois fiction, cartwheeling into the visual carnival of film and television.

Biographies like to find one feature—preferably a scandalous flaw—that provides the key to interpretation of the life of the subject. In the case of Robin Hood, concepts such as flexibility, multiplicity, dynamism, and endurance are all applicable but inadequate because they refer only to the technical structure of the myth. The key feature in the biography of Robin Hood is in its own way scandalous, because it insists on confrontation, if sometimes of a muffled kind, with the conservative forces of any period, political or financial, and is a feature that is usually revealed only in fugitive glimpses.

Robin Hood always represents resistance to authority; he is always a threat to somebody who has power. That may be powerfully euphemized, as when he resists only a bad king or when he is very much a self-helping gentleman, kind to the poor and to women, but also representing unchanging social order, as in Thomas Love Peacock or as played by Errol Flynn. Robin may be more overtly a threat to existing social order, as in the social bandit ballads in which killing the sheriff seems the right way to proceed (shades of 1381 there) or in *Robin of Sherwood,* in which working-class organization against an oppressive state seems the key feature—and, not surprisingly in 1984, the year of the defeated British miners' strike, needed some magic to make a success of it.

But Robin is no more than a focus of a dream of resistance; he is not the figure on the banners of revolution. The myth contains no plans for genuine redistribution, no new electoral system, no models of political organization that might actually work better. The Robin Hood myth does not surface in E. P. Thompson's exhaustive study on *The Making of the English Working Class* because that was a different kind of struggle: that was class war, fought out in discussions, planning, in hand-to-hand conflict with hegemonic law, not the simpler morale-boosting escapades that the Robin Hood tradition can provide. When the myth goes through periods of dynamic activity, it may indeed operate as a safety valve, as the reflex of genuine political resistance to oppression.

But that is not to say that the concept of resistance, however euphemized and carnivalized in ballads and plays, fiction and films, is not important both to people's concepts of freedom, and to the volatile history in which they live and which they remake. The concept of outlaw resistance has utopian exchange value, however it may be contained or even reversed in particular contexts. And one of the most striking—and perhaps even encouraging—aspects of the Robin Hood myth is that it is in fact increasingly worldwide; the figure has provided an internationally comprehended figure who stands for resistance to wrongful authority whether he is Ravi in India or Robin des Bois in France. As commerce and industrial production is international, so Robin Hood is a figure who can, on a worldwide basis, imply resistance or at least restraint to any forces that are inclined to operate like sheriffs on behalf of the monarchic power of international capitalism.

When Langland first mentions Robin Hood, he is an example of what a slothful person is interested in instead of his proper priestly duties. But neither in person nor as a myth could Robin Hood be accused of sloth. He combines vigor, movement, and youthfulness with his key feature of resistance to wrongful authority; and though there is certainly more to reform, restitution, and redistribution than running and jumping and looking good in tight clothing, the idea that such energies should be committed to some form of resistance is at once the central idea, the basis for endurance, and the strongest value of Robin Hood's mythic biography.

Notes

I. Bold Robin Hood

1. For the most recent discussion, see Richard Almond and A. J. Pollard, "The Yeomanry of Robin Hood and Social Terminology in Fifteenth-Century England," *Past and Present* 170 (2001): 52–77.

2. William Langland, *The Vision according to Piers Plowman: The B Version,* ed. George Kane and E. Talbot Donaldson (London: Athlone, 1975), Passus V, lines 394–95. There are no surviving songs or poems about Randolph, Earl of Chester, although such a figure was involved with Fulk Fitz Warren, an early thirteenth-century outlaw who, as discussed in chap. 2, pp. 63–64, may have influenced the "distressed gentleman" stage of Robin's biography.

3. Latimer told this story in a sermon preached before King Edward VI in 1549; he was referring to a period about ten years before. The passage is given in full in Jeffrey L. Singman, *Robin Hood: The Shaping of a Legend* (Westport, Conn.: Greenwood, 1998), 117.

4. For further references, see Singman, *Robin Hood,* 116–19.

5. See Stephen Knight and Thomas H. Ohlgren, eds., *Robin Hood and Other Outlaw Tales* (Kalamazoo: Western Michigan University Press, 1997), 24.

6. For a discussion of the Rutland Barnsdale and its possible significance, see Stephen Knight, *Robin Hood: A Complete Study of the English Outlaw* (Oxford: Blackwell, 1994), 29–30.

7. See Knight and Ohlgren, eds., *Robin Hood and Other Outlaw Tales,* 25–26.

8. The passage is to be found in the Parliamentary Rolls (*Rotuli Parliamentorum*) and is quoted by F. J. Child, *The English and Scottish Popular Ballads,* 5 vols. (Boston: Barker, 1904; reprint, New York: Dover, 1965), 3:41.

9. Reprinted in the list of such references assembled by Lucy Sussex and printed as an appendix to Knight, *Robin Hood: A Complete Study,* 263.

10. For a discussion of the proverbs, see R. B. Dobson and J. Taylor, eds., *Rymes of Robyn Hood: An Introduction to the English Outlaw* (London: Heinemann, 1976), appendix 3, 288–92.

11. On medieval archery, see Jim Bradbury, *The Medieval Archer* (Woodbridge: Boydell, 1985).

12. Joseph Ritson, ed., *Robin Hood: A Collection of All the Ancient Poems, Songs and Ballads Now Extant Relative to the Celebrated English Outlaw (To Which are Prefixed Historical Anecdotes of His Life)*, 2 vols. (London: Egerton and Johnson, 1795); for a discussion of the proverbs, see 1:lxxxvii–xci; for the comment on "Good even, good Robin Hood," see 1:lxxxvii.

13. This proverb was discussed on several occasions in *Notes and Queries* in the nineteenth century. The fullest answer, one supported by modern Yorkshire farmers, was H. Fishwick's view that this referred to a southeastern wind that followed a freezing period, as "although higher in temperature than a wind blowing directly from the east, its dampness is certainly more prejudicial to health, and it is often more boisterous and penetrating." "A Thaw Wind," *Notes and Queries*, 4th ser., 11 (1873): 390.

14. For the full passage and an illustration, see J. C. Holt, *Robin Hood*, 2d ed. (London: Thames and Hudson, 1990), 69–70.

15. See Philippa C. Maddern, *Violence and Social Order: East Anglia, 1422–1442* (Oxford: Clarendon Press, 1992), 108–9.

16. The petition against Marshall in the Court of Star Chamber is printed fully and discussed by Holt, *Robin Hood*, 147–49.

17. The Edinburgh Riot is discussed in Knight, *Robin Hood: A Complete Study*, 109.

18. See Singman, *Robin Hood*, 64.

19. For a discussion of this, see Knight, *Robin Hood: A Complete Study*, 99.

20. See ibid., appendix, 262–88.

21. For an up-to-date discussion of the early play-games in light of the new *Records of Early English Drama* documentation, see Alexandra F. Johnston, "The Robin Hood of the Records," in *Playing Robin Hood: The Legend and Performance in Five Centuries,* ed. Lois Potter (Newark: University of Delaware Press, 1998), 27–44, and Singman, *Robin Hood*, 61–103.

22. J. D. Stokes, "Robin Hood and the Churchwardens in Yeovil," *Medieval and Renaissance Drama in England* 3 (1986): 1–25.

23. Johnston, "Robin Hood of the Records," 33, 37–38; David Wiles, *The Early Plays of Robin Hood* (Cambridge: Brewer, 1981), 7–30.

24. Sir John Paston's comments are reprinted in Singman, *Robin Hood*, 63.

25. For a text and commentary on the play, see Knight and Ohlgren, eds., *Robin Hood and Other Outlaw Tales*, 269–80, where this is treated as "Scene One" of "Robyn Hod and the Shryff of Notyngham." A recent analysis of the play is by John Marshall, "Playing the Game: Reconstructing *Robin Hood and the Sheriff of Nottingham*," in *Robin Hood in Popular Culture,* ed. Thomas G. Hahn (Cambridge: Brewer, 2000), 161–74.

26. For text and commentary, see Knight and Ohlgren, eds., *Robin Hood and Other Outlaw Tales*, 269–80, where this is treated as "Scene Two" of the play "Robyn Hod and the Shryff of Notyngham."

27. Wiles, *Early Plays of Robin Hood*, 33.

28. See Holt, *Robin Hood*, 58–59.

29. Chaucerians have not noted that the rogue friar in the General Prologue to *The Canterbury Tales* has many of the characteristics of Friar Tuck (though his name is given as Huberd), and he begins his tale with a summoner meeting a forest yeoman from the North, with language strongly reminiscent of the Robin Hood ballads. I would argue that, as seems highly likely on general grounds, Chaucer knew some of the "rhymes of Robin Hood" mentioned by his contemporary Langland and here makes some use of them.

30. The influence of F.J. Child is behind this view; he said that the play of "Robin Hood and the Sheriff" was "founded on" the ballad without considering that the play survives from nearly two hundred years before the ballad; see *English and Scottish Popular Ballads*, 3:90. The title of J.M. Steadman Jr.'s essay, "The Dramatization of the Robin Hood Ballads," *Modern Philology* 17 (1919): 9–23, assumes the same order, and that has been the standard view of commentators, for no argued reason. Even a drama scholar like David Wiles assumes the priority of the ballads in saying that the early reference to the plays at Exeter "shows that the games followed quite closely upon the ballads," *Early Plays of Robin Hood*, 43. A discussion of the "Dating Controversy," which seriously questions the notion that the ballads have priority is by George Swan in "Robin Hood's 'Irish Knife,' " *University of Mississippi Studies in English*, n.s., 11–12 (1993–95): 51–80; see in particular 65–66.

31. Ritson says that the maxim "is of the highest authority in Westminster-hall where, in order to the decision [*sic*] of a knotty point, it has been repeatedly noted, in the most solemn manner, by grave and learned judges," 1:lxxix. The maxim is referred to as a classic case of a self-evident fact in W. Bolland's legal textbook *A Manual of Yearbook Studies* (Cambridge: Cambridge University Press, 1925), 107.

32. Douglas Gray, "The Robin Hood Poems," in *Robin Hood: Anthology of Scholarship and Criticism,* ed. Stephen Knight (Cambridge: Brewer, 1999), 3–37; see in particular 14.

33. Knight and Ohlgren, eds., *Robin Hood and Other Outlaw Tales,* 37, lines 1–8.

34. Kelly de Vriess, "Longbow Archery and the Earliest Robin Hood Legends," in *Robin Hood in Popular Culture*, ed. Hahn, 41–59; Dean A. Hoffman, " 'With the shott I wyll / Alle thy lustes to full-fyl': Archery as Symbol in the Early Ballads of Robin Hood," *Neuphilologische Mitteilungen* 86 (1985): 494–505.

35. For a discussion of tricksters, see *Mythical Trickster Figures: Contours, Contexts, and Criticism,* ed. William S. Hynes and William G. Doty (Tuscaloosa: University of Alabama Press, 1993).

36. Knight and Ohlgren, eds., *Robin Hood and Other Outlaw Tales,* 72, lines 320–23.

37. Ibid., 80–168, lines 1823–24.

38. For a discussion of the date of the *Gest,* see Knight, *Robin Hood: A Complete Study,* 46–48. While scholars in the past have felt that the *Gest* might have been put together as early as 1400, this opinion was based on a misreading of Child,

who merely said that the ballads on which it was based were probably from the later fourteenth century. The most recent studies of its language place it firmly in the fifteenth century, probably about the middle; see Masa Ikegami, "The Language and Date of 'A Gest of Robyn Hode,' " *Neuphilologische Mitteilungen* 96 (1995): 271–81.

39. Thomas H. Ohlgren, "The 'Marchaunt' of Sherwood: Mercantile Ideology in *A Gest of Robyn Hode*," in *Robin Hood in Popular Culture*, ed. Hahn, 175–90.

40. H. A. Kelly, in *Chaucerian Tragedy* (Cambridge: Brewer, 1997), 45, suggests that Bower's usage is one of the instances in which a commentator thinks "that tragedies could well be considered the source not of good and decent stories . . . but of bad and indecent jokes and humorous escapades." While this is an appealing way of dismissing the question of what Bower meant by a Robin Hood tragedy, it may not be justified. In Kelly's other examples of this reduced understanding of "tragedy" as something like "play" or "game," the word is not opposed to "comedy," and the suspicion must remain that Bower did have something gloomy in mind when he wrote "tragedies."

41. The hero's betrayal by a relative or close friend is one of the elements of the international hero archetype discussed by Lord Raglan in *The Hero* (London: Methuen, 1936).

42. For a discussion of these characteristic adjectives, see Knight and Ohlgren, eds., *Robin Hood and Other Outlaw Tales*, 85.

43. For the archery contest, see in Child, *English and Scottish Popular Ballads*, "Robin Hood and the Golden Arrow," ballad no. 152, and "Robin Hood and Queen Katherine," ballad no. 145 (also in *Robin Hood and Other Outlaw Tales*, ed. Knight and Ohlgren); for the king, "The King's Disguise and Friendship with Robin Hood," ballad no. 151; and for the sheriff, see the Forresters manuscript version of "Robin Hood and the Bishop," called "Robin Hood and the Sheriffe," in *Robin Hood: The Forresters Manuscript*, ed. Stephen Knight (Cambridge: Brewer, 1999), 23–33.

44. Gray, "Robin Hood Poems," 27.

45. Knight and Ohlgren, eds., *Robin Hood and Other Outlaw Tales*, 286.

46. Ibid., 290.

47. There is evidence that a friar appears in the plays in general. The well-known painted "Tollett" window at Minsterley, Shropshire, shows a friar dancing with a woman, and the friar and his girlfriend are referred to frequently; see Holt, *Robin Hood*, 160; Dobson and Taylor, eds., *Rymes of Robyn Hood*, 41 and 62. Some have thought that the woman he dances with here is Maid Marian (Dobson and Taylor, eds., *Rymes of Robyn Hood*, 214 n. 1), but she is just the traditional friar's robust girlfriend, who appears in Anthony Munday's play *The Downfall of Robert, Earle of Huntington* (see pp. 52–62) as Jinny, and probably surfaces in Shakespeare's *As You Like It* as Audrey, the homespun woman who is Touchstone's partner.

48. The only exception to this, according to Cyprian Blagden, were "exercises in economy on the part of the booksellers who, from time to time, and particularly towards the end of the century, used up old stock for printing more popular ballads." See "Notes on the Ballad Market in the Second Half of the Seventeenth Century," *Studies in Bibliography* 6 (1954): 161–80, 164 n. 2.

49. For an edition and discussion of the texts, see *Robin Hood: The Forresters Manuscript*, ed. Knight.

50. For a discussion of the period, see Stephen Knight, " 'Quite Another Man': Robin Hood and the Royal Restoration," in *Playing Robin Hood*, ed. Potter, 167–81.

51. Knight and Ohlgren, eds., *Robin Hood and Other Outlaw Tales*, 553.

52. The two common titles of this popular ballad refer to different class origins for the men rescued, either lower as "The Widow's Three Sons" or higher as "Three Squires." In other versions they do not fit these categories. As the class of the rescued men is not central to the narrative (though it is to its changing ideology), it seems best to describe the ballad functionally.

53. Knight and Ohlgren, eds., *Robin Hood and Other Outlaw Tales*, 518.

54. Child, *English and Scottish Popular Ballads*, 3:21.

55. Dobson and Taylor, eds., *Rymes of Robyn Hood*, 179.

56. For introductions to and texts of these outlaws' stories, see Thomas H. Ohlgren, ed., *Medieval Outlaws: Ten Tales in Modern English* (Stroud: Sutton, 1998).

57. Knight and Ohlgren, eds., *Robin Hood and Other Outlaw Tales*, 509, line 1.

58. Silent sings one line naming the three outlaws in the drinking scene in Shakespeare's *Henry IV, Part 2*, act 5, scene 3, line 100; notes usually attribute the line to "Robin Hood and the Pinder of Wakefield," but it occurs in a number of ballads.

59. Knight and Ohlgren, eds., *Robin Hood and Other Outlaw Tales*, 472, lines 41–44.

II. Robert, Earl of Huntingdon

1. Stephen Knight and Thomas H. Ohlgren, eds., *Robin Hood and Other Outlaw Tales* (Kalamazoo: Western Michigan University Press, 1997), 27.

2. Edward Hall, *The History of England during the Reign of Henry the Fourth and the Succeeding Monarchs to the End of the Reign of Henry the Eighth*, ed. Sir H. Ellis (London: Johnson, Rivington et al., 1809), 515.

3. Knight and Ohlgren, eds., *Robin Hood and Other Outlaw Tales*, 28.

4. Raphael Holinshed, *The History of Scotland*, in *Chronicles*, vol. 2 (London: Harrison, 1577), 202.

5. John Stow, *The Annales of England* (London: Newbery, 1592), 227.

6. F. J. Child records five surviving seventeenth-century versions of this ballad in *The English and Scottish Popular Ballads*, 5 vols. (Boston: Barker, 1904; reprint, New York: Dover, 1965), 3:115. The ballad also appears in the early garlands.

7. *George a Greene: The Pinner of Wakefield* appears in vol. 2 of the *Complete Works of Robert Greene*, ed. J. Churton Collins, 2 vols. (Oxford: Clarendon Press, 1905), but most recently scholars have regarded it as anonymous. See Edwin Davenport, "The Representation of Robin Hood in Elizabethan Drama: *George a Greene* and *Edward I*," in *Playing Robin Hood: The Legend as Performance in Five Centuries*, ed. Lois Potter (Newark: University of Delaware Press, 1998), 45–62; see in particular 47.

8. *George a Greene*, 2:99, lines 1081–83.

9. For a discussion of the Scottish relations of the tradition, see Lewis Spence, "Robin Hood in Scotland," *Chambers Journal* 18 (1928): 94–96.

10. Michael Shapiro, "Cross-Dressing in Elizabethan Robin Hood Plays," in *Playing Robin Hood*, ed. Potter, 77–90; see in particular 83.

11. George Peele, *The Dramatic Works: Edward I*, ed. F. S. Hook, vol. 2 of *The Life and Works of George Peele*, ed. Charles Tyler Prouty (New Haven: Yale University Press, 1961), 113, lines 1176–80.

12. For a discussion of these events—and the continuing playing of the Robin Hood games—see Jeffrey L. Singman, *Robin Hood: The Shaping of a Legend* (Westport, Conn.: Greenwood, 1998), 62–68.

13. David Wiles, *The Early Plays of Robin Hood* (Cambridge: Brewer, 1981), 54.

14. Though no broadside ballads survive from the sixteenth century, it is clear from the Sloane manuscript "Life of Robin Hood," written by about 1600 (see William Thoms, ed., *A Collection of Early English Prose Romances*, 2 vols. [London: Nattali and Bond, 1858], 2:124–37), that a number of the later surviving ballads were already well-known: instances are "Robin Hood's Progress to Nottingham," "Robin Hood and the Pinder of Wakefield," "Robin Hood and Allin a Dale" (using Scarlock as the hero), and "The Death of Robin Hood." It is clear that Anthony Munday, writing *The Downfall of Robert, Earle of Huntington* in 1598–99, is familiar with "Robin Hood Rescues Three Young Men."

15. For a discussion of some of the ways in which Munday "merges the strands" of the tradition and creates "an inherent mixing of genres," see Jeffrey L. Singman, "Munday's Unruly Earl," in *Playing Robin Hood*, ed. Potter, 63–76; see in particular 65–66.

16. The diary of Philip Henslowe, the owner-manager of the theater the Rose, indicates that in February 1598 he paid Munday £5 for "a playe boocke called the firste parte of Robyne hoode"; a little later Munday and Henry Chettle received money for the second play. Late in 1598 Chettle was paid for "mendyinge" the play "for the corte"; see Philip Henslowe, *Henslowe's Diaries,* ed. W. W. Greg (London: Bullen, 1908), 83, 84, 89. It is curious that Henslowe's father was a forester in Ashdown Forest.

17. Anthony Munday, *The Downfall of Robert Earle of Huntington;* see Knight and Ohlgren, eds., *Robin Hood and Other Outlaw Tales*, 296–401, lines 336–43.

18. Wiles, *Early Plays of Robin Hood*, 22.

19. Helen Cooper, *Pastoral: Medieval into Renaissance* (Cambridge: Brewer, 1977), 54. The French tradition tends to spell the name as Marion, while the majority of English, and eventually American, uses employ the spelling closer to the Latin original, Mariana; this version of the name will be used here unless a text has "Marion."

20. Lord Raglan, *The Hero* (London: Methuen, 1936).

21. Anthony Munday and Henry Chettle, *The Death of Roberte, Earle of Huntingdon;* see Knight and Ohlgren, eds., *Robin Hood and Other Outlaw Tales*, 402–40, lines 848–51.

22. David Bevington, *Tudor Drama and Politics* (Cambridge: Harvard University Press, 1968), 295.

23. The first suggestion to this effect was made in 1793 by a commentator known as "DH," probably the antiquarian Richard Gough, in a note in *Gentleman's Magazine* 63 (March 1793): 226.

24. See Malcolm A. Nelson, *The Robin Hood Tradition in the English Renaissance*, Salzburg Studies in English Literature, Elizabethan Series, vol. 14 (Salzburg: University of Salzburg Press, 1973), 124.

25. *Looke About You* (London: Ferbrand, 1600), 49.

26. For a discussion of this, see A. H. Thorndike, "The Relationship of *As You Like It* to the Robin Hood Plays," *Journal of English and Germanic Philology* 4 (1902): 59–69.

27. For a translation of and comments about Fulk's story, see Glyn S. Burgess, trans., *Two Medieval Outlaws: Eustace the Monk and Fouke Fitz Waryn* (Cambridge: Brewer, 1997), and Thomas E. Kelly, "Fouke Fitz Waryn," in *Medieval Outlaws: Ten Tales in Modern English,* ed. Thomas H. Ohlgren (Stroud: Sutton, 1998), 106–167.

28. The song "By Landsdale, mery Landsdale" starts with a "jolly miller" who had a son called "Renold." He went off to seek his fortune, and went to sleep. His father found him and gave him a bow, and Renold shot an armed man "at the half miles end":

And there of him they made
good yeoman Robin hood,
Scarlet, and little John, and little John, hey ho.

Thomas Ravenscroft, *Deuteromelia, or the Second part of Musicks melodie, or melodius Musicke* (London: Adams, 1609), n.p.

29. For a text and full discussion of the Fulk tradition, see Burgess, trans., *Two Medieval Outlaws.*

30. For details, see W. F. Prideaux, "Who Was Robin Hood?" in *Notes and Queries*, 7th ser., 2 (1886): 421–24, and Stephen Knight, "Rabbie Hood: The Colonial (and Postcolonial) Impact of Scotland on the Robin Hood Tradition," in *The Outlaw Tradition: New Interdisciplinarian Essays*, ed. Helen Phillips (Manchester: Manchester University Press, forthcoming).

31. For a text and commentary, see Matthew P. McDiarmid, ed., *Hary's Wallace (Vita Nobilissimi Defensoris Scoti Wilelmi Wallace Militis)*, 2 vols. (Edinburgh: Blackwood, for the Scottish Text Society, 1968).

32. See Prideaux, "Who Was Robin Hood?" and Knight, *Rabbie Hood,* for a discussion of the popularity of Robin Hood in Scotland before publication of the *Gest.*

33. William Warner, *Albions England* (London: Orwin, 1589; facsimile ed., Hildesheim: Olb, 1971), 121.

34. Michael Drayton, *Poly-Olbion*, vol. 4 of *The Works of Michael Drayton*, ed. J. William Hebel (Oxford: Blackwell, 1961), song 26, lines 300–301.

35. Julie Sanders, "Jonson, *The Sad Shepherd* and the North Midlands," *Ben Jonson Journal* 6 (1999): 49–68.

36. See *The Works of Ben Jonson,* ed. C. H. Herford and Percy and Evelyn Simpson, 10 vols. (Oxford: Clarendon, 1950), 2:216. In a recent study Anne Barton is more skeptical about a strong relationship between the two works; see *Ben Jonson, Dramatist* (Cambridge: Cambridge University Press, 1984), 341–42, but some apparent links remain.

37. The fullest study of the sources is in Herford, Simpson, and Simpson's introduction to the play, 2:216–17; a recent view stressing the English literary connections is by Anne Barton, *Ben Jonson, Dramatist,* 347–48.

38. See Stephen Knight, " 'Meere English Flockes': Jonson's Use of the English Robin Hood Tradition in *The Sad Shepherd,*" in *Robin Hood: Medieval and Post-Medieval,* ed. Helen Phillips (Cambridge: Brewer, forthcoming).

39. Ben Jonson, *The Sad Shepherd,* in *Ben Jonson's Plays and Masques,* ed. Robert M. Adams (New York: Norton, 1979), "Argument" to act 2, 290.

40. Lois Potter, introduction to "Part Two: Cultural Cross-Dressing," in *Playing Robin Hood,* ed. Potter, 91–99; see in particular 94.

41. Child discusses the matter in some detail; see *English and Scottish Popular Ballads,* 3:133 and 144–45; see also Joseph Ritson, ed., *Robin Hood: A Collection of All the Ancient Poems, Songs and Ballads Now Extant Relative to the Celebrated English Outlaw,* 2 vols. (London: Egerton and Johnson, 1795), 2:138, and for the "Forresters" version of the ballad, Stephen Knight, ed., *Robin Hood: The Forresters Manuscript* (Cambridge: Brewer, 1998), 98.

42. See the "Additions and Corrections" to Child, ed., *English and Scottish Popular Ballads,* 5:240.

43. Knight and Ohlgren, eds., *Robin Hood and Other Outlaw Tales,* 501–6, line 1.

44. For a new edition of and commentary on *Gamelyn,* see ibid., 184–226.

45. Ibid., 227–35, line 6.

46. Child, ed., *English and Scottish Popular Ballads,* 3:147.

47. Ibid., 3:147–50, in particular stanza 9c.

48. Knight and Ohlgren, eds., *Robin Hood and Other Outlaw Tales,* 529–40, in particular line 21.

49. Helen Phillips notes that her name may come from Clorinda, a warrior princess in Tasso's *Gerusalemme Liberata;* see "Forest, Town, and Road: The Significance of Places and Names in Some Robin Hood Texts," in *Robin Hood in Popular Culture,* ed. Thomas G. Hahn (Cambridge: Brewer, 2000), 197–214; see in particular 213.

50. In "Forest, Town, and Road" she suggests, in the context of other evidence, that "Robin Hood's move from Sherwood to Tutbury becomes a symbol of Charles II's uncontested return to England," 212.

51. Knight and Ohlgren, eds., *Robin Hood and Other Outlaw Tales,* 493–98, in particular lines 4–9.

52. Evelyn Perry discussed the ballad as an example of transvestism, in "Disguising and Revealing the Female Hero's Identity: Cross-Dressing in the Ballad

of 'Robin Hood and Maid Marian,' " in *Robin Hood in Popular Culture*, ed. Hahn, 191–96.

53. Knight and Ohlgren, eds., *Robin Hood and Other Outlaw Tales*, 602–25, lines 89–100.

54. J. C. Holt, *Robin Hood*, 2d ed. (London: Thames and Hudson, 1990), 151.

55. R. B. Dobson and J. Taylor, eds., *Rymes of Robyn Hood: An Introduction to the English Outlaw* (London: Heinemann, 1976), 26.

56. Singman, *Robin Hood*, 143. Singman sees this as an instance of the ballads being seen as merely foolish, but the king's remark has a conservative political edge.

57. Knight and Ohlgren, eds., *Robin Hood and Other Outlaw Tales*, 441–51, in particular lines 131–33.

58. For a discussion of the history of the text, see Lucy Toulmin-Smith's introduction to her edition: John Leland, *The Itinerary of John Leland, in England and Wales,* ed. Toulmin-Smith, 5 vols. (London: Bell, 1906–10).

59. For the comment on Barnsdale, see *Itinerary of John Leland*, ed. Toulmin-Smith, 4:13. The reference to Kirklees is in John Leland, *Collecteana*, ed. T. Hearne (Oxford: Sheldonian Theatre, 1774), 1:54. For a discussion, see Dobson and Taylor, eds., *Rymes of Robyn Hood*, 21 and 44; Holt, *Robin Hood*, 41–42.

60. Dobson and Taylor, eds., *Rymes of Robyn Hood*, 287.

61. Most sources give the date as 1665, but David Hepworth has established 1669 as correct; see "A Grave Tale," in *Robin Hood: Medieval and Post-Medieval*, ed. Phillips. Hepworth argues that the surviving copy of Johnston's drawing may have been changed by Stukeley, even to adding the names.

62. Knight and Ohlgren, eds., *Robin Hood and Other Outlaw Tales*, 625.

63. The epitaph, and a general discussion of these materials, is found in Holt, *Robin Hood*, 41–42.

64. Ibid., 43.

65. See Hepworth, "Grave Tale."

66. Holt, *Robin Hood*, 44.

67. *The Reliques of Early English Poetry,* ed. Thomas Percy, 4 vols. (London: Dodsley, 1765), 1:104.

68. As Richard Gough reported in *Sepulchral Monuments*, 2 vols. (London: Nichols, 1786), 1:cviii.

69. See the general introduction to Knight, ed., *Robin Hood: The Forresters Manuscript*, xi–xxi.

70. Thomas Hahn has reported on the "Lives" to a conference, and scholars look forward to his forthcoming edition of these elusive but popular texts.

71. Anthony Munday, *Metropolis Coronata: The Triumph of Ancient Drapery* (London: Purslowe, 1615).

72. See Alexandra F. Johnston, "The Robin Hood of the Records," in *Playing Robin Hood*, ed. Potter, 39.

73. *Robin Hood : An Opera* (London: Watts, 1730).

74. The author probably knew the name King Edward from the *Gest*, rather than from the plays of the 1590s that use it, *Edward I* and *George a Greene*, which were little known by 1730.

75. Moses Mendez, *Robin Hood: A New Musical Entertainment* (London: Cooper, 1751).

76. Ritson, ed., *Robin Hood*, 1:lxxii.

77. This figure is based on records at the British Library, the Bodleian Library, and the National Library of Scotland. It is much higher than that found in J. Harris Gable's *Bibliography of Robin Hood*, Studies in Language, Literature, and Criticism (Lincoln: University of Nebraska Press, 1939). But so many of the garlands and lives were appearing from small local publishers and so many were easily lost or destroyed, the actual figures are likely to be at least double those that are recorded.

78. Leonard McNally, *Robin Hood; or Sherwood Forest, A Comic Opera, as it is performed at the Theatre-Royal in Covent Garden* (London: Almon, 1784).

79. *Airs, Duets and Choruses in the Operatical Pantomime of Merry Sherwood or Harlequin Forester, now performing at the Theatre-Royal, Covent Garden* (London: Longman, 1795).

III. Robin Hood Esquire

1. Thomas Percy, ed., *Reliques of English Poetry: Consisting of Old Heroic Ballads, Songs, and other Pieces of our earlier Poets (Chiefly of the Lyric kind), Together with some few of later Date*, 4 vols. (London: Dodsley, 1765). For Percy's procedures and biography, see the introduction by Nick Groom to the facsimile edition (London: Routledge/Thoemmes, 1996). The first seven poems in his manuscript are Robin Hood ballads; they are all damaged by ripped pages. Editors have felt that the later "Robin Hood and Guy of Gisborne" might have had some lines missing after the first stanza, but in this part of the manuscript there are no signs of ripped pages, and it is possible to read the text as being complete; see Stephen Knight and Thomas H. Ohlgren, ed., *Robin Hood and Other Outlaw Tales* (Kalamazoo: Western Michigan University Press, 1997), 181.

2. Percy, ed., *Reliques*, 1:86.

3. Marilyn Butler, "Antiquarianism (Popular)," in *An Oxford Companion to the Romantic Age,* ed. Iain MacCalman (Oxford: Oxford University Press, 1999), 328–38.

4. Thomas Evans, ed., *Old Ballads, Historical and Narrative, With Some of Modern Date, Now First Collected, and Reprinted from Rare Copies,* 2 vols. (London: Evans, 1777). There was a second edition also in two volumes, in 1784, and a much augmented third edition, edited by his son Robert Evans, in four volumes, in 1810.

5. *Specimen of the Early English Poets,* ed. George Ellis (London: Edwards, 1790), is a collection of "all the most beautiful poems which had been published in this country during the Sixteenth and Seventeenth centuries" (i) and includes no

medieval texts. *Specimens of Early English Metrical Romances,* ed. George Ellis (London: Longman, Hunt, Rees and Orme, 1805), was fully devoted to medieval texts but did not include ballads.

6. Joseph Ritson, ed., *Robin Hood: A Collection of All the Ancient Poems, Songs and Ballads Now Extant Relative to the Celebrated English Outlaw,* 2 vols. (London: Egerton and Johnson, 1795); see preface, 1:i. He mentions Hawkins as a model on 1:iii.

7. Bertrand Bronson, *Joseph Ritson, Scholar-at-Arms,* 2 vols. (Berkeley: University of California Press, 1938), 1:217–18.

8. R. H. Evans, ed., *Old Ballads, Historical and Narrative,* 3d ed., 4 vols. (London: Evans, 1810), 2:87.

9. William Wordsworth, *Poetical Works of Wordsworth,* ed. Thomas Hutchinson, rev. ed. edited by Ernest de Selincourt (Oxford: Oxford University Press, 1936), 231.

10. Sir Walter Scott, *The Poetical Works of Sir Walter Scott,* ed. J. Logie Robertson (London: Oxford University Press, 1904), 258, canto 5, stanza 22.

11. See a letter to Charles Williams Wynne, December 30, 1804, National Library of Wales MSS 4811–15D. I am indebted for this reference to Dr. Gavin Edwards.

12. Elizabeth Villa-Real Gooch, *Sherwood Forest; or Northern Adventures,* 3 vols. (London: Highley, 1804), 1:vi and 1:14.

13. Brian Bailey, *The Luddite Rebellion* (Stroud: Sutton, 1998), 31; the other links between Ludd and Robin Hood are referred to on 20 and 69.

14. Lois Potter, "Sherwood Forest and the Byronic Robin Hood," in *Robin Hood in Popular Culture: Violence, Transgression, and Justice,* ed. Thomas G. Hahn (Cambridge: Brewer, 2000), 215–24.

15. I am indebted to Marilyn Butler for this interpretation.

16. Nicholas Roe, *John Keats and the Culture of Dissent* (Oxford: Oxford University Press, 1997), 140–55.

17. For a text of Reynolds's sonnets and a discussion of his exchange with Keats, see John Barnard, "Keats's 'Robin Hood,' John Hamilton Reynolds, and the 'Old Poets,' " in *Robin Hood: Anthology of Scholarship and Criticism,* ed. Stephen Knight (Cambridge: Brewer, 1999), 123–40; see in particular 125.

18. John Keats, *The Poems of John Keats,* ed. Miriam Allott (London: Longman, 1970), 301–4, particularly line 1.

19. Barnard, "Keats's 'Robin Hood,' " 127.

20. Ibid., 134.

21. Leigh Hunt, *Stories in Verse* (London: Routledge, 1855), 137.

22. These appear both in the Toll Booth riots (long before the Porteous rioters sacked the town jail, Robin Hood rioters had done so in 1561, an event that Scott refers to in *The Abbott,* 1820) and in the outlaws of the Vale of Belvoir whom Jeannie meets on her long trek to London. Scott knew Jonson's work, and there are some Robin Hood aspects in the character of George Robertson, at this stage the outlaws' leader, as well as in this slightly displaced setting for highway robbery.

23. For the original intention to call the hero Harold and Scott's change of mind, see Edgar Johnson, *Sir Walter Scott: The Great Unknown,* 2 vols. (London: Hamilton, 1970), 1:686. Scott commented on the source of the name Ivanhoe in his author's preface; see Penguin Classics edition, ed. A. N. Wilson (London: Penguin, 1986), 534. References in the text are to this edition.

24. See Christopher Hill, "The Norman Yoke," in *Puritanism and Revolution* (London: Secker and Warburg, 1965), 50–122.

25. A wand held up a circular, wreath-like target; a peg would pin a circular target—of cloth or skin—to a tree or butt. To break either would be to hit the center of the target. Curiously, there is one earlier instance of arrow-splitting, but as it occurs in the Forresters manuscript it seems most unlikely that Scott had ever seen it, and the fantasy development from splitting the wand or the peg to splitting the arrow was apparently created by two revisers of the tradition. In "Robin Hood and Queen Catherine," as the Forresters manuscript entitles the ballad, at the climax of the archery tournament:

Then shott Loxly for Our Queen
And cloue his Arrow in three.

(Stephen Knight, ed., *Robin Hood: The Forresters Manuscript* [Cambridge: Brewer, 1998], 59, lines 215–16.)

26. An unnamed "lieutenant" is mentioned in the outlaw band in chapter 32, but in chapter 41 Little John is said to have been in the North during all the action, so he cannot be the lieutenant.

27. See John Sutherland, *The Life of Walter Scott* (Oxford: Blackwell, 1995), 234.

28. *Robin Hood,* 2 vols. (Edinburgh: Oliver and Boyd, 1819), 1:55.

29. Sir Henry Newbolt argued for more influence than Peacock suggested, presumably deriving from prepublication revision; see "Peacock, Scott and Robin Hood," *Dalhousie Review* 4 (1925): 411–32. Christopher Dawson has argued that the resemblances are common to the literature of the period; see *His Fine Wit* (London: Routledge, 1970), 229–31.

30. Frances Brooke, *Marian, A Comic Opera* (London: Cadell, 1788).

31. Thomas Love Peacock, *Maid Marian,* ed. George Saintsbury (1895; reprint, London: Macmillan, 1959), 5.

32. The politics of the book are discussed by Marilyn Butler in " 'The Good Old Times': *Maid Marian,*" in *Robin Hood: Anthology of Scholarship and Criticism,* ed. Knight, 141–53.

33. Butler, " 'Good Old Times,' " 141–43 and 146–48.

34. George Saintsbury, introduction to Peacock, *Maid Marian,* xvii.

35. Auguste Thierry, *Histoire de la conquête de l'Angleterre par les Normans* (Paris: Firmin Didot, 1825); Edmond Barry, *Thèse de litterature sur les vicissitudes et les transformations du cycle populaire de Robin Hood* (Paris: Rignoux, 1832).

36. Pierce Egan, *Robin Hood and Little John, or the Merry Men of Sherwood Forest* (London: Forster and Hextall, 1840).

37. See Eve Kosofsky Sedgwick, *Between Men: English Literature and Male Homosocial Desire* (New York: Columbia University Press, 1985).

38. See Scott, *Ivanhoe,* ed. Wilson, 692.

39. Joachim H. Stocqueler, *Maid Marian, The Forest Queen* (London: Pierce, 1849.)

40. I am indebted for information about Stocqueler's life beyond his autobiography (*The Memoirs of a Journalist,* enlarged, rev. ed. [Bombay: The Times of India, 1873]) to the research of his descendant Peter Gill.

41. Bennet A. Brockman, "Robin Hood and the Invention of Children's Literature," *Children's Literature* 10 (1982): 1–14.

42. [George Emmett], *Robin Hood and the Outlaws of Sherwood Forest,* 3 vols. (London: Temple, 1869).

43. George Emmett, *Robin Hood and the Adventures of Merrie Sherwood,* 3 vols. (London: Hogarth, 1885); this is the same text, reset and with more sophisticated illustrations. It appeared in the "Hogarth House Library," along with adolescent titles such as *Midshipman Tom, Frank Fearless or the Cruise of the Firebrand,* and the less innocent-sounding *Tom Wildrake's Schooldays.*

44. Howard Pyle, *The Merry Adventures of Robin Hood, of Great Renown, in Nottinghamshire* (New York: Scribner, 1883), 289.

45. See the discussion of Pyle in Thomas Hahn and Stephen Knight, " 'Exempt Me Sire, I Am Afeard of Women': Gendering Robin Hood," in *The Outlaw Tradition: New Interdisciplinary Essays,* ed. Helen Phillips (Manchester: Manchester University Press, forthcoming).

46. Harry B. Smith and Reginald de Koven, *Maid Marian* (London: Hopwood and Crew, 1890), iv.

47. See Rudy Behlmer, "Robin Hood on the Screen: From Legend to Film," in *Robin Hood: Anthology of Scholarship and Criticism,* ed. Stephen Knight (Cambridge: Brewer, 1999), 441–60; see in particular 442.

48. For a discussion of this production, see Lois Potter, "The Apotheosis of Maid Marian: Tennyson's *The Foresters* and the Nineteenth-Century Theater," in *Playing Robin Hood: The Legend as Performance in Five Centuries,* ed. Lois Potter (Newark: University of Delaware Press, 1998), 182–204.

49. Alfred, Lord Tennyson, *The Foresters: Robin Hood and Maid Marian,* in *Tennyson: Poems and Plays* (London: Oxford University Press, 1965), 750; this edition has no line numbers, and references are to pages.

50. Lois Potter reports that this song was written as early as 1830; see Potter, "Sherwood Forest," 188.

51. For a discussion of these poets' contribution to the tradition, see Stephen Knight, *Robin Hood: A Complete Study of the English Outlaw* (Oxford: Blackwell, 1994), 209–14.

52. "Sherwood," from *Sherwood* (London: Watts, 1911); the poem is without line numbers.

53. Thomas Miller, *Royston Gower,* 3 vols. (London: Nicholson, 1838).

54. G. P. R. James, *Forest Days: A Romance of Old Times*, 3 vols. (London: Saunders and Otley, 1843).

55. "G. F.," review of *Robin Hood and Little John*, by Pierce Egan, *London and Westminster Quarterly* 33 (1840): 425–91.

56. Ritson did know the fragment of this ballad held in the British Library; he transcribes it in his introduction, 1:lxxvi–vii, and comments that it appears to be part of an outlaw story earlier than the *Gest,* but it was too fragmentary to reprint. The ballad was first printed by Robert Jamieson in *Popular Ballads and Songs,* 2 vols. (Edinburgh: Constable, 1806), 2:54–72, and then, a little less inaccurately transcribed, in C. H. Hartshorne, ed., *Ancient Metrical Tales* (London: Pickering, 1829), 179–97. An accurate version, corrected by Sir Frederick Madden, was added at the end of the second edition of Ritson's collection (London: Pickering, 1832), appendix 8, 221–36. Only in J. M. Gutch's edition of 1847 (see note 58), who called it "A Tale of Robin Hood," did the ballad become widely known.

57. See F. J. Child, ed., *The English and Scottish Popular Ballads,* 5 vols. (Boston: Barker, 1904; reprint, New York: Dover, 1965), 2:412–15; as Child notes, 2:412, Mrs. Brown of Falkland, the celebrated ballad-transmitter, appears to have adapted "Willie and Earl Richard's Daughter" to provide a ballad about Robin Hood's birth. Child suggests she was prompted by the presence of a character called "Brown Robin" in the related ballad "Rose the Red and White Lily" (2:415–24). Gutch published the latter ballad as being about Robin Hood.

58. Child, ed., *English and Scottish Popular Ballads,* 3:170; the ballad is reprinted in Knight and Ohlgren, ed., *Robin Hood and Other Outlaw Tales,* 628–32.

59. J. M. Gutch, ed., *A Lyttel Gest of Robin Hode, with Other Ancient & Modern Ballads and Songs Relating to this Celebrated Yeoman,* 2 vols. (London: Longman, 1847), 1:i.

60. Joseph Hunter, "The Great Hero of the Ancient Minstrelsy of England: Robin Hood, his period, real character etc., investigated," in *Critical and Historical Tracts,* vol. 4 (London: Smith, 1852), 28–38; see in particular 35–39.

61. Thomas Wright, "On the Popular Cycle of the Robin Hood Ballads," essay 17 in *Essays on the Literatures, Superstitions, and History of England in the Middle Ages,* 2 vols. (London: Smith, 1846), 2:164–211.

62. Stocqueler, *Memoirs of a Journalist,* 53; though the first book publication, this is an "enlarged, revised edition" because the memoirs first appeared in the newspaper and were elaborated in book form.

63. C. W. Brooks, C. L. Kearney, and Joachim Stocqueler, *Robin Hood and Richard Coeur de Lion* in *Plays* (London: Fairbrother, 1859).

64. F. R. Goodyer, *Once Upon a Time or A Midsummer Night's Dream in Merrie Sherwood. A Fairy Extravaganza* (Nottingham: Allen, 1868).

65. John Oxenford and G. A. MacFarren, *Robin Hood: An Opera* (London: Cramer, Beale and Chappel, 1860); *New and Original Grand Christmas Pantomime— Robin Hood* (Manchester: Theatre Royal Press, 1851).

66. See Marcus Smith and Julian Wasserman, "Travels with a Green Crayon," in *Robin Hood: Medieval and Post-Medieval,* ed. Helen Phillips (Cambridge: Brewer, forthcoming).

67. Henry Thoreau, "Walking," in *Excursions* (Boston: Tickner and Field, 1880), 164.

68. In chapter 8 of *Tom Sawyer* Tom leads an imitation of "Robin Hood and Guy of Gisborne," and he plays a version of "The Death of Robin Hood."

69. Alexandre Dumas, *Robin Hood: Prince des Voleurs* (Paris: Levy, 1872), and *Robin Hood le Proscrit* (Paris: Levy, 1873).

IV. Robin Hood of Hollywood

1. Kevin Harty, *The Reel Middle Ages: American, Western and Eastern European, Middle Eastern, and Asian Films about Medieval Europe* (Jefferson, N.C.: McFarland, 1999).

2. Thomas Hahn and Stephen Knight, " 'Exempt Me Sire, I Am Afeard of Women': Gendering Robin Hood," in *The Outlaw Tradition: New Interdisciplinary Essays*, ed. Helen Phillips (Manchester: Manchester University Press, forthcoming).

3. As Kevin Brownlow notes in *The Parade's Gone By* (London: Secker and Warburg, 1968), 290, this is from Charles Kingsley's "Old and New." The original text is in two long lines, not four short ones; see Charles Kingsley, *Poems,* 2 vols. (London: Macmillan, 1884), 2:99. The full text is:

See how the autumn leaves float by decaying,
Down the wild swirls of the rain-swollen stream.
So fleet the works of men, back to their earth again;
Ancient and holy things fade like a dream.

Nay! see the spring-blossoms steal forth a-maying,
Clothing with tender hues orchard and glen;
So, though old forms pass by, ne'er shall their spirit die,
Look! England's bare boughs show green leaf again.

I am indebted to Jeffrey Richards for the Brownlow reference.

4. See Brownlow, *Parade's Gone By,* 285, and Richard Schickel, *Douglas Fairbanks—The First Celebrity* (London: Elm Tree, 1976), 75.

5. Brownlow records that the film cost Fairbanks $1.4 million dollars and took in $2.5 million; see *Parade's Gone By,* 290.

6. Rudy Behlmer, "Robin Hood on the Screen: From Legend to Film," in *Robin Hood: Anthology of Scholarship and Criticism,* ed. Stephen Knight (Cambridge: Brewer, 1999), 441–60; see in particular 448.

7. Ina Rae Hark, "The Visual Politics of *The Adventures of Robin Hood,*" *Journal of Popular Fiction* 5 (1976): 3–17; see in particular 6.

8. See Behlmer, "Robin Hood on the Screen," 456.

9. Lardner's comments on this at a public talk were reported in the Melbourne *Age* on March 22, 1991; see Stephen Knight, *Robin Hood: A Complete Study of the English Outlaw* (Oxford: Blackwell, 1994), 235.

10. See Jeffrey Richards, "Robin Hood on Film and Television since 1945," *Visual Culture in Britain* 2 (2001): 65–80; see in particular 67.

11. Dudley Jones, "Reconstructing Robin Hood: Ideology, Popular Film, and Television," in *A Necessary Fantasy? The Heroic Figure in Children's Popular Culture,* ed. Dudley Jones and Tony Watkins (New York: Garland, 2000), 111–35; see in particular 125–28.

12. The song was used very little in the film, but clips from the film were used heavily in the song video. This suggests that the song gained from the film, rather than vice versa.

13. Kathleen Biddick, "The Return of Robin Hood," a section of the essay "English America: Worth Dying For?" in *The Shock of Medievalism* (Durham: Duke University Press, 1998), 74–75.

14. For a discussion of this film's perhaps surprisingly full relation to the tradition, see Stephen Knight, "*Robin Hood: Men in Tights*: Fitting the Tradition Snugly," in *Pulping Fictions,* ed. D. Cartmell et al. (London: Pluto, 1995); reprinted in Knight, ed., *Robin Hood: Anthology of Scholarship and Criticism,* 461–67.

15. Richards, "Robin Hood on Film and Television since 1945," 67.

16. Ibid., 77.

17. Charles A. Fenton, *S. V. Benét: The Life and Times of an American Man of Letters, 1898–1943* (New Haven: Yale University Press, 1958), 35–36.

18. Henry Gilbert, *Robin Hood and His Merry Men* (Edinburgh: Jack, 1912; rev. ed., Ware: Wordsworth, 1994), v.

19. J. Walker McSpadden and Charles Wilson, *Robin Hood and His Merry Outlaws* (London: Harrap, 1921), 9.

20. Roger Lancelyn Green, *The Adventures of Robin Hood* (London: Puffin, 1956).

21. *The Oxford Book of Ballads*, ed. Sir Arthur Quiller-Couch (Oxford: Clarendon, 1910). For a discussion of the origin of this spurious ballad, see chap. 3, n. 53.

22. Geoffrey Trease, *Bows against the Barons* (London: Lawrence, 1934), 21.

23. London: Lawrence and Wishart, 1948.

24. Carola Oman, *Robin Hood* (Dent: London, 1939), iv.

25. Antonia Pakenham, *Robin Hood* (London: Weidenfeld and Nicholson, 1957; rev. ed., London: Sidgwick and Jackson, 1978), 18.

26. Jay Williams, *The Good Yeomen* (London: Macdonald, 1965), 26.

27. The idea is mistaken: the Old English word was "heafod" and the "u" in the Middle English "heued" was pronounced as a "v."

28. Nicholas Chase, *Locksley* (London: Heinemann, 1983), 3.

29. Parke Godwin, *Robin and the King* (New York: Morrow, 1993), 8.

30. David Lampe, "The Heirs/Errors of *Ivanhoe*," in *Robin Hood in Popular Culture,* ed. Thomas G. Hahn (Cambridge: Brewer, 2000), 129–39; see in particular 136–39.

31. T. H. White, *The Sword in the Stone* (London: Collins, 1938); reprinted as the first book of *The Once and Future King* (London: Collins, 1948).

32. Robin McKinley, *The Outlaws of Sherwood* (London: Macdonald, 1989), 300.

33. Jennifer Roberson, *Lady of the Forest* (New York: Kensington, 1992), front cover.

34. Jennifer Roberson, *Lady of Sherwood* (New York: Kensington, 1999).

35. Roberson, *Lady of the Forest*, 746.

36. Gayle Feyrer, *The Thief's Mistress* (New York: Dell, 1996), 37.

37. Lampe, "Heirs/Errors of *Ivanhoe*," 138.

38. Theresa Tomlinson, *The Forestwife* (London: MacRae, 1993), back jacket.

39. Theresa Tomlinson, *Child of the May* (London: MacRae, 1998).

40. L. D. V. Owen, "Robin Hood in the Light of Research," *Times Trade and Engineering Supplement* 38, part 864 (1936): xxix.

41. J. C. Holt discusses the references in *Robin Hood*, 2d ed. (London: Thames and Hudson, 1990), 156–57.

42. David Crook, "Some Further Evidence concerning the Dating of the Origins of the Legend of Robin Hood," *English Historical Review* 99 (1984): 530–34; reprinted in Knight, ed., *Robin Hood: Anthology of Scholarship and Criticism*, 257–61.

43. See Holt, *Robin Hood*, 52.

44. J. C. Holt, "Robin Hood: The Origin of the Legend," in *Robin Hood: The Many Faces of That Celebrated Outlaw*, ed. Kevin Carpenter (Oldenburg: Bibliotheks- und Informationssystem der Universität Oldenburg, 1995), 27–34; see in particular 28.

45. J. C. Holt, "The Origins and the Audience of the Ballads of Robin Hood," *Past and Present* 18 (1960): 89–110; reprinted in Rodney Hilton, ed., *Peasants, Knights, and Heretics: Studies in Medieval English Social History* (Cambridge: Cambridge University Press, 1976), 236–57, and in Knight, ed., *Robin Hood: Anthology of Scholarship and Criticism*, 211–32; see in particular 211–12.

46. J. R. Maddicott, "The Birth and Setting of the Ballads of Robin Hood," *English Historical Review* 93 (1978): 276–99, reprinted in Knight, ed., *Robin Hood: Anthology of Scholarship and Criticism*, 233–55; see in particular 237.

47. John W. Walker, *The True History of Robin Hood* (Wakefield: West Yorkshire Printing, 1952), 8.

48. Percy Valentine Harris, *The Truth about Robin Hood* (Mansfield: Linney, 1951); see enlarged edition (1975), 78–79.

49. John Bellamy, *Robin Hood: An Historical Inquiry* (London: Croom Helm), 1985.

50. Graham Phillips and Martin Keatman, *Robin Hood—The Man behind the Myth* (London: O'Mara), 1995.

51. Graham Phillips, *The Search for the Grail* (London: Century, 1995), chaps. 14 and 15.

52. F. J. Child, ed., *The English and Scottish Popular Ballads*, 5 vols. (Boston, Barker, 1904; reprint, New York: Dover, 1965), 3:48.

53. Rodney Hilton, "The Origins of Robin Hood," *Past and Present* 14 (1958):

30–44; reprinted in Knight, ed., *Robin Hood: Anthology of Scholarship and Criticism*, 197–210; see in particular 197 and 199.

54. Maurice Keen, "Robin Hood—Peasant or Gentleman?" in *Past and Present* 19 (1961): 7–15; reprinted in Hilton, ed., *Peasants, Knights and Heretics*, 258–66.

55. Holt, "Origins and the Audience."

56. Eric Hobsbawm, *Bandits*, rev. ed. (London: Penguin, 1985).

57. When Hilton reprinted the Robin Hood essays from *Past and Present* in *Peasants, Knights and Heretics,* Keen, in an afterword (266) to his essay (see note 54), changed his support from Hilton to Holt, saying, "I do not believe that any attempt to relate the Robin Hood story to the social pressures of the Peasants' Revolt will stand up to scrutiny."

58. Peter Coss, "Aspects of Cultural Diffusion in Medieval England: The Early Romances, Local Society, and Robin Hood," *Past and Present* 108 (1985): 35–79; reprinted in abbreviated form, concentrating on the Robin Hood sequences, in Knight, ed., *Robin Hood: Anthology of Scholarship and Criticism*, 329–42; see in particular 341.

59. Richard Tardif, "The 'Mistery' of Robin Hood: A New Social Context for the Texts," in *Words and Worlds: Studies in the Social Role of Verbal Culture*, ed. S. Knight and S. Mukherjee (Sydney: Sydney Association for Studies in Society and Culture, 1983); reprinted in Knight, ed., *Robin Hood: Anthology of Scholarship and Criticism*, 345–61; see in particular 360.

60. "Robin Hood," in *Dictionary of National Biography,* ed. Leslie Stephen and Sidney Lee (London: Smith Elder, 1885–1910), vol. 26 (1891): 421–24; reprinted in Knight, ed., *Robin Hood: Anthology of Scholarship and Criticism*, 379–84; see in particular 379.

61. J. W. Hales and F. J. Snell, "Robin Hood," in *Encyclopedia Britannica*, 11th ed. (London: Cambridge University Press, 1910), 421.

62. Robert Graves, *The White Goddess* (London: Faber, 1948), 350.

63. Margaret Murray, *The God of the Witches* (London: Faber, 1931), 35–36.

64. Lord Raglan, "Robin Hood," a chapter in *The Hero* (London: Methuen, 1936); reprinted in Knight, ed., *Robin Hood: Anthology of Scholarship and Criticism*, 385–91; see in particular 389–90.

65. John Matthews, *Robin Hood: Green Lord of the Wildwood* (Glastonbury: Gothic Image, 1993), 100.

66. Lorraine Kochanske Stock, "Lords of the Wildwood: The Wild Man, the Green Man, and Robin Hood," in *Robin Hood in Popular Culture*, ed. Hahn, 139–49.

67. Joseph Falacky Nagy, "The Paradoxes of Robin Hood," *Folklore* 91 (1980): 198–210; reprinted in Knight, ed., *Robin Hood: Anthology of Scholarship and Criticism*, 411–25; see in particular 411.

68. Rodney Hilton's account of the audience is primarily a Marxist reading, and Richard Tardif's essay is a more nuanced account in that mode; Stuart Kane has

offered a gender-based reading in "Horseplay: Robin Hood, Guy of Gisborne, and the Neg(oti)ation of the Bestial," in *Robin Hood in Popular Culture*, ed. Hahn, 101–10. In the same volume the outlaw tradition is seen from a feminist viewpoint in Sherron Lux's "And the 'Reel' Maid Marian," 151–60, and Evelyn Perry's "Disguising and Revealing the Female Hero's Identity: Cross-Dressing in the Ballad of *Robin Hood and Maid Marian*," 191–96. The essay by Thomas Hahn and Stephen Knight (see note 2) also operates in the field of gender. Though they and Kane are aware of the possibility of Freudian readings, no full-scale interpretation following Freud or his successors, including Lacan, appears to have yet been offered, which seems surprising in the context of so much suggestive and potentially symbolic material.

Works Cited

Aires, Duets and Choruses in the Operatical Pantomime of Merry Sherwood or Harlequin Forester, now performing at the Theatre-Royal, Covent Garden. London: Longman, 1795.

Almond, Richard, and A. J. Pollard. "The Yeomanry of Robin Hood and Social Terminology in Fifteenth-Century England." *Past and Present* 170 (2001): 52–77.

Bailey, Brian. *The Luddite Rebellion.* Stroud: Sutton, 1998.

Barnard, John. "Keats's 'Robin Hood,' John Hamilton Reynolds, and the 'Old Poets.' " In Knight, ed., *Robin Hood: Anthology of Scholarship and Criticism*, 123–40. Originally published in *Proceedings of the British Academy* 75 (1989): 181–200.

Barry, Edmond. *Thèse de littérature sur les vicissitudes et les transformations du cycle populaire de Robin Hood.* Paris: Rignoux, 1832.

Barton, Anne. *Ben Jonson: Dramatist.* Cambridge: Cambridge University Press, 1984.

Behlmer, Rudy. "Robin Hood on the Screen: from Legend to Film." In Knight, ed., *Robin Hood: Anthology of Scholarship and Criticism*, 441–60. Originally published as " 'Welcome to Sherwood!' *The Adventures of Robin Hood* (1938)," in *Behind the Scenes*, 2d ed. (Hollywood: French, 1990), 61–86.

Bellamy, John. *Robin Hood: An Historical Inquiry.* London: Croom Helm, 1985.

Bevington, David. *Tudor Drama and Politics.* Cambridge: Harvard University Press, 1968.

Biddick, Kathleen. "The Return of Robin Hood." In *The Shock of Medievalism.* Durham: Duke University Press, 1988, 74–75.

Blagden, Cyprian. "Notes on the Ballad Market in the Second Half of the Seventeenth Century." *Studies in Bibliography* 6 (1954): 161–80.

Bolland, W. *A Manual of Yearbook Studies.* Cambridge: University of Cambridge Press, 1925.

Bradbury, Jim. *The Medieval Archer.* Woodbridge: Boydell, 1985.

Brockman, Bennet A. "Robin Hood and the Invention of Children's Literature." *Children's Literature* 10 (1982): 1–14.

Bronson, Bertrand. *Joseph Ritson, Scholar-at-Arms*. 2 vols. Berkeley: University of California Press, 1938.

Brooke, Frances. *Marian: A Comic Opera*. London: Cadell, 1788.

Brooks, C. W., C. L. Kearney, and J. H. Stocqueler. *Robin Hood and Richard Coeur de Lion* in *Plays*. London: Farebrother, 1859.

Brownlow, Kevin. *The Parade's Gone By*. London: Secker and Warburg, 1968.

Burgess, Glyn S., trans. *Two Medieval Outlaws: Eustace the Monk and Fouke Fitz Waryn*. Cambridge: Brewer, 1997.

Butler, Marilyn. "Antiquarianism (Popular)." In *An Oxford Companion to the Romantic Age*, edited by Iain MacCalman. Oxford: Oxford University Press, 1999, 328–38.

——. " 'The Good Old Times': *Maid Marian*." In Knight, ed., *Robin Hood: Anthology of Scholarship and Criticism*, 141–53. Originally published as part of " 'The Good Old Times': *Maid Marian* and *The Misfortunes of Elphin*" in *Peacock Displayed: A Satirist in His Context* (London: Routledge, 1979).

Carpenter, Kevin, ed. *Robin Hood: The Many Faces of That Celebrated Outlaw*. Oldenburg: Bibliotheks- und Informationssystem der Universität Oldenburg, 1995.

Chase, Nicholas. *Locksley*. London: Heinemann, 1983.

Child, F. J., ed. *The English and Scottish Popular Ballads*. 5 vols. Boston: Barker, 1904. Reprint, New York: Dover, 1965.

Cooper, Helen. *Pastoral: Medieval into Renaissance*. Cambridge: Brewer, 1977.

Coss, Peter R. "Aspects of Cultural Diffusion in Medieval England: The Early Romances, Local Society, and Robin Hood." *Past and Present* 108 (1985) 35–79. Robin Hood section reprinted in Knight, ed., *Robin Hood: Anthology of Scholarship and Criticism*, 329–43.

Crook, David. "Some Further Evidence concerning the Dating of the Origins of the Legend of Robin Hood." *English Historical Review* 99 (1984): 530–34. Reprinted in Knight, ed., *Robin Hood: Anthology of Scholarship and Criticism*, 257–61.

Davenport, Edwin. "The Representation of Robin Hood in Elizabethan Drama: *George a Greene* and *Edward I*." In Potter, ed., *Playing Robin Hood*, 45–62.

Dawson, Christopher. *His Fine Wit*. London: Routledge, 1970.

de Vriess, Kelly. "Longbow Archery and the Earliest Robin Hood Legends." In Hahn, ed., *Robin Hood in Popular Culture*, 41–59.

DH [Richard Gough]. "Note" on Huntington. *Gentleman's Magazine* 63 (March 1793): 226.

Dobson, R. B., and John Taylor, eds. *Rymes of Robyn Hood: An Introduction to the English Outlaw*. London: Heinemann, 1976.

Drayton, Michael. *Poly-Olbion*. Vol. 4 of *The Works of Michael Drayton*, edited by J. William Hebel. Oxford: Blackwell, 1961.

Dumas, Alexandre. *Robin Hood: prince des voleurs*. Paris: Levy, 1872.

———. *Robin Hood le proscrit*. Paris: Levy, 1877.

Egan, Pierce. *Robin Hood and Little John, or the Merry Men of Sherwood Forest*. London: Forster and Hextall, 1840.

Ellis, George, ed. *Specimens of Early English Metrical Romances*. London: Longman, Hunt, Rees and Orme, 1805.

———. *Specimens of the Early English Poets*. London: Edwards, 1790.

Emmett, George. *Robin Hood and the Adventures of Merrie Sherwood*. 3 vols. London: Hogarth, 1885.

[———]. *Robin Hood and the Outlaws of Sherwood Forest*. 3 vols. London: Temple, 1869.

Evans, R. H., ed. *Old Ballads, Historical and Narrative*. 3rd ed. 4 vols. London: Evans, 1810.

Evans, Thomas, ed. *Old Ballads, Historical and Narrative, With Some of Modern Date, Now First Collected and Reprinted from Rare Copies*. 2 vols. London: Evans, 1777.

Fenton, Charles A. *S. V. Benét: The Life and Times of an American Man of Letters, 1898–1943*. New Haven: Yale University Press, 1958.

Feyrer, Gayle. *The Thief's Mistress*. New York: Dell, 1996.

Fishwick, H. "A Thaw Wind." *Notes and Queries,* 4th ser., 11 (1873): 390.

Gable, J. Harris. *Bibliography of Robin Hood*. Studies in Language, Literature, and Criticism. Lincoln: University of Nebraska Press, 1939.

"G. F." Review of *Robin Hood and Little John*, by Pierce Egan. *London and Westminster Quarterly* 33 (1840): 425–91.

Gilbert, Henry. *Robin Hood and His Merry Men*. Edinburgh: Jack, 1912. Rev. ed., Ware: Wordsworth: 1994.

Gilliat, Rev. Edmund. *In Lincoln Green: A Merrie Tale of Robin Hood*. London: Seeley, 1887.

Godwin, Parke. *Robin and the King*. New York: Morrow, 1993.

Gooch, Elizabeth Villa-Real. *Sherwood Forest, or Northern Adventures*. 3 vols. London: Highley, 1804.

Gough, Richard. *Sepulchral Monuments*. 2 vols. London: Nichols, 1786.

Graves, Robert. *The White Goddess*. London: Faber, 1948.

Gray, Douglas. "The Robin Hood Poems." In Knight, ed., *Robin Hood: Anthology of Scholarship and Criticism*, 3–37. Originally published in *Poetica* (Japan) 18 (1984): 1–18.

Green, Robert Lancelyn. *The Adventures of Robin Hood*. London: Puffin, 1956.

Greene, Robert. *The Complete Works of Robert Greene*. Edited by J. Churton Collins. 2 vols. Oxford: Clarendon, 1905.

Groom, Nick. Introduction to Percy, *Reliques of Early English Poetry*.

Gutch, J. M., ed. *A Lytel Gest of Robin Hode, with Other Ancient and Modern Ballads and Songs Relating to This Celebrated Yeoman*. 2 vols. London: Longman, 1847.

Hahn, Thomas G., ed. *Robin Hood in Popular Culture: Violence, Transgression, and Justice*. Cambridge: Brewer, 2000.

Hahn, Thomas G., and Stephen Knight. " 'Exempt me Sire, I Am Afeard of Women': Gendering Robin Hood." In Phillips, ed., *The Outlaw Tradition: New Interdisciplinary Essays*.

Hale, J. W., and F. T. Snell. "Robin Hood." In *Encyclopaedia Britannica*. 11th ed. London: Cambridge University Press, 1910.

Hall, Edward. *The History of England during the Reign of Henry the Fourth and the Succeeding Monarchs to the End of the Reign of Henry the Eighth*. Edited by Sir H. Ellis. London: Johnson, Rivington et al., 1809, 515.

Hark, Ina Rae. "The Visual Politics of *The Adventures of Robin Hood*." *Journal of Popular Fiction* 5 (1976): 3–17.

Harris, Percy Valentine. *The True History of Robin Hood*. Mansfield: Linney, 1951.

Hartshorne, C. H., ed. *Ancient Metrical Tales*. London: Pickering, 1829.

Harty, Kevin J. *The Reel Middle Ages: American, Western and Eastern Europe, Middle Eastern, and Asian Films about Medieval Europe*. Jefferson, N.C.: McFarland, 1999.

Henslowe, Philip. *Henslowe's Diaries*. Edited by W. W. Greg. London: Bullen, 1908.

Hepworth, David. "A Grave Tale." In Phillips, ed., *Robin Hood: Medieval and Post-Medieval*.

Hill, Christopher. "The Norman Yoke." In *Puritanism and Revolution*. London: Secker and Warburg, 1965, 50–122.

Hilton, Rodney. "The Origins of Robin Hood." *Past and Present* 14 (1958): 30–44. Reprinted in Hilton, ed., *Peasants, Knights, and Heretics*, 221–35, and in Knight, ed., *Robin Hood: Anthology of Scholarship and Criticism*, 197–210.

——, ed. *Peasants, Knights, and Heretics: Studies in Medieval English Social History*. Cambridge: Cambridge University Press, 1976.

Hobsbawm, Eric. *Bandits*. 2d ed. London: Penguin, 1985.

Hoffman, Dean A. " 'With the shot y wyll / Alle thy lustes to full-fyl': Archery as Symbol in the Early Ballads of Robin Hood." *Neuphilologische Mitteilungen* 86 (1985): 494–505.

Holinshed, Ralphael. *History of Scotland*. In *Chronicles*, vol. 2. London: Harrison, 1577.

Holt, J. C. "The Origins and the Audience of the Ballads of Robin Hood." *Past and Present* 18 (1960): 89–110. Reprinted in Hilton, ed., *Peasants, Knights, and Heretics*, 236–57, and in Knight, ed., *Robin Hood: Anthology of Scholarship and Criticism*, 211–32.

——. *Robin Hood.* 2d ed. London: Thames and Hudson, 1990.

—— "Robin Hood: The Origin of the Legend." In Carpenter, ed., *Robin Hood: The Many Faces of That Celebrated Outlaw*, 27–34.

Hunt, Leigh. *Stories in Verse.* London: Routledge, 1855.

Hunter, Joseph. "The Great Hero of the Ancient Minstrelsy of England: Robin Hood, his period, real character etc., investigated." *Critical and Historical Tracts*, vol. 4. London: Smith, 1852, 28–38.

Hynes, William S., and William G. Doty. *Mythical Trickster Figures: Content, Contexts, and Criticism.* Tuscaloosa: University of Alabama Press, 1993.

James, G. P. R. *Forest Days: A Romance of Old Times.* 3 vols. London: Saunders and Otley, 1843.

Jamieson, Robert. *Popular Songs and Ballads.* 2 vols. Edinburgh: Constable, 1806.

Johnson, Edgar. *Sir Walter Scott: The Great Unknown.* 2 vols. London: Hamilton, 1970.

Johnston, Alexandra F. "The Robin Hood of the Records." In Potter, ed., *Playing Robin Hood*, 27–44.

Jones, Dudley. "Reconstructing Robin Hood: Ideology, Popular Film, and Television." In *A Necessary Fantasy? The Heroic Figure in Children's Popular Culture*, edited by Dudley Jones and Tony Watkins. New York: Garland, 2000, 111–35.

Jonson, Ben. *Ben Jonson's Plays and Masques.* Edited by Robert M. Adams. New York: Norton, 1979.

——. *The Works of Ben Jonson.* Edited by C. H. Herford and Percy and Evelyn Simpson. 10 vols. Oxford: Clarendon Press, 1950.

Kane, Stuart. "Horseplay: Robin Hood, Guy of Gisborne, and the Neg(oti)ation of the Bestial." In Hahn, ed., *Robin Hood in Popular Culture*, 101–110.

Keats, John. *The Poems of John Keats.* Edited by Miriam Allott. London: Longman, 1970.

Keen, Maurice. "Robin Hood—Peasant or Gentleman?" *Past and Present* 19 (1961): 7–15. Reprinted in Hilton, ed., *Peasants, Knights, and Heretics*, 258–66.

Kegami, Masa. "The Language and Date of 'A Gest of Robyn Hode.'" *Neuphilologische Mitteilungen* 96 (1995): 27–81.

Kelly, H. A. *Chaucerian Tragedy.* 2d ed. Cambridge: Brewer, 1997.

Kingsley, Charles. *Poems.* 2 vols. London: Macmillan, 1884.

Knight, Stephen. "'Meere English Flockes': Jonson's Use of the English Robin Hood Tradition in *The Sad Shepherd*." In Phillips, ed., *Robin Hood: Medieval and Post-Medieval*.

——. "'Quite Another Man': Robin Hood and the Royal Restoration." In Potter, ed., *Playing Robin Hood*, 167–81.

——. "Rabbie Hood: The Colonial (and Postcolonial) Impact of Scotland on the Robin Hood Tradition." In Phillips, ed., *The Outlaw Tradition: New Interdisciplinary Essays.*

——. *Robin Hood: A Complete Study of the English Outlaw.* Oxford: Blackwell, 1994.

——, ed. *Robin Hood: Anthology of Scholarship and Criticism.* Cambridge: Brewer, 1999.

——, ed. *Robin Hood: The Forresters Manuscript.* Cambridge: Brewer, 1999.

Knight, Stephen, and Thomas H. Ohlgren, eds. *Robin Hood and Other Outlaw Tales.* 2d ed. Kalamazoo: Western Michigan University Press, 2000.

Lampe, David. "The Heirs/Errors of *Ivanhoe.*" In Hahn, ed., *Robin Hood in Popular Culture*, 129–39.

Langland, William. *The Vision according to Piers Plowman: The B Version.* Edited by George Kane and E. Talbot Donaldson. London: Athlone, 1975.

Lee, Sir Sidney. "Robin Hood." In *Dictionary of National Biography.* London: Smith Elder, 1885–1910.

Leland, John. *Collecteana.* Edited by Thomas Hearne. Oxford: Sheldonian Theatre, 1776.

——. *The Itinerary of John Leland in England and Wales.* Edited by Lucy Toulmin-Smith. 5 vols. London: Bell, 1906–1910.

Looke About You. London: Ferbrand, 1600.

Lux, Sherron. "And the 'Reel' Maid Marian." In Hahn, ed., *Robin Hood in Popular Culture*, 151–60.

Maddicott, J. M. "The Birth and of the Ballads of Robin Hood." *English Historical Review* 93 (1978): 276–99. Reprinted in Knight, ed., *Robin Hood: Anthology of Scholarship and Criticism*, 233–55.

Marshall, John. "Playing the Game: Reconstructing *Robin Hood and the Sheriff of Nottingham.*" In Hahn, ed., *Robin Hood in Popular Culture*, 161–74.

Matthews, John. *Robin Hood: Lord of the Wildwood.* Glastonbury: Gothic Image, 1993.

McDiarmid, Matthew, P., ed. *Hary's Wallace (Vita Nobilissimi Defensoris Scoti Wilelmi Wallace Militis).* 2 vols. Edinburgh: Blackwood, for Scottish Text Society, 1968.

McKinley, Robin. *The Outlaws of Sherwood.* London: Macdonald, 1989.

McNally, Leonard. *Robin Hood; or Sherwood Forest, A Comic Opera, as it is performed at the Theatre-Royal in Covent Garden.* London: Almon, 1782.

McSpadden, J. Walker, and Charles Wilson. *Robin Hood and His Merry Outlaws.* London: Harrap, 1921.

Mendez, Moses. *Robin Hood: A New Musical Entertainment.* London: Cooper, 1751.

Miller, Thomas. *Royston Gower.* 3 vols. London: Nicholson, 1838.

Muddock, Joyce, R. *Maid Marian and Robin Hood: A Romance of Old Sherwood Forest*. London: Chatto and Windus, 1892.

Munday, Anthony. *The Downfall of Robert, Earle of Huntington*. In Knight and Ohlgren, eds., *Robin Hood and Other Outlaw Tales*, 296–401.

——. *Metropolis Coronata: The Triumph of Ancient Drapery*. London: Purslowe, 1615.

Munday, Anthony, and Henry Chettle. *The Death of Robert, Earle of Huntington*. London: Leacke, 1601; reprint, London: Malone Society, 1967.

Murray, Margaret. *The God of the Witches*. London: Faber, 1931.

Nagy, Joseph Falacky. "The Paradoxes of Robin Hood." *Folklore* 91 (1980): 198–214. Reprinted in Knight, ed., *Robin Hood: Anthology of Scholarship and Criticism*, 411–25.

Nelson, Malcolm A. *The Robin Hood Tradition in the English Renaissance*. Salzburg Studies in English Literature. Elizabethan Studies, vol. 14. Salzburg: University of Salzburg Press, 1973.

New and Original Grand Christmas Pantomime—Robin Hood. Manchester: Theatre Royal Press, 1851.

Newbolt, Sir Henry. "Peacock, Scott and Robin Hood." *Dalhousie Review* 4 (1925): 411–32.

Noyes, Alfred. *Sherwood*. London: Watts, 1911.

Ohlgren, Thomas H. "The 'Marchaunt' of Sherwood: Mercantile Ideology in *A Gest of Robyn Hode*." In Hahn, ed., *Robin Hood in Popular Culture*, 175–90.

——, ed. *Medieval Outlaws: Ten Tales in Modern English*. Stroud: Sutton, 1998.

Oman, Carola. *Robin Hood*. London: Dent, 1939.

Owen, L. D. V. "Robin Hood in the Light of Research." *Times Trade and Engineering Supplement* 28, part 864 (1936): xxix.

Oxenford, John, and G. A. MacFarren. *Robin Hood: An Opera*. London: Cramer, Beale and Chappel, 1860.

Pakenham, Antonia. *Robin Hood*. London: Weidenfeld and Nicholson, 1957. Rev. ed., London: Sidgwick and Jackson, 1978.

Peacock, Thomas Love. *Maid Marian*. London: Hookham, 1822. Edited by George Saintsbury. London: Macmillan, 1895. Reprint, London: Macmillan, 1959.

Peele, George. *The Dramatic Works: Edward I*. Edited by F. S. Hook. Vol. 2 of *The Life and Works of George Peele*, edited by Charles Tyler Prouty. New Haven: Yale University Press, 1961.

Percy, Thomas, ed. *Reliques of English Poetry: Consisting of Old Heroic Ballads, Songs, and other Pieces of our earlier Poets (Chiefly of the Lyric kind), Together with some few of later Date*. 4 vols. London: Dodsley, 1765. Facsimile ed. with an introduction by Nick Groom, London: Routledge/Thoemmes, 1996.

Perry, Evelyn. "Disguising and Revealing the Fame Heroic Identity: Cross-Dressing in the Ballad of 'Robin Hood and Maid Marian.'" In Hahn, ed., *Robin Hood in Popular Culture*, 191–96.

Phillips, Graham. *The Search for the Grail*. London: Century, 1955.

Phillips, Graham, and Martin Keatman. *Robin Hood—The Man behind the Myth*. London: O'Mara, 1995.

Phillips, Helen. "Forest, Town, and Road: The Significance of Places and Names in Some Robin Hood Texts." In Hahn, ed., *Robin Hood in Popular Culture*, 197–214.

——, ed. *The Outlaw Tradition: New Interdisciplinary Essays*. Manchester: Manchester University Press, forthcoming.

——, ed. *Robin Hood: Medieval and Post-Medieval*. Cambridge: Brewer, forthcoming.

Potter, Lois. "The Apotheosis of Maid Marian: Tennyson's *The Foresters* and the Nineteenth-Century Theater." In Potter, ed., *Playing Robin Hood*, 182–204.

——. "Part Two: Cultural Cross-Dressing." In Potter, ed., *Playing Robin Hood*, 91–99.

——. "Sherwood Forest and the Byronic Robin Hood." In Hahn, ed., *Robin Hood in Popular Culture*, 315–24.

——, ed. *Playing Robin Hood: The Legend as Performance in Five Centuries*. Newark: University of Delaware Press, 1998.

Prideaux, W. F. "Who Was Robin Hood?" *Notes and Queries*, 7th ser., 2 (1886): 421–24.

Pyle, Howard. *The Merry Adventures of Robin Hood, of Great Renown, in Nottinghamshire*. New York: Scribner, 1883.

Raglan, Lord. *The Hero*. London: Methuen, 1936.

Ravenscroft, Thomas. *Deuteromelia, or the Second part of Musicks melodie, or melodius Musicke*. London: Adams, 1609.

Richards, Jeffrey. "Robin Hood on Film and Television since 1945." *Visual Culture in Great Britain* 2 (2001): 65–80.

Ritson, Joseph, ed. *Robin Hood: A Collection of All the Ancient Poems, Songs and Ballads Now Extant Relative to the Celebrated English Outlaw (To Which Are Prefixed Historical Anecdotes of His Life)*. 2 vols. London: Egerton and Johnson, 1795. 2d ed., London: Pickering, 1832.

Roberson, Jennifer. *Lady of Sherwood*. New York: Kensington, 1999.

——. *Lady of the Forest*. New York: Kensington, 1992.

Robin Hood. 2 vols. Edinburgh: Oliver and Boyd, 1819.

Robin Hood: An Opera. London: Watts, 1730.

Saintsbury, George. Introduction to 1895 edition of Peacock, *Maid Marian*.

Sanders, Julie. "Jonson, *The Sad Shepherd* and the North Midlands." *Ben Jonson Journal* 6 (1999): 49–68.

Schickel, Richard. *Douglas Fairbanks: The First Celebrity*. London: Elm Tree, 1976.

Scott, Sir Walter. *The Abbot*. Edinburgh: Constable, 1820.

———. *Ivanhoe*. Edinburgh: Constable, 1820. Edited by A. N. Wilson, London: Penguin, 1986.

———. *The Poetical Works of Scott*. Edited by J. Logie Robertson. London: Oxford University Press, 1904.

Sedgwick, Eve Kosofsky. *Between Men: English Literature and Homosocial Desire*. New York: Columbia University Press, 1985.

Singman, Jeffrey L. *Robin Hood: The Shaping of a Legend*, Westport: Greenwood, 1998.

Smith, Harry B., and Reginald de Koven. *Maid Marian*. London: Hopewood and Crew, 1890.

Smith, Marcus, and Julian Wasserman. "Travels with a Green Crayon." In Phillips, ed., *Robin Hood: Medieval and Post-Medieval*.

Southey, Robert. Letter to Charles Williams Wynne, December 30, 1804. National Library of Wales MSS 4811–15D.

Spence, Lewis. "Robin Hood in Scotland." *Chambers Journal* 18 (1928): 94–96.

Steadman, J. M., Jr. "The Dramatization of the Robin Hood Ballads." *Modern Philology* 17 (1919): 9–23.

Stock, Lorraine Kochanske. "Lords of the Wildwood: The Wild Man, the Green Man and Robin Hood." In Hahn, ed., *Robin Hood in Popular Culture*, 239–49.

Stocqueler, Joachim H. *Maid Marian, The Forest Queen*. London: Pierce, 1849.

———. *The Memoirs of a Journalist*. Enlarged, rev. ed. Bombay: Times of India, 1873.

Stokes, J. D. "Robin Hood and the Churchwardens of Yeovil." *Medieval and Renaissance Drama in England* 3 (1986): 1–25.

Stow, John. *Annales of England*. London: Newbery, 1592.

Sutherland, John. *The Life and Times of Sir Walter Scott*. Oxford: Blackwell, 1995.

Swan, George. "Robin Hood's 'Irish Knife.' " *University of Mississippi Studies in English*, n.s., 11–12 (1993–95): 51–80.

Tardif, Richard. "The 'Mistery' of Robin Hood: A New Social Context for the Texts." In *Words and Worlds: Studies in the Social Role of Verbal Culture*, edited by Stephen Knight and S. N. Mukherjee. Sydney: Sydney Association for Studies in Society and Culture, 1983, 2130–45. Reprinted in Knight, ed., *Robin Hood: Anthology of Scholarship and Criticism*, 345–61.

Tennyson, Alfred, Lord. *Tennyson: Poems and Plays*. London: Oxford University Press, 1965.

Thierry, Auguste. *Histoire de la conquête de l'Angleterre par les Normans*. Paris: Firmin Didot, 1825.

Thoms, William, ed. *A Collection of Early English Prose Romances.* 2 vols. London: Nattali and Bond, 1858.

Thoreau, Henry. *Excursions.* Boston: Tickner and Fields, 1880.

Thorndike, A. H. "The Relationship of *As You Like It* to the Robin Hood Plays." *Journal of English and Germanic Philology* 4 (1902): 59–69.

Tomlinson, Theresa. *Child of the May.* London: MacRae, 1998.

——. *The Forestwife.* London: MacRae, 1993.

Trease, Geoffrey. *Bows against the Barons.* London: Lawrence, 1934. 2d ed., London: Lawrence and Wishart, 1948.

Walker, John W. *The True History of Robin Hood.* Wakefield: West Yorkshire Printing Co., 1952.

Warner, William. *Albions England.* London: Orwin, 1589. Facsimile ed., Hildesheim: Olb, 1971.

Wiles, David. *The Early Plays of Robin Hood.* Cambridge: Brewer, 1981.

Williams, Jay. *The Good Yeomen.* London: Macdonald, 1956.

Wordsworth, William. *Poetical Works of Wordworth.* Edited by Thomas Hutchinson. Rev. ed. edited by Ernest de Selincourt. Oxford: Oxford University Press, 1936.

Index

Page references followed by an "f" indicate figures.